PEOPLE IN CITIES

Recent publications from SAUS

PEOPLE IN CITIES
A transatlantic policy exchange

**Edited by Robin Hambleton
and Marilyn Taylor**

S·A·U·S

First published in Great Britain in 1993 by

SAUS Publications
School for Advanced Urban Studies
University of Bristol
Rodney Lodge
Grange Road
Bristol BS8 4EA

Telephone (0272) 741117
Fax (0272) 737308

© SAUS 1993

British Library Cataloguing in Publication Data
A catalogue record for this book is available from the British Library

SAUS Study 11

ISBN   1 873575 59 9
ISSN   0268-3725

The School for Advanced Urban Studies is a centre for research, post-graduate and continuing education, and consultancy at the University of Bristol.   The School's focus   is   the   analysis,   development   and implementation of policy in the fields of employment, health and social care, housing, social management, and urban change and government. Its aim is to bridge the gaps between theory and practice, between different policy areas, and between academic disciplines. SAUS is committed to the wide dissemination of its findings and in addition to courses and seminars the School has established several publications series: **SAUS Studies,   Occasional   Papers,   Working   Papers,   Studies   in Decentralisation   and   Quasi-Markets,   DRIC   Reports   and   SAUS Guides and Reports**.

SAUS is working to counter discrimination on grounds of gender, race, disability, age and sexuality in all its activities.

CONTENTS

ACKNOWLEDGEMENTS

The idea for the conference on which this book is based was developed with William Plowden of the Harkness Fellowships. Our particular thanks are due to him and the Harkness Fellowships for giving us the opportunity to bring this body of material together, for organising the conference with us and providing financial support. Thanks are also due to the Department of the Environment for their participation in the conference and for their financial support. For their hard work in putting together the papers for the book and their patience during the publication process we thank the Harkness fellows and other contributors. Finally we would like to express our appreciation of the work of the publications staff - Alison Shaw, Jane Raistrick and Julia Mortimer - for producing the finished document.

NOTES ON THE CONTRIBUTORS

Jon Bright is Director of Field Operations for Crime Concern, the crime prevention organisation set up in 1988. Before taking up this post, he was coordinator of NACRO's Safe Neighbourhood Unit for six years. The Unit pioneered multi-agency approaches to crime prevention and community safety on local authority housing estates. In 1990 he was awarded a Harkness Fellowship to study crime prevention in the USA.

Richard Bolsin is Head of Education Support Services for Kent County Council. In 1990-91 he held a Harkness Fellowship at the Center for International Studies, University of Pittsburgh and examined how partnerships between public and private sectors in US cities can contribute towards improving education standards and quality. He has published various articles on this subject.

Steve Bullock is a deputy chair of the Association of Metropolitan Authorities and was Leader of the London Borough of Lewisham for five years until 1993. He has a particular interest in the political management of public bodies and led Lewisham's successful bid to become a City Challenge Pacemaker. He is currently involved in the development of training programmes for elected members.

Nicholas Falk is a director of the Urban and Economic Development Group which he founded in 1976. He held a Harkness Fellowship at Stanford Business School in 1967-69.

Robin Hambleton is Professor of City and Regional Planning at the University of Wales, Cardiff, and has a long-standing interest in transatlantic policy transfer and has written widely on the subject. He held a Fulbright Fellowship at the Institute of Urban and Regional Development, University of California, Berkeley in 1988, and in 1990 he published *Urban government in the 1990s: lessons from the USA*.

Kevin Lavery is Head of Corporate Team at Westminster City Council. Previously he has worked for Kent County Council, the London Borough of Bexley and the Association of District Councils. In 1991 he gained a scholarship from Save and

Prosper and the Society of Local Authority Chief Executives to examine 'strong mayor' and 'council-manager' forms of government in the USA. To this end he spent a six week period in Phoenix, Seattle and Washington DC.

Philip Leather is a senior research fellow at the School for Advanced Urban Studies, University of Bristol. His main research interest is housing renewal policy and he has carried out research on comparative housing conditions and renewal policies in Europe and the USA with Sheila Mackintosh.

Sheila Mackintosh is a research fellow at the School for Advanced Urban Studies, University of Bristol. She specialises in housing renewal policy. With Philip Leather she has carried out comparative research in this area in Europe and the USA.

Penny Morris is a research fellow in communications skills at Cambridge University School of Clinical Medicine and founder of COMNET, the UK network for communication in health care. She was a Harkness Fellow in 1990-91 and studied patients' contributions to health professionals' training throughout the USA.

Sandra Newton is a civil servant presently working as head of small firms policy at the Department of Trade and Industry. She was a Harkness Fellow between August 1990 and March 1991, researching in six cities mainly in the north east and south of the USA. the project was stimulated in part by a German Marshall Employment Fellowship in 1988 and work done in a range of national and diocesan committees for the Church of England.

Alex Norman is Emeritus Professor at the University of California at Los Angeles and also works as an independent consultant.

Kurt L. Schmoke was first elected mayor of Baltimore City in 1987, becoming the city's first elected African-American mayor. Now serving his second term of office, his commitment to creative strategies for urban renewal has remained a focal point of his tenure as mayor. In 1977 he joined President Carter's White House Domestic Policy Staff, and in 1978 he returned to Baltimore to become an assistant United States attorney. In 1982 he was elected state's attorney for Baltimore City, where he served until becoming mayor.

Karamjit Singh is one of the eleven full-time members of the Police Complaints Authority and has previously worked in local government, voluntary and academic sections. In 1990 he was awarded a Harkness Fellowship and studied police-community relations in the USA.

Marilyn Taylor is a lecturer in the management of health and social care at the School for Advanced Urban Studies at the University of Bristol. She brought with her 21 years of experience in the fields of community development and the voluntary sector and has worked with many community projects in inner cities and outer estates.

PREFACE

This book is based on the proceedings of a conference organised jointly between Bristol University's School for Advanced Urban Studies (SAUS) and the Harkness Fellowships, a programme of graduate scholarships funded by The Commonwealth Fund of New York. Several of the papers were presented by earlier Harkness Fellows. The reasons for the involvement of SAUS are obvious enough. It may be worth explaining how the Harkness Fellowships come into the picture.

The Harkness programme started in 1925. It now offers fellowships to graduates from three countries (the United Kingdom, Australia and New Zealand) to visit and study in the United States of America (USA). Mr Harkness' basic objective was to strengthen ties between the countries concerned. In achieving that objective, the programme aims to bring about changes of three kinds: in the fellows themselves, in the countries from which they come and to which they return and in the country in which they spend their fellowships. The intention is that they should act as transmitters, in both directions, of ideas and information. They should take to the USA knowledge and understanding of some issue at home, in which they are interested and about which they may be concerned. In the USA they should discover how Americans think about the issue, how they deal with it, whether our experiences are interesting and relevant to them, whether there is scope for pooling ideas and, more generally, whether American approaches to the topic shed some light on American attitudes and society at large. Back home after this experience, they should be better placed to influence our own thinking and actions related both to the specific issue and perhaps more broadly.

Since the UK Harkness programme was remodelled in 1990, it has been focused around three broad themes. These were chosen, after much discussion on both sides of the Atlantic, because they were incontestably important to both countries and because they were or could be subjects of a common language. These themes are at present defined as people in cities, human resources in the 21st century, and promoting good health. The debate about each of the three has, if anything, intensified since they were first chosen.

This is certainly true of cities. The long-term future of cities such as London or New York, Liverpool or Detroit is itself a matter of debate. In addition, in increasingly urban societies both the successes and the failures of those societies are often most conspicuously displayed in cities - sometimes immediately next to each other, as on London's South Bank where concert or theatre-goers now must skirt the teeming cardboard cities of the dispossessed. How a society regards and deals with such contrasts can say a great deal about its basic values: its attitudes to wealth and poverty, to human rights and entitlements, and to the role of government.

Those who are selected as Harkness Fellows are likely to have something interesting to say to their American hosts. On their return, they are encouraged to do all that they can to spread or to draw on what they have learned in the USA. They may do this through academic research, or journalism, or directly through making or implementing policy. The point is that they should disseminate and apply the fruits of their experience as widely as possible. This of course is not a matter simply of describing, still less extolling, US practice. It means using the USA as a context in which to compare approaches and as a vantage point from which to assess our own. More generally, it means being open-minded towards the whole process of international comparison and of believing it to be intrinsically helpful in understanding ourselves and the problems that we face.

This is why the Harkness programme was involved in the Bristol seminar and why several earlier fellows contributed papers to it. We believe that the results successfully achieve the aims set out above. We are grateful to Robin Hambleton and Marilyn Taylor at SAUS for making the seminar possible and for inviting us to collaborate with them. 'People in cities' remains one of the programme's themes; we are confident that Harkness Fellows will continue to have a lot to say on this important subject.

William Plowden
Senior Adviser, UK Harkness Fellowships

11 June 1993

one

TRANSATLANTIC POLICY TRANSFER

Robin Hambleton and Marilyn Taylor

Introduction

Anglo-American dialogue in the field of public policy is nothing
new. On the contrary there has been a considerable amount of
exchange over the years, and policy ideas have moved freely back
and forth across the Atlantic. This dialogue has tended to take
place at two levels.

On the one hand, much of the practical exchange of ideas and
experience has been between individuals and/or small groups.
Contacts are made, visits are arranged, mutual learning takes place
and the transatlantic explorers return to their home country to make
whatever use they can of what they have discovered. This model
can be enormously powerful for the individuals involved. But it is
not easy for those who participate in such exchanges to translate
what they have learned into appropriate initiatives in their home
country. When they return they may feel isolated, they may find
colleagues are unsympathetic to the imported ideas, and they
almost certainly lack advice on how to make international policy
transfer work on the ground.

On the other hand, there is an increasingly active cross-national
academic exchange of ideas and approaches. The field of
comparative government and politics is well established and
numerous texts are available which attempt to compare and contrast
alternative approaches in different countries - not just to understand
the variety of political systems but also to formulate and test
hypotheses about the political process (Hague and Harrop, 1987;
Heidenheimer et al, 1990). Whilst most of this literature is

restricted to comparison of national politics and government, there has in recent years been a welcome growth of interest in comparative urban policy and city government. Several of these texts focus on Anglo-American comparisons (Barnekov et al, 1989; Hambleton, 1990; Keating, 1991; Logan and Swanstrom, 1990; Wolman and Goldsmith, 1992). These various cross-national studies are useful in providing frames of reference within which discussion of the possibilities for urban policy transfer can take place. However, a limitation is that, with some exceptions, they tend to be written at a fairly general level. As a result, it may be difficult for the busy policy maker to see what relevance the discussions have for decision making in the here and now.

This book, which is concerned with policies for people in cities, attempts to make connections between these two realms. It seeks to make a contribution both to the academic discourse about urban policies and urban governance and also to pressing public policy debates about alternative strategies for improving the quality of life in cities. At one level it offers a series of cross-national reflections on the nature of urban governance, on the way the institutional context shapes policies and on the importance of taking account of the cultural differences between countries when considering policy transfer. At another level, it provides a string of grounded discussions of the effectiveness of various policies in practice. What policies for people in cities are being pursued in the USA? How are these policies performing? What are the possibilities for cross-national policy transfer? These are the sort of questions addressed in subsequent chapters.

In October 1991, with the support of the Harkness Fellowships, a transatlantic conference was organised at the School for Advanced Urban Studies, University of Bristol. Most of the chapters in this book first appeared as papers at the conference which set out to raise the quality of debate about the effectiveness of US policies for cities and to explore the relevance of US approaches for UK policy making in the 1990s. The conference, which was well attended by senior policy makers from central and local government and elsewhere, generated a good deal of useful discussion and it was felt that steps should be taken to disseminate the findings to a wider audience. Contributors agreed to revise their papers and, to strengthen the collection, we commissioned two additional chapters: Chapter 2 by Mayor Kurt Schmoke of Baltimore on city leadership and urban regeneration and Chapter 11 by Philip Leather and Sheila Mackintosh on neighbourhood housing renewal.

In this opening chapter we outline some of the main dimensions of the debate about policies for people in cities and about the potential for cross-national policy transfer. Three general points should be made at the outset. First, all of the chapters were written before the election of President Clinton in November 1992. At the national level new US policies for cities are beginning to emerge and we return to this point in the final chapter. Second, the focus of this collection is on the possibilities for transfer from the USA to the UK. This is not to imply that policy transfer in the opposite direction is unimportant - on the contrary the process is clearly two-way. Nevertheless, whilst we hope that this book will be of interest to American colleagues, the main aim of the contributions is to offer insights for those concerned with UK public policy. Third, consistent with our desire to link the worlds of academia and practice, the authors of various chapters write from a diversity of perspectives and in a variety of styles. There are chapters by leading city politicians in both the UK and the USA, by a variety of policy professionals (working in and outside the public sector) and by American and British academics. No claim is made that the book offers a comprehensive review of all policies for cities. Inevitably, there are omissions. We do, however, believe that the contributors address some of the most pressing issues now confronting those concerned with formulating policies for people in cities.

The book is structured around the following four cross-cutting themes.

Part 1   *Strategic leadership and political management*

Local government has a crucial orchestrating role to play in future policy making for cities and the first three chapters explore new possibilities for urban leadership and urban management.

Part 2   *Working across the boundaries*

Few now argue that the public sector working in isolation can be effective in addressing urban problems. Successful strategies involve working across the boundaries of the public, private and voluntary sectors. Three very different chapters explore this theme in some depth.

Part 3   *Crime and policing*

Urban disorders in both the UK and the USA have catapulted law and order onto the public policy agenda. The two chapters on crime and policing deal with aspects of US policing which have been neglected in ongoing media coverage of urban unrest.

Part 4   *Community renewal and empowerment*

At root many of the problems encountered in cities can be traced to the fact that many citizens feel powerless to influence events. It follows that effective strategies need to empower citizens - to give them a genuine role in decision making - and three chapters explore different aspects of this theme.

Cross-national comparisons

The inner cities of the UK are, as in the USA, the pressure points of our society. As the economy has moved from rural to urban to industrial to post-industrial, it is in the inner cities that the effects of economic restructuring have been most sharply felt. Whether they are seen through the eyes of a Hogarth or a Dickens, a Charles Booth or a Seebohm Rowntree, or now on our television screens and in the pages of the press, the images of the inner city have overwhelmingly been those of despair (the term 'inner city' is not used to describe Knightsbridge or Kensington). But to see inner areas simply as problem areas is to deny their considerable and often wasted potential. Apart from their central location, they have many other advantages: "The diversity of their populations, the size of their markets, the cultural assets of their buildings and institutions and the frequent breadth of their economies" (Solesbury, 1986, p 400). Urban policy, while triggered by the all too visible crises of the inner city, should be a constant search for ways of releasing that potential.

In addressing inner city issues, the UK has often looked to the USA for ideas: from the US War on Poverty of the 1960s to current debates about community development corporations and the possibility of strengthening city leadership by introducing the 'strong mayor' form of local government. Some argue that, as central government policy moves away from welfare provided by the state towards market models, it is fruitful to examine the experience of the USA (Hambleton, 1990). Certainly, a good deal of transatlantic urban policy transfer seems to be taking place. But is this desirable? If it is, how far is it possible to transfer policies developed under US conditions to the UK? What lessons - good and bad - can we learn from the USA? At the outset, we want to stress that it is unhelpful to adopt a stance which is 'for' or 'against' US models. Such a stance is simplistic if not crass. The reality of the US experience is complex and subtle; in some respects US policies for cities are bold and imaginative, in other ways US models are disturbing, even alarming. It follows that the aim of cross-national comparison should be to examine the evidence with care to identify lessons, whether negative or positive, which can enhance understanding as well as inform debate about the future direction of policy. There can be no substitute for careful analysis of what policies work in what contexts and why.

Critics of inner city policies in the 1960s and 1970s argue that the UK ignored the reservations that US advisers expressed about the way the policies were being transferred at that time (Loney, 1983). Today, too, it is possible to argue that too much has been based on too little - that ideas and policies have been borrowed on the basis of anecdote rather than analysis (Wolman, 1992). Inevitably, visits to any other country to look at what seem to be promising initiatives expose policy makers to showcase examples, enthusiasts and advocates rather than to the complex reality of policy implementation. City councils and chambers of commerce, once absorbed by the hype of 'civic boosterism', cannot be expected to draw attention to policy failure or neglect. When enthusiasm becomes an important element of policy implementation, dispassionate analysis is often the casualty.

Despite the rhetoric about US urban 'success stories', evidence about the actual impact of US urban regeneration schemes is far from comforting (Barnekov et al, 1989; Hambleton, 1990, 1991). Thus, areas of astonishing urban devastation often lie only a few minutes' walk from the show-piece 'renaissance' sites. For example, the gleaming downtown development areas of St Louis are scarcely any distance from the urban dereliction to the north or across the Mississippi in East St Louis. Another example is provided by Houston, the 'oil capital of the world'. Here, unrestrained free enterprise has brought rapid expansion over the past 20 years but also air and water pollution, development chaos, transport and traffic seizure along with familiar social costs

(Feagin, 1988). Evidence of this kind does not mean that there is no value in looking at these policies. Failure, as Wolman (1992) points out, can tell us what approaches to avoid. It can also help us to determine what aspects of a policy need to be changed if it is to succeed.

Cross-national policy transfer is a fascinating but treacherous field. Not only do the differences between governments have to be taken into account, but local differences within any one country can be substantial: an example from one city may not work in another. In his analysis of US city government, Sharpe remarks:

> Nowhere is this more true than in the United States where each state has evolved over a lengthy period its own inimitable style of urban government and where, within each state, urban areas have adopted different forms so that even within one state more variety may be apparent than in other national systems. (Sharpe, 1973, p 3)

In these circumstances, we must guard against generalising too freely. Major political, cultural, social, economic, racial, legal, historical and geographical differences need to be recognised.

Notwithstanding these reservations there are three good reasons for engaging in systematic comparison of public policies (Heidenheimer et al, 1990):

- to look for guidance in designing better policies;

- to gain a deeper understanding of how government institutions and political processes operate as they deal with concrete problems;

- to understand the growing interdependence between countries that is a hallmark of our times.

A fourth argument for examining US trends is purely practical. Whether or not there are far-reaching differences between UK and US society, it remains the case that specific policies or ideas can be transferred across the Atlantic. Indeed this kind of policy transfer has been taking place for many years. So how can this process be made more systematic?

Inner cities - defining 'the problem'

The problems of inner city areas are well documented and do not need rehearsing here in any great detail. High unemployment rates, poor housing, declining services, high levels of crime, racial tension and high dependence on income support leave communities struggling against impossible odds. Welfare agencies report high case loads, people with skills and resources move out, and high stress causes family and community breakdown.

People in cities come from all walks of life. But with increasing home ownership and gentrification of the more desirable locations, people who have little or no choice are likely to find themselves trapped in particular parts of the city and the divide between those who 'have' and those who 'have not' acquires geographical as well as financial dimensions. There has been talk here, as in the USA, of a growing underclass, defined by its exponents as people who are beyond the reach of welfare services and who no longer accept the norms of society at large (Murray, 1990). Nor is urban stress confined to the inner cities: the marginalisation of inner city populations to outer estates, often inaccessible and devoid of facilities, has exacerbated the experience of alienation and added isolation to the problems experienced by inner city residents.

This brief description would be familiar to most US colleagues. There, too, economic change is having an increasingly uneven impact and social divisions *within* cities are growing. Indeed it can be argued that social polarisation has gone much further. A recent study of poverty rates in the USA provides startling evidence which shows that the gap between the rich and the poor is very wide and is growing remorselessly. Figures published by the US Committee on Ways and Means indicate that:

> Between 1979 and 1989, while the richest 20% of the population had gained substantially in their income (by more than 20%, when adjusted for household composition, federal income taxes, and the cash value of benefits in kind), the poorest 20% experienced a reduction of 2%. (Townsend, 1992, p 19)

This study showed that poor households with children did much worse with some experiencing an 18% drop in their cash income during this 10 year period.

Policy responses to these problems have been based on a variety of explanations of the inner city 'problem': individual pathology, alienation and, more recently, theories of an underclass; multiple deprivation and the need for positive discrimination to equip the disadvantaged to compete; system dysfunction and the need for corporate planning and social engineering; lack of investment and the need for economic development; and adaptation of cities to global shifts, with some commentators arguing that we are witnessing a fundamental transformation in the nature of urban governance from managerialism to entrepreneurialism (Harvey, 1989).

The policy response

In the 1960s and 1970s the political language was of deprivation and disadvantage. Positive discrimination sought to redress the balance through the targeting of particular areas and groups. A variety of special programmes emerged which resulted in a modest redistribution of resources. The Urban Programme, the Community Development Projects, the Inner Area Studies and the Comprehensive Community Programme represented a range of rational 'social engineering' approaches, from community development, through research to better understand and target social problems, to corporate planning between central and local government and other actors (Hambleton, 1978). The Urban Programme provided funds in partnership with local authorities for smaller-scale locally initiated projects.

Most were pilot programmes. Only the Urban Programme, the most extensive of the programmes, survives today, and even this programme was subjected to dramatic expenditure cuts in November 1992 (Hambleton, 1993). The Community Development Projects and the Inner Area Studies came to the conclusion that inner city problems had structural roots and required major policy change at national and international level, not piecemeal local programmes (Loney, 1983). The Community Development Projects' critical analysis caused particular disquiet and embarrassment among government sponsors at the time, but its insistence on the structural nature of local problems is largely accepted today.

Rising unemployment and economic recession could only worsen the plight of the inner cities. The urban unrest of the early 1980s (riots in St Paul's, Bristol, in 1980 followed by major troubles in numerous cities in 1981) gave a new spur to inner city policy. However, under a new government, committed to rolling back the frontiers of the welfare state and to a new set of solutions, the emphasis shifted to wealth creation and private sector led strategies (Stewart, 1987).

The Conservative government removed restrictions on development and wooed private industry to invest in the inner cities, in the style of the Victorian city fathers. The priorities of the Urban Programme were recast, with an emphasis on economic rather than social objectives. The role of local authorities was reduced with the setting up of task forces and urban development corporations: a move which undermined the powers of local government (Colenutt and Tansley, 1990).

Inner city policy received a boost after the 1987 elections when inner cities were given high priority in a post-election speech by Margaret Thatcher, then prime minister. Early 1988 saw the high-profile launch of the Action for Cities programme by central government (Cabinet Office, 1988). This saw the private sector as playing the key role in regenerating inner cities and stressed the theme 'helping businesses to succeed'. However, critics argued that new strategies were in fact a restatement of existing programmes.

In November 1990 Margaret Thatcher was ousted as prime minister. On taking over the leadership John Major brought Michael Heseltine back into government and, during his second spell as Secretary of State for the Environment, he appeared to press for a more conciliatory approach towards local government. Thus, Heseltine's City Challenge initiative of May 1991 invited selected local authorities to draw up programmes of action 'to tackle their key neighbourhoods' and to bid for central government funds. Private sector involvement remains a key criterion for the assessment of these bids and there is a strong emphasis on lateral working across the public, private, voluntary and academic communities.

The general shift in urban policy from social to economic regeneration in the UK followed closely on a similar change in the USA, with 'privatism' as the dominant ideology:

> Privatism stresses the social as well as economic importance of private initiative and competition, and it legitimises the public consequences of private action. Its legacy is that both personal and community well-being are evaluated largely in terms of fulfilment of private aspirations and the achievements of private institutions. (Barnekov et al, 1989, p 1)

The dominant ideology in the USA during the 1980s was, as in the UK, that of the 'new right' (Green, 1987; King, 1987). This argues that high levels of public expenditure 'crowd out' resources from the private sector of the economy. This view is, of course, contested by opposition parties who argue that the emphasis on paving the way for the private sector has gone too far. Having said that, all the main parties now agree that the private sector has a very important role in urban regeneration. This theme of engaging the private sector is explored in several chapters: in Chapter 2 Kurt Schmoke discusses private sector participation in urban regeneration projects in Baltimore; in Chapter 5 Nicholas Falk examines various forms of public/private sector partnership; and in Chapter 7 Richard Bolsin considers how businesses can work with local schools.

In both the USA and the UK, there has been a proliferation of urban initiatives. Some have been imported to the UK, others have been exported to the US. For example, the UK urban development grants (which were later renamed city grants) were closely modelled on the US urban development action grants originally launched by the Carter administration in 1977. The dominant features of US urban policy in recent years have been twofold: the rise of urban growth coalitions, often led by business elites, which act in partnership to tackle regeneration; and civic boosterism, or place marketing. The latter involves aggressive marketing of the city as a 'commodity' in an attempt to build a climate of business confidence and following this up with financial incentives to attract private sector investment. The cost effectiveness of this approach is questioned by academics on both sides of the Atlantic (Cummings, 1988; Hambleton, 1990; Logan and Swanstrom, 1990).

The policy setting: a changing institutional environment

Solutions to the inner city 'problem' are shaped by the overall policy framework set down by higher levels of government. In the US context there are, of course, two levels of government above the level of the city - the state level and the federal level. During the 1980s the Reagan administration pursued a policy, not of federal intervention, but of federal policy withdrawal. A consequence of this is that, in many parts of the country, the states have become more heavily involved in urban policy making. The US strategy of reducing central government interference is seen as leading to better programme coordination and more efficient use of resources. The contrast with the growth in the last decade or so of Whitehall intervention in British local government could hardly be more striking.

Economic regeneration in the UK has taken place in the context of central government policies which seek, first, to transfer service delivery to independent providers and, second, to restrict state responsibility for financing public services, placing more responsibility on the individual, the family, the community and business. These are all policies which borrow heavily from US models.

These moves towards market models are creating a new institutional environment. In the 1960s inner city policies revolved around local government. Now a range of independent providers, central government agencies, opted out services, management and employee buy-outs and public/private hybrids are emerging. Local industry is being encouraged to play a greater role across the board and the financial institutions have been urged to adopt a more imaginative approach.

However, to suggest that the buck has been passed from the public sector to the private and voluntary sectors is to over-simplify. Rein has commented on the "third terrain" that exists, both in the UK and the USA, between government and private institutions, a terrain that is both public and private: "Perhaps modern industrial society is best characterised by the expansion of this fuzzy and ill-defined territory" (Rein, 1989, p 51). To understand this new territory, he argues, is essential to future policy. In our view, this expansion could offer the possibility of a more flexible and diverse response. Or it could lead to fragmentation, duplication and wasted energies.

In the USA contracting with voluntary organisations is fairly common, particularly in the fields of recreation, health, human services, arts/culture and employment/training, although there are marked variations across the country. In the UK there is widespread concern that, as voluntary organisations become increasingly involved in the contract culture, they will lose their independence.

The role of government has changed but not disappeared. At best government is released, as another US commentator suggests, to do what it does best: "raising resources and setting societal policies through a democratic political process, while utilising the private sector for what it does best - organising the production of goods and services" (Salamon, 1989, pp 10-11). This "third-party government", he suggests, requires new forms of public management: "Instead of command and control ... bargaining and persuasion.   Instead of the clarification of directives ... the manipulation of incentives" (Salamon, 1989, p 13). In this sense, it reflects trends in management in the private sector towards decentralisation and federalism with a small strategic centre and leadership which offers incentives rather than commands (Handy, 1989).

If the resources available through this new institutional environment are to be used to best advantage to provide a better quality of life, there will need to be some orchestration. This offers a positive new role for local government in the UK and there has been much talk of the 'enabling authority'. Rather than "working within the boundaries" of the public sector, local authorities are increasingly "working across the boundaries" of the public, private and voluntary sectors (Stewart and Taylor, 1993). This, of course, has been a key theme in recent central government policy towards local government.   The government consultation paper on the internal management of local authorities in England rightly points out that: "The people who run local councils increasingly need different skills to meet the challenge of their developing role as enablers rather than providers" (Department of the Environment, 1991, p 2). But enabling requires resources and authority which, because of the centralisation of power in Whitehall, urban authorities find to be in short supply. Will local governments of the future be encouraged to play a leadership role? Or will other local actors be competing for this role?

In the USA local government retains an essential role, both as financier and as planning authority.   In Boston, for example, developers of downtown sites are required to make a contribution towards housing and job training in the city, through a linkage programme, which stipulates proportional payments into a housing and a jobs fund. British local authorities do not have the legal framework to do this, and many urban authorities feel hampered by financial restraint and the prospect of council tax capping.

Massive cuts in central government financial support to local government in the 1980s are common to both countries.   Indeed, the spending cuts imposed in some US cities are far worse than anything in the UK and a growing number of cities are in a state of financial collapse: for example, East St Louis. City authorities are having to manage with less, are under growing pressure to privatise many of their services and are being urged to become more entrepreneurial.

There are four important differences between local governments in the two countries. First, US local government is *more diverse*, and in a sense this adds to the complexity of the institutional environment. There are, to British eyes, a staggering 83,000 local governments in the USA: city governments, cities, counties, towns and townships as well as school districts and special districts for all sorts of purposes from sewage disposal to mosquito abatement. Of the 83,000, some 39,000 are general local authorities, which are most nearly comparable with UK local authorities for they are elected, and raise and spend funds on a range of functions.

Second, US city governments usually *separate legislative from executive power*. As discussed more fully by Lavery in Chapter 4 there are two main forms - mayor-council and council-manager - and two broad types of mayor-council government. In both mayor-council types voters elect the council members to serve on the council and the individual politician to serve as mayor. The weak mayor type gives the mayor relatively unimportant administrative powers relative to the council. Under the strong mayor arrangement the mayor has formidable administrative powers: he or she can veto legislation passed by the council, hire and fire chief officers and set the budget. The council-manager form is rather different. The council acting rather like a board of directors lays down the policies and expects all executive action to be taken by the city manager and his or her staff. The distinction between the mayor-council and the council-manager forms is, however, starting to blur as the latter are introducing elected mayors alongside the city manager.

A third difference relates to the *nature of local politics*. In US local government personality can be very important because in local elections candidates are not identified by party on the ballot. Indeed, in many municipalities elections are 'non-partisan'. In 'partisan' systems candidates are chosen by primary elections open to any declared member of the party - no dues or formal membership are required (Stoker and Wolman, 1992).

It is clear that the strengthening of party politics in local government in the UK during the 1980s is quite different from US experience. The ideological intensity and general polarisation of party political activity at local level often surprises American visitors. This polarisation of local government is likely to be lasting, according to the Widdicombe Report (1986, p 15). US city councils are, by contrast, much less likely to be riven with ideological conflicts. In Chapter 3 Steve Bullock offers a series of reflections on the nature of city leadership in the UK context which suggests that US models will need considerable adaptation if they are to be successfully imported.

However, it is also possible to suggest that city politics in the UK is moving towards a US form in the sense that party politics is becoming more pluralistic. The electorate is certainly more heterogeneous that it was 10 years ago - class is no longer the only important political cleavage. According to surveys, a smaller proportion of the electorate identifies with any one political party. There is a larger floating vote and British people are increasingly ready to protest and assert themselves politically on single issues that concern them (Young, 1984). Organisations based around neighbourhood, ethnicity, gender and specific issues (such as homelessness or transport policy) are increasingly active.

Finally, the *systems for financing local government* are rather different. While property taxes are central in the USA, some councils generate funds from local sales taxes, hotel room taxes and local income taxes and so on. Budget restraint comes from below, as in the case of the famous voter-initiated Proposition 13 in California, rather than from above through local tax capping. In essence Proposition 13 stated that, for both houses and businesses, property taxes should be limited to 1% of the total value of the property. Many other states emulated the Californian initiative and this has eroded a key source of income for many US city councils (Hambleton, 1990, pp 37-42).

Before leaving this discussion of the changing institutional environment it is important to flag another difference between the US and British policy setting. In urging individuals and businesses to give more to charity and invest more in their communities, the UK government seeks to emulate the philanthropic tradition of the USA. Certainly, there may well be scope for increased giving from these sources but the philanthropic tradition is a great deal stronger in the USA than in this country. As Sandra Newton explains in Chapter 6 the role of the church is crucial in this.

The policy setting: community resources, consumerism and citizenship

The crucial inner city resource is its population - a reality often overlooked in development policies which have often displaced indigenous populations or benefited outsiders to the detriment of the original residents (Hausner and Robson, 1985). Labelled as 'the problem', people in cities are too frequently ignored in the formulation of policies affecting their communities. But it has often been the insensitivity of institutions - public and private - which has aggravated the difficulties people already experience: the departure of an important industry; housing developments which fail to take people's needs into account; or transport decisions which isolate a community with few cars.

To focus on the indicators of disadvantage in inner cities is to compound the stigmatisation and intensify the problems of the people who live there. The investment of the 1970s and early 1980s showed how community energies can be released, derelict areas transformed, employment prospects improved, community buildings developed as the centre of local activities and services, and confidence regained (Taylor, 1988). Employers who want a pool of locally trained labour and a workforce which is committed to the community, developers who want to attract new investment into the area, social work agencies who want to generate networks of community care, probationers who want to rehabilitate offenders within the community and police who want to prevent criminal activity; all have been able to work more sensitively and effectively in partnership with community networks to the benefit of each partner.

Many UK community initiatives developed against a background of local and central government funding, particularly through the Community Programme of the then Manpower Services Commission. Funding to *all* voluntary organisations from central and local government nearly doubled over the first two terms of the Conservative administration and, as one of the authors has argued elsewhere, community based empowerment organisations benefited considerably from the battle between central and local government of the early 1980s (Taylor, 1992).

However, during the second and third terms of the Conservative government, spending on the voluntary sector by local authorities has struggled to keep up with inflation (see, for example, Charities Aid Foundation, 1991, p 88). Some metropolitan authorities, and hence inner cities, have been particularly hard hit, first by central government capping of local tax revenues and, more recently, by the introduction of new forms of local taxation (the 'poll tax' and, in 1993, the council tax). Meanwhile, grants through non-departmental public bodies have declined dramatically, largely because of the disappearance of the Community Programme and cutbacks in its successor, Employment Training. And we have already referred to the drastic November 1992 cuts in Urban Programme funding.

Yet again, this is a scenario that has echoes in the USA where federal funding was cut back during the Reagan administration. Local administrations were able to pick up some of the pieces and the continued availability of the community development block grant has benefited some areas. But public money for community organising, as opposed to community housing and economic developments, is now increasingly hard to come by.

The overriding ideology shaping UK central government policy is that individuals will gain more control over the environment they live in and the services they use through the operation of the market. If there is adequate competition and choice, individuals will go for the services they prefer and those which do not pass muster will go the wall. Service consumers will now have the option of 'exit' to another provider (Hirschman, 1970), assuming of course that they have the information on which to make choices and the advocacy to make them stick.

There are a number of problems with this analysis. First, not all services are open to choice - public goods, such as the environment, are consumed by all of us and there are limitations on our exit option. Second, giving choice to some consumers may leave less choice for others - rising home ownership, for example, has accompanied a steep rise in homelessness.

Many people in inner cities would be more appropriately described as recipients of services rather than consumers, in that they lack choice. Because of poverty or lack of mobility they have little or no choice over the services they use. Indeed the fact that they use particular services demonstrates their lack of choice. Such service recipients, who do not have the 'exit' option need to be able to influence services through, to use Hirschman's term, 'voice'. That is, they need to be able to express their dissatisfaction directly and effectively to those providing services or, more radically, to exercise direct control over the running of these services themselves.

It is arguable whether contracting out can make this possible. Another American author argues that:

> the contract relationship offers a major advantage over the public sector, in that it allows both exit and voice mechanisms to be activated, in the event that the service quality declines or does not meet the contractor's specifications. (de Hoog, 1985)

The user has access to the purchaser, through the democratic process. It is also possible for the purchaser to specify some form of consumer involvement and redress in the contract, or for consumers to be involved in management (as are parents, at least, in opted out schools). There is a problem, however, in that a presumption of the contract model is that the needs of the service can be fully specified before the contract is let. This is difficult and works against innovation during the contract period.

The second problem is that choice depends on the variety that is made available to choose from. An older person from a minority ethnic background may be offered a variety of choices by a meals on wheels service. But if he or she follows a particular religious diet and this is not catered for, he or she has no choice. Putting services out to contract does not in itself provide choice, especially where it is the purchaser rather than the consumer who is selecting the contractor. The option of 'voice' needs to be available if people in cities are to influence the overall pattern of provision that is made available in their area. In doing so, they begin to cross the line from being consumers to being citizens with an interest wider than their own service consumption (Hambleton and Hoggett, 1990, pp 21-24; Taylor et al, 1992).

Services do not operate in isolation. The quality of life in an inner city area will depend on the interaction between different services and between different institutions, rather than on any one service. If people in cities are to influence this, two things are needed. First, as has been indicated, some mechanism is needed to orchestrate the energies and interests of different players in the inner city arena and, second, channels are needed through which people in cities can influence this mechanism. If, as suggested earlier, it is government which is best placed to provide the orchestration, the democratic process provides, in theory at least, the channel through which people can exercise their voice. How far this is true in reality in a situation where the role of local government - and hence of local democracy - is under great pressure is an issue which deserves far greater attention.

'Consumerism' and the changes that have gone with it, represent a bold step forward from the bureaucratic paternalism which has characterised professionalised public services in both the UK and the USA for so many years. A risk, however, is that by concentrating on people as consumers rather than as citizens, we may move into an era of new style 'managerial paternalism'. Local government is about more than providing services, it is about the development of citizenship. Many councils on both sides of the Atlantic recognise this and are putting energy into reform strategies which put the emphasis on community development by, for example, strengthening public involvement in local government, decentralising decision making, and introducing neighbourhood policies and programmes (Carmon, 1990).

Several chapters explore the importance of developing strategies in concert with local people. In Chapter 8 Jon Bright stresses this in relation to youth crime prevention and, in Chapter 9, Karamjit Singh suggests that policing strategies must stem from community consultation and enjoy community support if they are to hope to be effective. In Chapter 10 Alex Norman extends the discussion by exploring the role that community development can play in inner city areas and subsequent chapters examine community involvement in neighbourhood housing renewal (Philip Leather and Sheila Mackintosh in Chapter 11) and health care (Penny Morris in Chapter 12).

Planning for the future

Inner cities, both in the UK and the USA, will be affected in the future by population trends which suggest an increasing imbalance between the economically active and inactive populations. For example, within the growing older population the proportion of frail older people is increasing. Trends towards more single person households, higher divorce rates and more single parent families will put more pressure on housing and support services. If current experience is anything to go by, the closure of mental hospitals and institutions for people with learning difficulties is likely to bring more vulnerable people onto inner city streets. Rising homelessness and the current recession with the increase in jobless totals will also continue to put pressure on inner city populations.

Inner cities in the UK are likely to be influenced by European developments as decisions about the economy are increasingly taken in Brussels. Some inner cities have already acted as magnets to people from marginal areas in the UK looking for work. Will they be joined by people from beyond the UK and what are the implications of this? Within cities, people already marginal to the workforce may find themselves even more marginalised. Supranational changes in the institutional environment create new challenges for those working at the local level in local government, in local firms, and in the voluntary and community sectors (Baine et al, 1991). The influence of multinational industry remains paramount as city leaders and managers compete for capital investment and tourism across the globe. There is already a depressing similarity in city centre developments as supposed formulas for success are copied from country to country.

Centralising economic forces are, however, balanced by decentralising forces as new technology makes single site, mass production less necessary. Self-employment in the UK is on the increase and trade union membership is decreasing. Multinational industries are decentralising and giving more decision-making power to subsidiary parts of the organisation. The diversification of politics that was referred to earlier is an interesting parallel to this. Commercial decentralisation could well increase opportunities to involve local businesses in local initiatives. But, as better off people are offered more choice about the way they work and where they work, inner cities which were based on major centralised industrial developments may well find themselves increasingly isolated from the economic mainstream. The development of out-of-town supermarkets, shopping malls and business parks (all first developed in the USA) are examples of the way in which investment is moving away from inner areas in many cities.

A number of other changes are in progress which will affect the future urban policy agenda. Here just three are mentioned. First, many cities in their search for new roles in an era of deindustrialisation have turned to the arts and culture as vehicles for urban regeneration. The dominant approach has been to use the arts as a catalyst for economic promotion and development. However, the effectiveness of this model is being questioned and an alternative approach to 'cultural planning' is being developed in some cities (Griffiths, 1993). Such policies focus sharply on the day-to-day quality of life in the contemporary city and address concerns like the fear of walking alone on the streets, the mistrust of strangers, the decline of conviviality, the sameness of city centres, the disappearance of vibrant public spaces and the squalor of the public realm (Comedia, 1991). This approach has less to do with the construction of grand cultural buildings and much more to do with the details of urban design and street furniture, policies for street lighting and night-time public transport, creative support to locally based 'cultural industries' and the recreation of a welcoming public realm.

A second trend which we see emerging in the 1990s is a growing recognition of the need to engage in the strategic planning of whole cities. In this area it is probably the case that cities in Europe are ahead of their US counterparts. The notion of strategic planning is more highly developed in the UK context and debates about the need for 'sustainable development' are certainly more advanced than in the USA, although the strategic metropolitan counties were abolished in the mid 1980s. There is no room for complacency but at least in Europe there is an agenda of environmental issues - the European Community *Green paper on the urban environment* (Commission of the European Communities, 1990) - which many cities are beginning to address.

The third trend relates to the growing social polarisation within cities. The way that economic change is having an increasingly uneven impact on cities was mentioned earlier. In September 1991, 10 years after Michael Heseltine, then Secretary of State for the Environment, announced his private sector orientated inner city policy to the House of Commons, there were outbreaks of public disorder in peripheral and inner estates in a number of cities: including the Meadowell estate in North Tyneside, the Elswick and Scotswood area of Newcastle, and the Lawrence Weston estate in Bristol. In 1992 there were further incidences of unrest in Wood End, Coventry; in the Ordsall area of Salford; in Hartcliffe, Bristol; and in Blackburn, Burnley and Huddersfield. Whilst the scale of the devastation does not begin to compare with the destruction in Los Angeles in April 1992, these troubles are significant because they are the latest in an increasingly long line of periodic disturbances in disadvantaged areas which began to occur in the 1980s. Clearly a key task for urban policy in the 1990s is to reduce the social and economic divisions found within cities. Without specific initiatives there is a danger that civilised living will collapse in at least parts of some UK cities.

Conclusion

To conclude this chapter we return to the theme of cross-national policy transfer introduced earlier. Wolman (1992) has provided a helpful checklist of factors which should be taken into account in transferring lessons from one country to another. He argues that the 'recipient' country should assess:

● how similar the problem in the originating country is to their own;

● how successful the policy was in the originating country;

● how the policy setting in the originating country compares to their own.

These three questions are examined in more detail in Chapter 13, drawing on the material presented in the body of the book. For the moment, in relation to the first point it has already been suggested that many of the social and economic problems faced by inner cities in the UK and the USA are, broadly speaking, similar. They raise important questions about how rapid economic change can be handled, how the social tensions created by economic restructuring can be dealt with and who should take responsibility. We have also argued that the dominant ideology which shapes the definition of the problem has been similar in both countries. In this context we have identified the empowerment of people in cities as citizens and consumers as a key factor which should be taken into account in urban policy evaluation.

In relation to the second point, it has been suggested that showcase US urban regeneration projects cannot be considered entirely successful. Indeed, they may reinforce the problems faced by the casualties of economic change. But there is much to be learned from failure as well as success and policies do not have to be considered on an all-or-nothing basis. It has also been suggested that some features of US approaches appear to be full of potential. For example, local authorities have more autonomy, there is great diversity in the form of local government, and there is a good deal of working across the boundaries of the public, private and voluntary sectors.

In relation to the third point about the policy setting, whilst some significant differences have been noted, it has been suggested that an explosion of institutional forms and a blurring of sectors is common to both countries. Historically the institutional and cultural context has been very different but there are, we contend, elements of convergence. There are, however, important differences in the relationship between national and local government in the two countries and in the traditions of local government itself. In this context, leadership in the new, rather than the old, management language is needed - inspiration and orchestration rather than uniformity and control.

References

Baine, S., Benington, J. and Russell, J. (1991) *Changing Europe: challenges facing the voluntary and community sectors in the 1990s*, London: Community Development Foundation.

Barnekov, T., Boyle, R. and Rich, D. (1989) *Privatism and urban policy in Britain and the US*, Oxford: Oxford University Press.

Cabinet Office (1988) *Action for cities*, London: HMSO.

Carmon, N. (ed) (1990) *Neighbourhood policy and programmes*, London: Macmillan.

Charities Aid Foundation (1991) *Charity trends: 14th edition*, Tonbridge: Charities Aid Foundation.

Colenutt, B. and Tansley, S. (1990) *Inner city regeneration: a local authority perspective*, First year report on the urban development corporations, Manchester: Centre for Local Economic Strategies.

Comedia (1991) *Out of hours: a study of economic, social and cultural life in twelve town centres in the UK*, London: Comedia.

Commission of the European Communities (1990) *Green paper on the urban environment*, Brussels: Commission of the European Communities.

Cummings, S. (ed) (1988) *Business elites and urban developments: case studies and critical perspectives*, Albany: State University of New York Press.

de Hoog, R. (1985) 'Human services contracting: environmental, behavioural and organisational conditions', *Administration and Society*, vol 16, no 4, pp 427-54.

Department of the Environment (1991) *The internal management of local authorities in England: a consultation paper*, London: HMSO.

Feagin, J.R. (1988) 'Tallying the social costs of urban growth under capitalism', in S. Cummings (ed) *Business elites and urban development*, Albany: State University of New York Press, pp 205-34.

Green, D.G. (1987) *The new right: the counter-revolution in political, economic and social thought*, Brighton: Wheatsheaf.

Griffiths, R. (1993) 'The politics of cultural policy in urban regeneration strategies', *Policy and Politics*, vol 21, no 1, pp 39-46.

Hague, R. and Harrop, M. (1987) *Comparative government and politics: an introduction*, London: Macmillan.

Hambleton, R. (1978) *Policy planning and local government*, London: Hutchinson.

Hambleton, R. (1990) *Urban government in the 1990s: lessons from the USA*, Bristol: SAUS Publications, School for Advanced Urban Studies, University of Bristol.

Hambleton, R. (1991) 'American dreams, urban realities', *The Planner*, 28 June, pp 6-9.

Hambleton, R. (1993) 'Issues for urban policy', *Town Planning Review*, vol 64, no 3, July.

Hambleton, R. and Hoggett, P. (1990) *Beyond excellence: quality local government in the 1990s*, working paper 85, Bristol: SAUS Publications, School for Advanced Urban Studies, University of Bristol.

Handy, C. (1989) *The age of unreason*, London: Business Books.

Harvey, D. (1989) 'From managerialism to entrepreneurialism: the transformation of urban governance in late capitalism', *Geografiska Annaler*, 71B, pp 3-17.

Hausner, V. and Robson, B. (1985) *Changing cities*, London: Economic and Social Research Council.

Heidenheimer, A.J., Heclo, H. and Teich Adams, C. (1990) *Comparative public policy*, New York: St. Martin's Press.

Hirschman, A.O. (1970) *Exit, voice and loyalty: responses to decline in firms, organisations and states*, Harvard University Press.

Keating, M. (1991) *Comparative urban politics: power and the city in the United States, Canada, Britain and France*, Aldershot: Edward Elgar.

King, D.S. (1987) *The new right: politics, markets and citizenship*, London: Macmillan.

Logan, J.R., and Swanstrom, T. (eds) (1990) *Beyond the city limits: urban policy and economic restructuring in comparative perspective*, Philadelphia: Temple University Press.

Loney, M. (1983) *Community against government: the British community development project 1968-78*, London: Heinemann Educational Books.

Murray, C. (1990) *The emerging British underclass*, Choice in Welfare series no 2, London: IEA Health and Welfare Unit.

Rein, M. (1989) 'The social structure of institutions: neither public nor private', in S.B. Kamerman and A.J. Kahn (eds) *Privatisation and the welfare state*, Princeton, New Jersey: Princeton University.

Salamon, L.M. (1989) *Beyond privatisation: the tools of government action*, Washington DC: The Urban Institute Press.

Sharpe, L.J. (1973) 'American democracy reconsidered', parts 1 and 2, *British Journal of Political Science*, vol 3, pp 1-28 and 129-67.

Solesbury, W. (1986) 'The dilemma of inner city', *Public Administration*, vol 64, pp 389-40.

Stewart, M. (1987) 'Ten years of inner cities policy', *Town Planning Review*, vol 58, no 2, pp 129-45.

Stewart, M. and Taylor, M. (1993) *Local government community leadership*, Luton: Local Government Management Board.

Stoker, G. and Wolman, H. (1992) 'Drawing lessons from US experience: an elected mayor for British local government', *Public Administration*, vol 70, pp 241-67.

Taylor, M. (1988) *Releasing enterprise: voluntary organisations and the inner city*, London: National Council for Voluntary Organisations.

Taylor, M. (1992) 'Moving towards the market' in R. Kramer, L. Salamon and B. Gidron (eds) *Government and the non-profit sector: emerging relationships in welfare states*, San Francisco: Jossey Bass.

Taylor, M., Hoyes, L., Lart, R. and Means, R. (1992) *User empowerment in community care: unravelling the issues*, Studies in Decentralisation and Quasi-Markets working paper no 11, Bristol: SAUS Publications, School for Advanced Urban Studies, University of Bristol.

Townsend, P. (1992) 'The power of one', *New Statesman and Society*, 18 September, pp 18-20.

Widdicombe, D. QC (1986) *The conduct of local authority business*, Cmnd 9797, London: HMSO.

Wolman, H. (1992) 'Understanding cross-national policy transfers: the case of Britain and the US', *Governance: an international journal of policy and administration*, January, pp 27-45.

Wolman, H. and Goldsmith, M. (1992) *Urban politics and policy: a comparative approach*, Oxford: Blackwell.

Young (1984) 'Political attitudes', in R. Jowell and S. Witherspoon (eds) *British social attitudes: the 1985 report*, London: Gower.

part one

STRATEGIC LEADERSHIP AND POLITICAL MANAGEMENT

two

LEADERSHIP IN CITIES
A view from the USA

Kurt L. Schmoke

Introduction

I recently told a congressional panel that I am partisan about only one thing: US cities. Unfortunately, for the last 10 years, cities have had few, if any, partisans among the USA's national leaders. Major urban funding programmes have been cut or eliminated. In Baltimore, since 1982, direct federal grants for elementary and secondary education fell from $40.2 million to $27.4 million, community development block grants dropped from $31.3 million to $13.9 million, and federal revenue sharing went from $25.3 million to zero.

So these have not been the best of times for US cities. But they have not been the worst of times either. Cities are finding ways to rejuvenate themselves, in the way wild flowers manage to spring up even in the most desolate of inner city areas. Moreover, with the change in national leadership, cities now have a friend in Washington. President Clinton has called cities places of expanding opportunity. This is a striking difference from the last 12 years, when cities were viewed primarily as repositories of the poor.

I will talk about the rejuvenation of cities shortly. But first I want to introduce a message I have frequently given in the USA. That is the connection between the health of cities and national security.

Cities and national security

The end of the cold war means that the chances of armed conflict and nuclear war are greatly reduced. Both Europe and the USA are safer now than at any time since World War II. But the cold war diverted billions of dollars from domestic priorities to military hardware. Now it is time to put some of that money back into cities, not only because cities need the money, but because national security - whether in the USA or Europe - will, in large measure, be based on economic power. The engines for this economic power are cities.

Europe has done a much better job than the USA in supporting its cities. I frequently point out that London is not closing its libraries, Berlin is being rebuilt and most European countries pride themselves on, and carefully manage, their cities.

The same has not been true for the USA. That is why I have argued strenuously that congress and the president should recognize that US cities are not obsolete. They are the primary source of workers, capital, research facilities and technical expertise. Cities are also key transportation hubs, exchange points for information and people, university and research centres, and the primary source of new labour. All of which make cities indispensable at a time when economic security is national security.

Taking initiatives at local level

The interesting question about cities is, if the national government is not going to take care of these tools for national and economic security, who is? In Baltimore, the answer has been community groups, businesses and local governments working together to build better schools and neighbourhoods, to speed physical development downtown, to bring minorities into the economic mainstream and to carry on a spirit of self-help in the face of what had been national neglect.

I am, as I frequently like to say, an optimist about cities. Cities are wounded because they are cash poor and the repository of every major social problem from crime to substance abuse to poverty. But as Shakespeare said, the people are the city. And in Baltimore it is people - highly motivated, well organized, with a broad array of skills - who are leading the city's regeneration.

The jewel in the crown of Baltimore's neighbourhood revitalization is a community called Sandtown-Winchester, in which 300 new homes for low and moderate income families are being built at a cost of $24 million. This project actually got its intellectual start in Israel where I visited Kiryat Gat, a city that had been physically and spiritually renewed.

I wanted to see a similar renewal in West Baltimore, and so did a lot of other people and organizations. Among them were BUILD, a multiracial, community-based church and labour organization, and the Enterprise Foundation, a non-profit development company led by Jim Rouse, one of the USA's foremost urban developers. Rouse developed Baltimore's Inner Harbor and the downtowns of several other US cities. He has now turned his outstanding talents to building low and moderate income housing.

As quoted in a recent *Philadelphia Inquirer* article, a researcher at the Urban Institute reportedly said that Jim Rouse and I are "testing a prototype". Actually, the entire Sandtown community is testing a new prototype based on two simple ideas.

First, simply building housing is not enough. Urban revitalization must address the underlying problems of poor neighbourhoods. That means crime, schools, health, adolescent pregnancy and so forth. Housing is just the skeleton. Freedom from despair and poverty is what makes a community an organic, functioning, life-sustaining place. Second, the people who live in the community must lead that march to freedom.

That is what is happening in Sandtown-Winchester. Federal, state and local money and the kind of technical expertise available from the Enterprise Foundation are building the 3,200 homes. But it is the persistence, thinking, organizing and leadership of the people who actually live in Sandtown that are making this project a US success story.

Sandtown already includes a $3 million prenatal care and follow-up outreach which is funded in part by a private foundation and the National Institute of Health. A $2.7 million youth opportunity unlimited programme helps the young people of Sandtown-Winchester with job training, education, and recreation. Several private developers are training young people in Sandtown-Winchester to work in construction. The Baltimore Partnership for Drug-Free Neighbourhoods has a $500,000 grant to develop drug prevention strategies. With government and private sector support, playgrounds are being repaired, trees are being planted and a newsletter is being published. Together, these and other community improvement programmes are putting a beating heart back into Sandtown-Winchester - the kind of heart without which no urban rejuvenation can succeed.

Henry Cisneros, the new Secretary of Housing and Urban Development, recently visited Sandtown-Winchester and expressed his deep admiration for the progress being made there and for the people who live there. I hope that President Clinton and Secretary Cisneros will give us the opportunity to build other Sandtown-Winchesters in Baltimore and will use our model on urban rejuvenation in other US cities.

I started with Sandtown-Winchester because it illustrates the basic elements of a national human services agenda that I believe is absolutely necessary to revitalizing urban communities. Specific jewels such as Sandtown are not enough. There has to be a crown too - a larger overall policy that individual projects fit into.

A policy for cities

The overall policy for cities mentioned above might have three elements.

- Federal non-categorical grants that give cities the flexibility to target resources where they are needed should be provided. That is an idea that mayors all over the world understand.

- Focus should be kept on neighbourhoods and the people who live in them. The histories of those neighbourhoods and the memories and dreams of the people who live in them should be built on. Urban regeneration must be made less bureaucratic and more the product of consensus, partnership and team building.

- Services should be integrated, combining physical development with educational and social services.

To these three elements, I would add the following: a renewed focus on job training; planning ahead for the fact that our population is getting older; using schools as the pivotal neighbourhood institution for providing not only education, but also health care and other family services; developing programmes that are inclusive in that they teach people to do things for themselves; and doing all this with a large measure of private sector support.

What kind of private support is available and how can it be enlisted? An examination of how the private sector has been involved in Baltimore's rejuvenation may throw some light on this question. The history goes back several decades. The Greater Baltimore Committee, which consists of the city's leading businesses, was a driving force behind the rebuilding of downtown Baltimore. What are now Charles Center and the Inner Harbor are in large measure the creation of a public/private partnership. Downtown is now a huge economic and cultural asset for the city. But the work of the business and non-profit sector is not finished. They have to be as equally committed to rebuilding neighbourhoods and social institutions as they were to rebuilding downtown - not simply as a gesture of decency but as a gesture of common sense about our economic future.

The response of the private sector

An example of private sector response is that of the Community Development Financing Corporation (CDFC), an entity created two years ago to loan money for the rehabilitation of vacant houses, of which Baltimore has about 5,000. About three-quarters of the corporation's initial $40 million capitalization came from private lending institutions. Without that money, the corporation would not have got off the ground. As it is, CDFC has already financed the rehabilitation of hundreds of homes, many occupied by low and moderate income families.

A second example of how the private sector has been brought into the city's revitalization is the school/business partnership programme. We now have about 300 school/business partnerships. These businesses understand that future workers and the city's future tax base are in our schools today. So many of these businesses willingly provide equipment, including computers, scholarships and incentives, tutoring, books, career counselling, mentoring and other services. These business partners and their contributions are critically important, especially at a time when the city's schools have a demonstrably unequal share of state education funding, a matter that will soon be a subject of litigation. Also this partnership programme is by no means ad hoc; it has an advisory committee and several sub-committees made up of school and business representatives.

The third example of private sector participation also relates to education. Baltimore has signed a contract with a private company to run nine of its schools. The company has succeeded in other cities and will work in close partnership with the school board, principals, teachers and parents. I think the private sector, with its experience in business management, needs to be more frequently used in traditional government functions, such as education. The privatisation of education is an experiment in Baltimore. It has some opposition, but I am confident that it will succeed and will be only one of many moves towards the provision of private sector government services.

A fourth example of enlisting private sector support and involvement is, in my view, the most important. It has been a top priority to bring minorities and women into the economic mainstream, and I have challenged the private sector to make this mission an important one. Let me first say as a general proposition, that urban regeneration, without a strong minority business community is impossible. Baltimore is already more than 50% non-white. Our tax base, our schools, our ability to control crime, our children's future all depend on the wide availability of economic opportunity. With that in mind, the private sector can make no greater contribution to the renewal of our city than sharing economic power.

Access to the economic mainstream for minorities has come slowly, but it has come. The city is now fully enforcing Ordinance 610 which grants minority enterprises 20% of all city contracts. This ordinance faced several legal obstacles put in its way by a Supreme Court case called *Richmond v. Croson*. In that case the court invalidated a Richmond, Virginia ordinance that set aside a certain percentage of city contracts for minorities. The court found the Richmond law was too rigid and that there had not been a sufficient showing of past discrimination. Unlike many other cities that abandoned similar laws after *Croson*, Baltimore made some adjustments and then successfully defended the ordinance against five separate legal challenges. It is now being fully enforced.

Armed with Ordinance 610, I have over the last several years challenged the private sector to follow the lead of the city: that is, affirmatively hire a certain percentage of minorities to work on private development projects. The challenge is working. Inner Harbor East is a commercial and residential project with a potential value of $300 million. The developers have agreed to abide by the provisions of Ordinance 610.

The same is true for several other large projects. The word is getting around. Bringing minorities into the economic mainstream is not only just, it is good business practice. It means a greater pool of talent, better labour relations, more competition, a larger tax base which creates downward pressure on the property tax rate, less crime and more tourism. In other words, minority hiring is a, if not the, cornerstone of urban regeneration in US cities.

I should add that this basic goal has been taken beyond encouraging the private sector to follow the guidelines of Ordinance 610. In 1992, in a speech to the Greater Baltimore Committee, I challenged them to find new ways to help minority businesses. They have since responded with a plan to pair new minority-owned businesses with established businesses in mentoring relationships.

I have also made inclusiveness a guiding principle of our new 20 year strategy for downtown development. And the downtown partnership, which is a quasi-governmental agency that oversees the maintenance of downtown, is putting together its own plan to help minority businesses in the downtown area.

Conclusion

An article in the July issue of *Atlantic Monthly* posited that the USA has embarked on the "suburban era". This article takes the familiar tack that cities are politically weak and economically obsolete. I reluctantly agree with the first proposition. Over the last two decades, cities have become politically weaker. However, that may now be changing. President Clinton was strongly supported by people living in cities, and that support helped him to carry some states. As for economics, cities matter. I think the USA's slow rate of growth over the last five years is partly attributable to the neglect of cities. This neglect has cost the USA far more than it has saved. Urban crime, drug addiction, homelessness, unemployment and adolescent pregnancy are draining billions of dollars from the US economy.

So I return to where I began: the need for a national policy to rejuvenate cities. State and local government can do more: they can become more efficient; they can find new ways to provide services, including greater reliance on the private sector; they can mobilize the community to do more for itself. But none of this alone, or together, can substitute for a national government that recognizes its own self-interest in helping cities, and its moral obligation to the millions of its citizens who live in cities. In other words, urban regeneration in Baltimore and other cities is moving forward on the strength of those who live in, work in and love cities. With a new federal partner, we will be able to speed the day when that rejuvenation is complete.

three

LEADERSHIP IN CITIES
A view from the UK

Steve Bullock

Cities, large or small, are not natural phenomena. They exist as the result of many individual decisions and acts of will. As the great cities increasingly operate on a world stage while smaller cities seek distinctive regional roles it becomes ever clearer that they need leadership which provides a vision of what the city could become. However, there is a gap between the leadership which provides vision and the leadership which can make vision into reality and this is the area with which this paper is concerned. I will attempt to identify some of the tasks for city leadership and to look at some of the possible sources of that leadership.

To state that citics need leadership is not to prescribe the form, nature or source of that leadership. There is, however, a widely held view that elected local authorities have a special responsibility to provide leadership. This view was strongly held by the former Secretary of State for the Environment, Michael Heseltine, and his City Challenge initiative put this into practice. I will look at how local government attempts to provide leadership, the obstacles placed in its way and also how individual leaders may approach the task. Finally some consideration will be given to how leadership might be strengthened by learning from experience elsewhere.

Who leads?

Cities have many leaders. Some have a role in relation to the city as a whole; others to only a part of it. At the most basic level, leadership involves speaking on behalf of the city. In a fragmented city like London, from which I will inevitably draw many examples, even securing agreement on this advocacy role is not straightforward.

Elected borough councils and their leaders and have a key role to play. Many of the boroughs have the characteristics of small cities in their own right and local leaders who are providing the drive and vision required to halt decline and create the partnerships on which future success can be built. Indeed London has no fewer than 32 elected leaders (one for each London borough) not to mention the Lord Mayor of the City of London whose writ extends no further than the 'square mile' itself. These individual authorities do come together to speak collectively but in recent years this has been based on party divisions with two rival groups both claiming to be the 'voice of London'. In the absence of a regional tier of government it might be expected that national government would fill the vacuum but no individual minister can be identified who has responsibility for London; nor is there any parliamentary committee with such a role.

It is little wonder that others have stepped forward to fill this gap.   Stephen Hayklan, chair of the London region of the Confederation of British Industry (CBI) states:

> Accordingly business people want to demonstrate their preparedness to provide the leadership and vision needed to maintain and enhance London's international competitive status. (Confederation of British Industry, 1991)

However, it should be said that there was little evidence during the 1980s that the private sector was likely to be a source of leadership for the whole city, however effective its leadership within particular areas of business activity.

Equally London, like any great city, has within it a myriad of communities who define themselves by religion, race or geographical location. These communities have their own leaders and any attempt to provide city-wide leadership which ignores them will be disadvantaged. However, there has been little indication that the gulf between community leadership and city leadership is easily bridged.

Since the general election of April 1992 a cabinet subcommittee has been created to deal with London and a junior minister given specific responsibility for transport in the capital. However, the secretive nature of cabinet committees and the lack of dialogue with London's elected representatives or community groups does not indicate that London's leadership vacuum can be filled in this way. The government has now established a new body called the London Forum which consists only of business nominees. However, a linked grouping, London First, although set up by the private sector has been extended to include other interests including local authorities.

It is almost certainly the case that London's lack of leadership is a rather extreme case although other cities do experience the same phenomena, albeit less starkly. Vancouver, for example, appears at first sight to have a coherent city leadership provided by the mayor and city council. However, closer examination reveals that this is confined to the downtown area, which visitors might think of as Vancouver but which the 1.2 million people who live in the Greater Vancouver area outside the formal boundary of Vancouver see very differently. A recent study concluded that Vancouver's future problems, particularly population growth, could not be resolved by existing municipalities but needed powerful leadership which would coincide with the economic and ecological reality of the area (Y See Lig and Artibise, 1991). It is not my purpose to identify a precise form of city-wide government for large cities but rather to examine how leadership operates within cities and draw conclusions which will be valid at the level of the individual borough and the whole city.

Locally elected leaders?

If the responsibility for city leadership does fall on elected municipalities it is worth considering what those municipalities exist to do. Is leadership their principal role or does it arise out of other functions? Equally, do changes to function affect the ability to provide leadership? The clearest distinguishing factor in this context is also the most obvious. The very process of election provides a legitimacy and a universality to local authorities which is unique.

The process of local democracy is, as yet, flawed, as evidenced by low turn-outs at local elections. At the 1990 council election the turn-out in Lewisham was 46%, by no means the lowest in London. By contrast the intensity of the general election campaign produced a turn-out of over 70% in the same area. In 1985 the government of the day asked David Widdicombe QC to head a committee of inquiry into the way local government conducted its business. At the start of the report the committee states:

> Our terms of reference assume the continued existence of democratic local government. This principle, to which we all firmly subscribe, has been the starting point for our work and our recommendations are all intended as a means of strengthening the democratic process at local level. (Widdicombe, 1986)

While it is debatable whether his report achieved its stated objective, those aspirations are still widely accepted.

Insofar as local authorities exist principally to provide services, they are not particularly different from other service providers such as the health service or transport undertakings. In recent years local authorities have placed a great deal of emphasis on service delivery issues. New management approaches have been adopted as authorities have striven for quality, value for money and 'more for less'. This approach has met with varying degrees of success with authorities like York, Norwich, Middlesbrough and Lewisham among others adopting a leadership role for local government in general. However this approach does not necessarily translate into a wider city leadership role. York, Norwich and Middlesbrough are clearly identifiable cities but the city council is not responsible for delivering either of the two largest local authority services, education or social services. Lewisham by contrast is much harder to locate geographically yet does provide those services.

From 1979 onwards, there has been an unresolved conflict between central and local government not only about finance but also about the role of local government which has been increasingly constrained by legislation. By the mid 1980s some city authorities were responding to this by asserting an overtly political stance which brought the conflict with central government into sharp focus. This stance did not find support from local populations generally and resulted in the status of local government falling. A general decline in service quality, not as a result of financial restriction but because of waste, inefficiency and restrictive practices, compounded this. The emphasis on service issues described earlier was to a great extent a response to this and it was perhaps inevitable that during such a period of 'getting back to basics' the leadership role of local authorities would be neglected or at least underplayed. However, such a role has been played historically and examples abound, the best known of which are probably Joseph Chamberlain in Birmingham and Herbert Morrison in London. Stewart sets this out clearly:

> Local authorities have a capacity for voice, not merely in setting out the objectives which their own activities are designed to meet, but in giving expression to the general problems and issues facing the community or communities that make up their area. A local authority can be an advocate for those who live and work within its area. (Stewart and Game, 1991)

If it is accepted that local authorities have not only a responsibility to provide city leadership but have, by attending to the quality of directly managed services, earned the right to exercise that leadership, how can they do so? What does city leadership entail and what difficulties are encountered?

The local authority as leader

The prerequisite of leadership is a clear picture of the needs and resources, strengths and weaknesses of the city. The authority can only create a vision if the vision relates to the present reality of the city as experienced by those who live and work there. Lewisham cannot realistically aspire to a future based on, say, a mix of finance sector employment and tourist based enterprise. Both things can and do play a role but will be limited by the borough's history and its geography. A vision which is clearly appropriate to Lewisham will gather more support than one which is over-generalised. For example, Y See Lig and Artibise (1991) identify a future for Vancouver based on the key relationship between its economy and its, as yet, unspoilt environment. The threat to that environment can be turned into a niche for Vancouver as a world leader in reconciling the demands of the two. Lewisham's vision may be a little more prosaic but is uniquely Lewisham's. The borough's greatest asset is its people. The majority have always had to find work beyond the borough boundary and this is unlikely to change. Our vision is of a city which is an attractive place to live, which offers the opportunity to its inhabitants to acquire the skills they need to meet employers' needs inside or outside the borough, and in that way to reverse years of decline.

It is difficult to evaluate the local authority leadership role without considering the specific tasks of leadership and the individuals who must carry out those tasks. Above all it is, in the UK system, the leader of the council who is the key individual. The leader does not operate alone: the chief executive has a distinct role and within their areas of concern so do committee chairs and chief officers. But it is the leader who sets the tone and must articulate the shared vision. The style adopted by individual leaders will vary but it is possible to identify common tasks.

I will argue that effective leadership can only be achieved if leaders address four areas. Each area must be addressed and preferably in sequence. However leaders will frequently have to deal with all four areas at once. The areas are:

● town hall politics;

● the local authority as an organisation;

● community leaders and opinion formers;

● the community at large.

Many of the failures of local authority leadership can be traced to attempts to provide leadership for the community at large without having achieved a degree of success in the earlier stages. The newly elected leader will, in most cases, have a low public profile and attempts to provide leadership for a whole city without first seeking to establish a relationship with the other leaders of the community are doomed to fail.

Town hall politics

Taking each area in turn, leaders' problems start rather than end when they succeed in being elected to office by their fellow councillors. During the early months in office leaders inevitably find they are 'tested' by colleagues, council officers and community groups as well as political opponents. It is vital that such tests are dealt with satisfactorily as no leader who is insecure on the political level will be able to exert leadership of the authority as a whole.

Speaking from personal experience, within months of becoming leader my party lost a vote in the council chamber for the first time in many years. Several months' work went into recovering the position in order to take the same issue back to council and obtain a majority. Failure to do this would have encouraged further attempts to undermine my position, while my success left members and officers in no doubt as to who was in charge.

The local authority as an organisation

The second stage is the key to effective city leadership. First, the leader must make clear what the respective roles of the leader and chief executive are to be. I would argue strongly that the politically elected leader must take responsibility for developing the authority's own image as well as the wider vision. There needs to be a clear line drawn between the political and operational management of the authority. Leaders must be seen to accept ultimate responsibility for the conduct of the authorities' business albeit not the day-to-day operations. By so doing leaders establish themselves as being on an equal footing with other leaders and potential partners.

Community leaders and opinion formers

This is perhaps illustrated most clearly in relation to the private sector. If firm links and lasting partnerships are to be built, elected leaders need to establish themselves as solid figures with a status which can be readily understood by those unfamiliar with the arcane world of UK local government. The frequent confusion between the roles of the UK mayor and the leader serve to illustrate the difficulty of this task. Throughout most of mainland Europe the mayor is also the leading local political figure and any potential employer or development looking to build links with the local authority would seek out the mayor. This often happens here as well, sometimes with unfortunate consequences. Most town halls have stories about unwitting visitors who are most impressed by the welcome to the mayor's parlour only to find that when the key question is asked they are told: "Oh I don't know anything about that; you'll have to talk to the leader!".

The community at large

European colleagues seeking to establish political links have on occasions been disappointed by UK responses simply because their approaches have been made to the mayor - who is non-political - rather than the leader. Mayors are high profile, easily identified figures because of the position they hold, and the annual change, far from undermining this, adds to the regard for the office. In contrast there is no formal role for leaders, who need to carve out their own distinctive role through their own efforts.

This brings considerable benefits if it can be achieved. The acceptance by not only the private sector but also community leaders, tenants' representatives, church leaders and local media of the leader as a substantial figure with something important to say provides the platform for the leader, and through him/her the authority, to address the wider community. It also provides a foundation from which to call on their support when trying to persuade central government to fund particular local initiatives.

There is not, of course, a simple progression from one of these areas of leadership to the next. It may be necessary to operate in one area before a leader feels properly secure in another. For example, leaders of hung authorities constantly face problems at the political level and must find ways to accommodate or contain the threat posed by instability. It is also possible for leaders to fail to maintain a balance between the areas identified here. The first priority has to remain the authority itself and leaders need to be clear what areas of work they will give priority to over time. The foregoing approach can be illustrated by looking at where a leader needs to build relationships. Initially the following would be on most leaders' agendas:

- political colleagues;
- senior staff;
- party representatives;
- council employees and their union representatives;
- other organisations working directly with the council;
- health authorities, police, councils for racial equality, tenants' associations;
- neighbouring local authorities;
- local media.

Only if a leader has coped with the myriad aspects of building those relationships - not only as a councillor but also as a counsellor, adviser, caseworker, publicist and advocate - as well as developing policies and strategies, can work take place effectively on a wide front, involving groups and individuals who do not see themselves as having a direct relationship with the council. In many ways the distinguishing characteristic of the groups just described is that if the leader ignores them they will come and find him/her. Genuine leadership for the whole area can only be achieved by reaching out beyond those groups to churches, local businesses and employers, distinct communities and other agencies who operate in the area.

Finally, it may be possible to address audiences beyond the borough boundary whether regional, national or international. I will now look at some of the difficulties encountered in attempting effective leadership.

Obstacles to effective city leadership in the UK

There is a deep-rooted tradition in the UK of unsalaried public service, at least at the local level. Widdicombe's (1986) report identified the increasing number of leading councillors who were involved in full-time duties. Among larger authorities 50% had one or more full-time councillors. However, the changes proposed and later enacted in modified form for members' remuneration fall well short of allowing salaries to be paid.

A recent Audit Commission management paper (1990) identified one aspect of the role of councillors as being to function as board members - this role was perceived as becoming more complex. The paper described members' remuneration at an average of £2,000 for a 17 hour week as 'very cheap'. When comparing UK city government with the US models this lack of financial compensation, let alone a living wage, is one of the most striking differences. This situation is not an accident of history but a conscious attempt by national politicians to downgrade the role of local politicians. While Secretary of State for the Environment, Michael Heseltine was an exception and his view that our cities need paid, directly elected mayors is well known. However, opposition from MPs is widespread, despite the fact that many launched their careers in local government. Tony Banks MP, quoted by Langton, said recently:

> The mayor would be someone with political power outside the House of Commons. And governments, as we saw with

the GLC [Greater London Council], do not like something
emerging from outside their own ranks. (Langton, 1991)

Langton went on to point out the fear of MPs that the local paper
might call mayors for comment on important issues more often than
the MPs themselves. Tony Banks, along with Michael Heseltine,
remains one of the few MPs who appear willing to countenance
elected mayors.

The conflict between the Greater London Council (GLC) and
central government which led to its abolition is symptomatic of the
antipathy to effective local government. The GLC was abolished
not for its failures but for its successes, which challenged central
government's own approach. The deliberate downgrading of local
government is greatly aided by poor quality and biased reporting of
local government issues both nationally and locally. Newspapers
take great delight in producing melodramatic headlines of two
sorts. In the first instance there is a broad brush approach which
seeks to smear all councils. A recent article in the *Independent*
newspaper had the headline "Renewable energy plans hindered by
councils". Careful reading of the article reveals that one MP had
claimed that some county councils were blocking schemes because
of public fears about the visual impact of some schemes. Local
newspapers by contrast delight in stories about financial 'crisis' yet
never deign to point out that local government achieves a budgetary
accuracy the private sector can only dream about. Nor are local
government's successes given attention. My own authority took no
losses following the recent Bank of Credit and Commerce
International (BCCI) collapse because a prudent investment policy
had identified BCCI as a bad risk. Many other authorities did the
same. Press comment dealt only with the handful of authorities
who got it wrong.

Local government suffers from a generalised public view that
councils are bureaucratic, inefficient or bungling. However,
individual authorities have been able to overcome this, not least by
paying attention to the quality of their communications with their
customers. Opinion surveys clearly demonstrate not only
differences in the way they are perceived between authorities but
that the public perception of individual authorities can change,
indeed that the perception of specific services can change. Surveys
carried out for my own authority showed that while in 1987 only
39% agreed with the statement 'The council is efficient/well run',

by 1991 the figure had risen to 56%. Taking refuse collection as an example of an individual service, we introduced a wheeled bin service and, as a result, net satisfaction rose from 63% to 79%. The comparison between a London borough and a city like Vancouver is an instructive one. The origins of the system of local government for the two are broadly the same and councillors from each would not feel out of place if transported to the other council chamber. The ways in which the two have developed, however, are very different.

Vancouver has a population of about 500,000 compared to Lewisham's 230,000. Unlike Vancouver, Lewisham is a unitary authority with responsibility for education, recreation and providing housing for rent. Nevertheless Mayor Gordon Campbell has a status in Vancouver which a borough leader could not achieve, however successful in carrying through the programme described earlier. This status arises only in part from the perception, however inaccurate, of Vancouver as a self-contained city. More importantly his administration not only has the freedom to act in the interests of the city as a key agent for its growth and development but is expected to do so by other levels of government. The mayor works full-time and the other institutions of the city look to city hall for leadership. Such notions are gaining currency among UK authorities but are still viewed in many quarters as dangerously radical!

If the key issue for those trying to provide leadership in cities is the economic well-being of those cities, it is clear that the most effective UK leaders have a vision and ability which is a match for their US or European counterparts. However, the obstacles placed in their way make it increasingly difficult to turn vision into a realistic programme of action.

The success of a number of French cities in recent years in identifying a role and marketing themselves is in no small part due to central government providing the space in which effective local leadership could evolve. To achieve the same result in the UK would require a change of heart by central government. There are specific financial restrictions placed on UK cities, in particular the central control of both spending and revenue raising, which limit their ability to achieve change or even promote their cities effectively.

The degree of central financial control which exists has grown over the past decade and has considerable significance for the operation of local democracy. The proportion of local authority expenditure financed locally fell dramatically with the replacement of domestic rates by the poll tax. This meant that the marginal cost of local decisions was greatly magnified. In 1989/90, 57% of local expenditure was raised locally. In 1992/93 this had fallen to 21%. This situation is likely to worsen now that council tax is in operation. It is clear that expecting local taxpayers to bear a 5% increase in taxation for each 1% increase in expenditure on local services is something which will require leadership skills of an extraordinary kind. Thus gearing produces a self-imposed limit on local budgets. However, an additional layer of control has been placed on top of this through the mechanism of 'capping'. This has, in effect, given the Secretary of State for the Environment the power to set upper limits for council budgets.

Nor has this been treated as a reserve power for use in extreme or unusual circumstances. It has been used each year on a variety of authorities. There are equally draconian but even more complex constraints on capital investment by local authorities. Experience elsewhere offers alternatives which illustrate the greater room for manoeuvre enjoyed by European and US municipalities and their leaders. In the USA where, as in the UK, central government has sought to limit local spending, new ways to fund capital projects have been developed. In particular municipal bonds have proved successful (Berger, 1991).   In the area of revenue funding, Germany provides an interesting case with the apportionment of revenue between tiers of government enshrined in law. The Länder (regional authorities) have access to six separate taxes while other taxes - including income tax - are shared between central government and the two tiers of local government. Crucially this split is a right and not subject to policy direction.

I will now consider how the UK system has been changing and what might happen in the future.

Where now for city leadership?

The time is right for local government to recognise that its formal structures no longer bear much relevance to the real decision-making processes.   In many authorities the council meetings themselves have long since ceased to be meaningful. This may even be the case in some hung authorities which have developed effective joint working. In authorities dominated by a single party it is also well known that key decisions are taken by the party groups. The growing complexity of local government, however, is increasingly leading to the creation of forms of executive government which bear little or no relation to formal structures. Taking my own authority as an example, a cabinet style system has evolved with committee chairs meeting together to consider and advise on major issues. In some authorities this has gone further and been formalised, although the present rules which outlaw one party committees can make this problematic.

The recent consultation paper on internal management (Department of the Environment, 1991) has led to intense discussion of potential changes to UK local government and to consideration of alternatives which draw heavily on experience elsewhere. There is a relatively broad consensus that the present system is flawed. However, no consensus exists on how improvements can be made. Central government in the practical aspects of its consultation paper seems wedded to a 'top down' approach. The issue is not only whether elected mayors, city managers or some form of executive are introduced but also how the processes of democracy can be strengthened. One aspect of the consensus referred to above relates to the present committee system which seems increasingly unwieldy and outdated. However, any of the changes mentioned should not necessarily mean the end of committee-based local government. Rather, a more effective system which is better focused and encourages participation beyond the council is needed. The re-election of a Conservative government in the general election of 1992 makes the search for such a system yet more urgent. The constraints which have been placed on local authorities in relation to service provision will remain, while the movement away from direct provision to operating through contracts or agents will grow. In these circumstances the leadership role for local authorities described earlier must be given a higher profile. There are three challenges to local authorities which can be identified in this context:

● strengthening democracy;

● maintaining and improving quality of services for local communities;

● building partnerships within and beyond the local community.

In this context authorities will increasingly need to create structures which foster active involvement by citizens. It is inevitable that this will involve decentralisation. The Tower Hamlets neighbourhood system offers one example where a very great degree of political and managerial devolution has occurred. Other authorities have followed slightly less dramatic but no less innovatory approaches, and Middlesbrough and Islington both offer ideas worth pursuing. More recently Bradford has introduced an extensive structure intended to facilitate community involvement.

My own authority introduced neighbourhood housing committees several years ago but these are increasingly seen as transitional bodies which will only achieve lasting acceptance if their role is widened and their autonomy increased. Such committees have clearly provided opportunities for much greater involvement by the local tenants, but the continued existence of a full range of powerful central committees not only creates demands on the time of elected members which are difficult to meet but also creates confusion about the power of the neighbourhood committees. Such committees should foster community leadership at neighbourhood level, but for this to be effective authorities need to identify and eliminate constraints on such leadership.

Turning to the issue of quality, local authorities need to get the basics of service delivery right. A great deal has been learned about how to achieve this, not least by devolving managerial responsibility. Authorities have also learned how to operate through contracts effectively. However, ahead lies the challenge of applying these lessons to a range of services where quality can be a more subjective issue. There can be no shirking of this challenge because failure to maintain quality will undermine the efforts to strengthen democracy referred to earlier.

Quality is not, of course, merely a matter of concern in respect of the services provided on our behalf by the council itself. Local communities rely on services provided by a variety of agencies. In pursuing a leadership role the authority should concern itself with those services and strive to create a working relationship with those service providers. In Lewisham we have created a quality commission consisting of back-bench councillors with the power to investigate and scrutinise specific aspects of council services, either by service or on a cross-departmental basis. We intend to use this approach to look also at services provided elsewhere in the borough. To do this effectively will mean establishing not only the credentials of the quality commission but working relationships at all levels.

It is, perhaps, in the area of partnerships that Michael Heseltine's legacy is most clearly seen. The City Challenge approach to urban regeneration is a flawed one but it is undeniable that it has released energies and brought into being partnerships which can only be of benefit to the communities concerned. In Lewisham we were successful in the first round of bidding in no small part because of the support for the bid from parts of the community quite distinct from, even critical of, the authority itself. The process of transforming the bid into a practical programme of regeneration led by a genuine partnership involving in our case councillors, tenants, community service groups, local business, police and educational and training bodies, is by no means an easy one and in this phase it is appropriate for an established local leader, in this case myself, to chair the board of the new partnership body. However, in future years this body should distance itself farther from the council and carve out its own role in providing community leadership.

Conclusions

Dynamic, visionary city leadership by local authorities is possible, as experience elsewhere demonstrates. It is needed in the UK if our cities are to survive and compete with their European counterparts and in London's case, the rest of the world. The individuals with the skills and vision exist and are willing to serve. Indeed they will go on striving to provide leadership in the present difficult circumstances but changes are needed if their chances of success are to be enhanced. These must include:

● an efficient process for executive government at the local level;

● an effective way to involve all councillors and the wider community in the democratic process;

● adequate remuneration and support for leading city councillors;

● a change of attitude to city governments - partnership cannot be a one way process.

When Secretary of State for the Environment, Michael Heseltine, challenged local authorities to take responsibility for the success or failure of their areas, that was a challenge authorities readily accepted, but it remains to be seen whether the present secretary of state's stated desire to work with local government will extend to removing the obstacles created by central government to successful city leadership.

References

Audit Commission (1990) *We can't go on meeting like this - the changing role of local authority members*, London: Audit Commission.

Berger, S. (1991) 'Market forces and public investment', *Local Government Chronicle*, 6 September.

Confederation of British Industry (1991) *A London development agency: optimising the capital's assets*, A CBI London region discussion paper.

Department of the Environment (1991) *The internal management of local authorities in England: a consultation paper*, London: HMSO.

Langton, J. (1991) 'Who'll rule London?', *Sunday Telegraph*, 13 October.

Stewart, J. and Game, C. (1991) *Local democracy - representation and elections*, Luton: Local Government Management Board.

Widdicombe, D. QC (1986) *The conduct of local authority business*, Cmnd 9797, London: HMSO.

Y See Lig, M. and Artibise, A.F.J. (1991) *From desolation to hope: the Pacific Fraser region in 2010*, Vancouver: University of British Columbia.

four

LOCAL GOVERNMENT US STYLE

Kevin Lavery

Introduction

Local government in the UK is big business. Annual budgeted expenditure in 1991/92 was £62 billion, 26% of total public expenditure. Nearly 2.3 million people (full-time equivalents) work in local authorities, 8% of the national workforce. Many more thousands rely for their livelihoods on local authority contracts. Local authorities help ensure that a wide range of services are provided, such as education, policing, fire, roads, social services and housing. All of these services are important and some are essential for a modern, civilised and democratic nation.

Throughout the 1980s the world of UK local government underwent rapid and unprecedented change. Government legislation in education, social services, housing, competition and finance transformed the role of local government. The expectations of the consumers of local government services also rose. During a period of rapid change it is essential for local authorities to respond positively if they are to secure the best possible services with the available resources.

A fundamental and far reaching review of UK local government commenced in 1991 following the appointment of Michael Heseltine as Secretary of State for the Environment. The review examined the purpose, functions, structure, financing and organisation of local government. A number of questions underpinned the element of the review which covered internal organisation, including:

- how can the quality of leadership be improved?

- how can local politicians become more accountable?

- how can the community profile of local politicians be increased?

- can local government become more business-like in its decision making and service delivery?

- what could be done to enhance the involvement of ordinary people in local government?

The possibility of introducing US style full-time elected mayors with substantial executive powers was suggested by Mr Heseltine. The US city manager system, where a small board of elected politicians delegate full operational authority to a professional manager, was commended by Michael Portillo, then Minister for Local Government.

This chapter focuses on the issue of internal organisation of local government. In particular, it examines the two major forms of government in US cities: the 'council-manager' and 'strong mayor' systems. It seeks to understand:

- the policy setting for US local government;

- how the mayor and manager systems operate in Phoenix and Seattle;

- whether and how they contribute to 'good government';

- how they affect the quality of city management;

- which elements could be transferred to UK local government.

It is based on information gathered on the cities of Phoenix and Seattle during a six week study tour of the USA during June and July of 1991.

Local government in the USA

It is difficult to generalise about US local government. Because the USA is a federal country local authorities are creations of their parent state. Moreover many authorities, especially the cities, have their own charters which provide them with a unique range of powers and duties. This makes for a rich, diverse and complex pattern of local government. The main areas of variations are described below.

● *Size*

Whilst most US local authorities are much smaller than their UK counterparts there is an enormous variation in size. For example, the County of Loving (Texas) has a population of less than 200 whereas the City of New York serves well over seven million people.

● *Range of functions*

Once again there is considerable variety from authorities with a single function, such as water or education, to multi-purpose authorities. A large and powerful city or county might be responsible for services such as policing, fire, parks, housing, highways and public utilities. A few cities, such as New York and Baltimore, run the education service. Compared to the UK public protection services have a higher profile and welfare services a lower profile.

● *Types of authority*

The main types of authority are counties, townships, municipalities, cities, school districts and other special districts covering, for example, sewage disposal. Several layers of local government in one area is not uncommon.

● *Finance*

There is no uniform system of local taxation. Property taxes predominate but there are also local sales and income taxes. Generally, compared to the UK, a greater proportion of revenue is raised locally.

● *Forms of government*

There are three main types of government in local authorities:

(i) The commission - this is where the power of the local authority is vested in an elected commission of usually three to seven members. The commissioners divide the functions of the authority by departments and each commissioner heads a department. The commission type has experienced a steady decline in favour but is still found in some counties and small cities.

(ii)   The council-manager - here an elected council ranging in size from five to nine members appoints a professional manager to be responsible for running the local authority. The councillors meet infrequently to decide policy and the manager has full delegated authority for operational management.

(iii)   The mayor-council - this is a simplified form of US federal and state government. The mayor is an independently elected chief executive. In the strong mayor form the mayor shares responsibility for policy making with the council but is totally responsible for administration. The mayor appoints departmental heads, proposes the budget and is the dominant force in the council. In the weak mayor form the mayor lacks administrative power and several of the senior officers are filled by direct election or appointed by the council.

● *Party politics*

In most US local governments (75% of US cities over 50,000) party politics is legally banned - candidates for office are not identified by political party on the ballot. This is called the non-partisan system and it is almost universal in council-manager local governments.

● *Elections*

In two-thirds of cities council members are elected 'at large', ie by the entire city. In the remainder council members are elected on a district basis or a mixture of at large and district.

● *Councils*

Irrespective of the form of government US city councils are much smaller than their UK counterparts.

It is important to appreciate the evolution of forms of city government in the USA. In the late 19th century the weak mayor system was most common. Urban squalor and corruption and incompetence in city government led to the emergence of a reform movement. The early reformers criticised the weak mayor system for its fragmentation and lack of leadership. This led to the development of strong mayor and commission systems. As the reform movement developed it became increasingly concerned with the politicisation of city government (especially machine politics) and the lack of good management. This produced pressure for:

- a strong appointed executive to ensure high standards of management;

- a non-partisan system to remove party politics from local affairs;

- 'at large' elections to avoid parochialism.

Gradually this became known as the council-manager plan. The reform movement became known as the National Municipal League and promoted the council-manager form with a model charter. The organisation is now called the National Civic League and it still promotes a model charter, albeit with some amendments since the early years. Staunton, Virginia, became the first council-manager city in 1908 and in 1914 Dayton, Ohio, became the first big city with a council-manager plan. Today the council-manager and mayor forms of government are the most common. The mayor form is dominant in the very smallest and largest cities whilst the council-manager form is slightly more common in cities with populations of 25,000-500,000. Notable examples of each form of government include New York and Boston as strong mayor cities, Portland (Oregon) as a commission city and San Diego and Dallas as council-manager cities.

In the late 20th century there has been some convergence between manager and mayor forms of government. Strong mayor systems have been criticised for lacking internal leadership and quality management. It is now common for such cities to appoint a chief administrative officer or deputy mayor to oversee the day-to-day running of the city. By contrast, council-manager cities have been criticised for lacking political leadership. Nearly all council-manager cities now have a mayor, of whom more than two-thirds are directly elected. It is also becoming more common, especially in the larger cities, for council-manager mayors to have their own staff and some powers (eg responsibility for proposing the budget and some veto powers).

US cities face a similar range of challenges and problems to their UK counterparts. Two issues are, however, qualitatively different and need to be understood. First, local government is much more fragmented in the USA, particularly between the core city and its hinterland. Metropolitan Chicago, for example, contains well over 1,000 local governments. This makes coordination nigh impossible. Fragmentation tends to be greatest in the large and old industrial metropolitan areas of the north east and mid west. Many cities are seeking ways of reducing fragmentation. The two most common methods are annexation and joint agreements. Annexation is most common in the south and west and is where a city expands its boundary to reflect growth. A number of joint agreements have been reached to ensure coordination of, for example, transport and planning. The best example is the Minneapolis-St Paul Regional Council. Underpinning all of these moves is a growing recognition that a range of issues require sub-regional responses and consequently the future of the suburbs is inevitably linked to those of the core cities. As one US mayor said: "you can't be a suburb of nowhere" (Barrett and Greene, 1991).

Second, US cities are suffering from a fiscal squeeze unheard of in the UK. New York and Washington DC have both been shedding staff in their thousands. Philadelphia is virtually bankrupt whilst Bridgeport, in affluent Connecticut, filed for bankruptcy in June. The underlying causes of the squeeze are suburbanisation, the nature of local taxation and recession. The tax base of core cities is diminishing because of a flight to the suburbs of people, employment and shopping. Whilst there is no uniform system of local taxation, compared to the UK a greater proportion of revenue is raised locally. Finally, some of the key taxes, especially sales and business taxes, are closely linked to the state of the economy. The heavy emphasis on local taxes and their volatility has obvious disadvantages but the system provides a strong incentive for cities to introduce policies to support the local economy. The cities in the mid west and north east are experiencing the greatest fiscal problems.

Phoenix and Seattle

As I have mentioned, this chapter is based on studies of local government in Phoenix and Seattle conducted during the summer of 1991. Phoenix had a population of 1,000,000 whilst Seattle had just over 500,000. Both cities had grown dramatically in recent years and their economies were amongst the strongest in the USA. Their main functions included police, fire, parks, highways and transportation. Significantly, both cities ran major utilities, most notably waste collection, water and sewerage. Seattle even ran the electricity company, known as City Light, whilst Phoenix ran an international airport and a cable television station. Neither city was responsible for education which was handled by separately elected school boards. Seattle's school board had the same boundary as the city council whereas Phoenix contained 28 separate school districts. The cities were involved in the provision of social services (known as 'human services') but it was a more limited role than a UK council. This was due to the smaller role of the welfare state in the USA and because county councils in both cities had the major role in community medical care and hospital care for those without insurance. The total annual operating budget for both cities was in the range of £0.5-0.8 billion. Phoenix had 12,000 staff whilst Seattle had 10,000.

There was a county tier of government in both cities. Maricopa County covered metropolitan Phoenix whereas King County covered metropolitan Seattle. Maricopa and King Counties had more limited remits than their English and Welsh counterparts. They provided some county-wide services such as courts, prisons and the sheriff's office as well as local services such as police, fire and parks in 'unincorporated' areas, ie those areas not incorporated into a city. In Maricopa around 170,000 people lived in unincorporated areas with over 400,000 in King County.

The majority of revenue was raised locally in both cities: 56% in Phoenix and 95% in Seattle. Local sales tax was the most important tax in Phoenix with other significant taxes on property and utilities. The city also received a proportion of state income, sales and vehicle licence taxes. State and federal grants were relatively small (eg in 1990 they amounted to $65 million for Phoenix). Seattle also had significant business, utility and property taxes. In both cities the utility companies were self-funding through user charges.

The two cities had contrasting policy priorities. Phoenix's top priorities were to maintain and improve public safety and to develop the downtown with more hotels, retailing and cultural facilities. In part, this was about creating a stronger sense of pride and identity but was also a way of raising city revenue. The city was also trying to strengthen the neighbourhoods. Seattle was renowned for its progressive social and environmental policies. The city had maintained the level of human services despite a dramatic reduction in federal support throughout the 1980s. It was also undertaking major initiatives on low cost housing, neighbourhood revitalisation and social support for education (eg free school meals for under-privileged children). It had an extensive public transport system and an award winning recycling programme.

Phoenix and Seattle were regarded as model councils in the USA. The business journal, *Financial World*, recently examined the quality of management in the big 30 US cities.   It rated Phoenix top of the group, closely followed by Seattle.   Other better known cities such as New York, Detroit and Philadelphia were not so well regarded.   Phoenix was seen as a national leader on competitive tendering and efficiency improvements.

City managers and strong mayors

Phoenix had a council-manager form of government where a small board of elected officials delegate operational authority to an appointed professional manager.   The system resembled a business: the electors were the shareholders, the council the board of directors and the city manager the salaried chief executive.   The council comprised eight councillors elected by district and a mayor elected by the entire city.   All elected officials served a two year term and the mayor chaired the council.   The council determined policy, appointed the city manager and kept his performance under review.   The city manager, Frank Fairbanks, 'served at the council's pleasure' which meant that he could be dismissed at any time.   The city manager had hiring and firing powers over all other staff, had complete authority to implement council policy, and proposed the annual budget.

Seattle had a strong mayor.   Norm Rice was a full-time elected mayor with powers to hire and fire senior executives, manage the city, propose the budget and veto council decisions.   Seattle also had a council of nine elected councillors, all of whom were elected at large for a four year term.   The council determined policy, confirmed mayoral appointments and reviewed the performance of the executive.   The council has its own staff of some 45 officers. Seattle's system of government was described as 'strong mayor, strong council'.   It was modelled on the US federal government with a separation of the executive (the mayor) and the legislative (the council) branches.   Unusually, Seattle also had three elected officials: an attorney, a treasurer and a comptroller.

There were three fundamental differences between the manager and strong mayor forms of governments. First, the powers of the mayor. Seattle's mayor had considerably more formal policy making and executive responsibilities than his Phoenix counterpart, Paul Johnson. Norm Rice hired and fired senior executives, proposed the budget and could veto council decisions - the council had to reconfirm a decision with at least two-thirds support to override a veto. Paul Johnson had few formal powers other than setting the agenda for council meetings, chairing them and nominating people to serve on citizen panels. A second difference was the relationship between the mayor and the council. Seattle's mayor was not a member of the council, and this was fairly common amongst strong mayor cities. Phoenix's mayor headed the council whilst Seattle's council elected a president from within its own ranks. Finally, the head of the executive in Seattle (the mayor) was elected whilst the equivalent post in Phoenix (the manager) was appointed by local elected officials.

Much of the debate about the US local government experience has focused on the difference between manager and mayor systems (Tranter, 1991). Despite these differences Phoenix and Seattle shared many common features. Both cities had directly elected mayors, although Seattle's mayor enjoyed more formal power than his Phoenix counterpart. Both cities had appointed heads of the executive, because Seattle had a 'deputy mayor' who handled the day-to-day management of the city. They had considerably fewer councillors than is the norm in the UK. Phoenix had nine councillors (including the mayor) for a city the size of Birmingham whilst Seattle had ten councillors (including the mayor) for a city larger than Sheffield. By contrast, Kent county council has 99 councillors for an area with a population in excess of 1.5 million. Politics in both cities were non-partisan by law. Finally, there was extensive public participation. It was common to have public hearings on draft council proposals at an early stage. Referenda were held and citizens had the right to place propositions on the annual ballot. There was also a plethora of citizen panels which advised the councils on policy and practice. This involved a great number of people in council affairs who would not otherwise get involved in politics. Neighbourhood and voluntary groups were also active.

Good government

Understanding governmental systems says little about their impact on the wider world. It is therefore crucial to examine whether the council-manager and strong mayor systems help or hinder 'good government'. This was achieved by evaluating Phoenix and Seattle against five desirable elements of 'good government': accountability, leadership, partnership within the council, closeness to citizens and competence.

Directly elected mayors - irrespective of the form of government - were highly visible and helped focus public attention on local issues. Mayors were generally regarded as being responsible for running city government and their re-election hopes hinged more on local performance than national factors. As a result local accountability was enhanced. UK council leaders are far more anonymous and parties less accountable compared to directly elected mayors. However, non-partisan mayors tended to promote the cult of personality and issues of style rather than policies and ideas. Moreover, it was difficult to unseat an incumbent mayor. Aspiring mayors required a good campaign team, advertising and endorsements from key groups. Crucially, the incumbent mayor had the great advantage of being familiar to the voters. What tended to happen in Phoenix and Seattle was that serious challenges to the mayor came from high profile councillors rather than complete outsiders.

The attributes of dynamic and purposeful leadership were identified as:

- *inspiring rather than commanding* - encouraging and communicating to gain support and goodwill, especially important in an enabling context;

- *leading rather than being led* - challenging the voters and staff to ensure that the council faces the difficult issues;

- *looking inwards and outwards* - staff should not be ignored and need to know their part in the bigger picture.

Leadership quality should not be confused with a governmental system and formal power should not be equated with actual power. It is possible to have a strong leader without formal powers and a weak leader with considerable power. Dynamic leaders require influence, communication skills, vision, charisma and management skills more than formal power. The study confirmed this thesis because the Phoenix and Seattle mayors were both dynamic and purposeful leaders despite the variation in their formal powers. Partnership amongst elected officials, and between elected and appointed officials, is vital to good government. There was more conflict between the mayor and the council in Seattle than in Phoenix, and this was a feature of the strong mayor system. The institutional separation of mayor and council in Seattle created two competing power bases. The council reacted to proposals which it had little or no involvement in drawing up. Conflict was accentuated where there were aspiring mayors on the council: in order to establish their own identity and approach they had to distinguish themselves from the mayor's proposals. In Phoenix the council and mayor developed proposals and made decisions together. The likelihood of conflict was also reduced by the Phoenix mayor's consensus style: typically he asked for views before declaring his own favoured position. The previous Phoenix mayor had a much more combative approach. Phoenix had also developed a strong bond between the mayor/council and the officers. This helped ensure that the organisation was equipped to deliver the political vision. In theory a political/managerial partnership is the trademark of a strong mayor system. Unfortunately, in practice, strong mayors and/or the managerial appointments do not always have the necessary managerial skills. Creating a partnership between the mayor, the council and the executive was firmly on Norm Rice's agenda. In his 18 months of office he had made greatest progress in building a partnership with the council.

On the face of it US local government appears remote from citizens: US city councillors cannot act as local representatives because of their small numbers and electoral turn-outs are as low as in the UK. A closer examination in Phoenix and Seattle revealed greater genuine openness and participation in local government than is usually the case in the UK. Moreover, citizens had a real impact on city government, especially through referenda and pressure group politics. Neighbourhood and business interests were active in both cities. There were even so called 'good government groups', known as the 'Go Gos'. A good example was the Municipal League in Seattle. It was a 70 year old organisation which was staffed by paid professionals and had a small but influential membership of around 1,500 people. The League developed from the reform movement. It was a self-appointed watch-dog on the city. Amongst other things it reviewed candidates for office, conducted research on major issues, provided public education through briefs and workshops and rewarded good public service.

There are three underlying reasons why citizens' views were taken seriously. First, the US legal system provides citizens with a wealth of opportunities to challenge the decisions of public bodies. Litigation was commonplace. Second, the referenda system means that specific actions and decisions of councils were genuinely open to challenge through the ballot box. Finally, citizens are much more prepared to challenge authority than their UK counterparts. In these circumstances it was not surprising that councils were prepared to listen and committed to achieving consensus.

Did extensive citizen involvement promote good government? It certainly acted as a check on the council, built commitment and provided some good ideas. Unfortunately, a large number of people still remained untouched by the council. Citizen involvement also had other drawbacks. The most obvious was that it slowed down decisions. It also gave 'nimbyism' (not-in-my-backyard) full reign, as much of the citizen involvement was negative in nature - stopping things happening. Two good examples were Seattle's proposal to redevelop the Pike Market Place and Phoenix's attempts to build a major sports stadium. Through referenda the former was stopped and the latter shackled. There were a few examples where referenda had been positive. One was where a group of Phoenix citizens succeeded in introducing a district election system for council members by placing the issue on the annual ballot. The most serious drawback, however, was that the process could easily become an end in itself.

Attempting to please all the interest groups could become an excuse for avoiding the challenges and difficult choices. This certainly happened during budget reduction exercises. Citizen involvement, therefore, required courageous leadership to ensure that the real issues were addressed rather than ignored.

The calibre of elected officials (ie elected mayors and councillors) in both cities was high with the majority having an educated, professional and/or business background. However, high calibre was not simply a result of paying councillors. Generous staff support helped but, more fundamentally, local government was held in higher esteem than in the UK. The non-partisan system was a major reason for this because people who were not politically active were attracted to enter office.

The council-manager system promoted managerial competence more than the strong mayor system. Phoenix had a tradition of officer excellence for which it had secured a national reputation. For example, the previous city manager was named as the top US city manager in 1986 by *City and State* magazine. Considerable care was taken when recruiting senior staff and once in post there was a systematic appraisal process related to pay: the 'Performance Achievement Programme'.

Seattle's mayor was elected on political rather than managerial grounds. There was, therefore, no guarantee that the mayor would be a good manager. New mayors usually took some time to learn how to manage the council bureaucracy. In any event the mayor was too busy to manage the city on a day-to-day basis. He therefore relied on key appointments such as the deputy mayor, but also others such as the budget director and the personnel director. It was usual for all of these general management post-holders to enter the administration with the mayor. Consequently they too had a learning curve. Moreover, these appointments had not always been made on the basis of managerial qualities - a former mayor had even appointed his brother as the deputy mayor! However, as a generalisation the managerial quality of senior executives in Seattle and Phoenix was high. Finally, there were no effective mechanisms in place for encouraging good performance in Seattle. This had been recognised by the mayor who was introducing accountability contracts with department heads. There were no plans to link performance to pay, however, even for top management.

Quality of strategic management

Central to the study was an assessment of what contributes to effective strategic management. This assessment was based on experience of Kent County Council, but it does not imply that Kent is the perfect model. Kent has introduced a simple approach to manage change at corporate level. It is called 'strategic management', the process of balancing the organisation's 'performance requirement' with the 'capability to respond'. The performance requirement is about where the organisation wants to be. It is determined by external change (eg new legislation, demography), customer needs, and the priorities of members and officers. Capability is concerned with the resources (finance, people, land and buildings and information), appropriate structures and processes, and the values and attitudes needed to achieve the tasks in hand. The aim of strategic management is to balance the performance requirement and the capability to respond. Table 1 below shows a range of possible relationships.

Table 1:   Strategic management achieving a balance

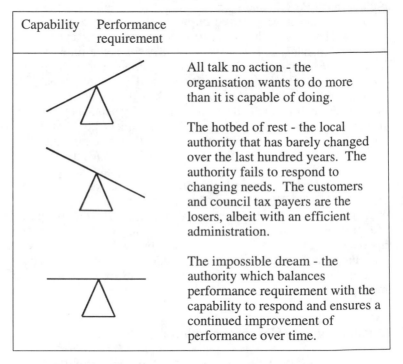

Capability	Performance requirement	
		All talk no action - the organisation wants to do more than it is capable of doing.
		The hotbed of rest - the local authority that has barely changed over the last hundred years. The authority fails to respond to changing needs. The customers and council tax payers are the losers, albeit with an efficient administration.
		The impossible dream - the authority which balances performance requirement with the capability to respond and ensures a continued improvement of performance over time.

A centralised power structure is a key feature of both strong mayor and council-manager systems - the mayor and the manager respectively control the executive. This is in sharp contrast to the UK system where chief officers are appointed by councillors not the chief executive. The accountabilities of chief officers here are also blurred because they have a reporting relationship both to the chief executive and a committee. In theory a centralised power structure should make it easier for a local authority to act as one organisation and this is critical to good strategic management. Does it work in practice?

This study used a set of critical success factors to evaluate the effectiveness of strategic management (Lavery and Hume, 1991). These factors are called the six Ps and are identified in Table 2. Each city was assessed against these factors and their comparative ratings are shown on a point scale of 1 to 5 (1 is very effective and 5 is poor). Phoenix deserved its reputation as one of the best managed cities in the US. It had a comprehensive range of management processes which were used prudently, an effective partnership between the mayor and manager, and a track record in improving efficiency. It had not identified low priority areas but this was understandable given its growth culture. Its biggest weakness was the absence of a genuine medium-term plan.

It is harder on the evidence to justify Seattle's high rating as a well managed city. It lacked many basic management processes and there was clearly scope for improving efficiency. The mayor had only been in office for 18 months, however, and had already instituted a range of changes to improve management - there were changes in senior executives, accountability contracts for senior executives were being introduced and the officer structure was being rationalised. Seattle's strength was the mayor's political vision and the innovative policies on education and human services. However, there is a long way to go and it remains to be seen whether the mayor and his staff will deliver their aspirations.

Centralised finance and personnel controls featured strongly in Phoenix and Seattle. Devolution of management responsibility has been used extensively in the private sector and has shown that making people personally responsible promotes a sense of ownership and improves performance. The mass of personnel and financial rules and regulations tended to smother initiative and led to frustration which was evident when talking to service directors. These centralised systems made it difficult for managers to manage. The fear of corruption appeared to underpin centralisation.

Table 2:   Quality of strategic management

	Phoenix	Seattle
Processes: local authorities require corporate processes for assessing needs, determining direction, deciding priorities, allocating resources, monitoring and managing performance. Phoenix had the most solid processes in place with systematic budget review and performance monitoring related to individual targets and appraisals. Seattle lacked the processes but this was being addressed. Neither city had medium-term planning which made it difficult for them to 'downsize' during a fiscal squeeze.	2	4
Policy: budget decisions should be policy led and the authority should have a corporate vision. Both cities were policy led. Seattle, in particular, was developing innovative policies, especially on education and human services.	2	1
Practicality: the practical arrangements to implement policy objectives need to be carefully considered, eg money, manpower, property and information.	2	3
Pain: strategic management should make a difference to how and what decisions are made rather than be a purely cosmetic exercise. It is not possible to do everything therefore priorities have to be set - low as well as high. Consequently there will be losers as well as winners. Phoenix had been more prepared to address the 'pain issue'. Seattle had, for example, responded to the recession with a series of 'one off' cost savings. Such measures (eg vacancy freezes) were blunt and merely delayed decisions on where permanent reductions should be made.	3	4

| | 4 | 2 |

Pragmatism: it is important to avoid becoming obsessed with means and processes at the expense of problems and solutions. Processes should also be built around people, encouraging ideas and recognising that judgements are needed. Seattle was the more exciting, interesting and pragmatic, in part because it lacked the desirable management processes. Phoenix often did things 'too well' and processes sometimes took over without a clear view on what was to be achieved. In both cities there was a sufficient concentration of power to produce clear decisions.

| | 1 | 3 |

Productivity: because resources will always be limited, local authorities should improve efficiency wherever possible to maximise service quality and range. Phoenix had the best track record on productivity. The difference was evident in the responses to their 1991 budget shortfalls - Phoenix's was made up by efficiency savings whereas Seattle's relied more on increased taxes and book-keeping measures. Phoenix had also pioneered competitive tendering which had saved $20m per annum.

Other shared features of city management included the following.

● General managers - there was much greater pluralism in US city management. A Master's degree in public administration was a required qualification for anyone wishing to become a city manager. More significantly it was common for managers to spend time in a variety of departments (eg the budget department and a service department). In Phoenix the city manager had a general deputy - the assistant city manager - and five deputy city managers who were responsible for the strategic management of the city's 26 departments. Each deputy was responsible for three to five departments, and their portfolios were changed every two to three years. This promoted general management skills amongst the top executives.

- Tenure for senior officers - it is difficult for a UK local authority to shed its senior officers and this can be a problem when a new direction is needed. In the USA change at top management level was commonplace and easy. This was because senior officers usually did not have contracts; hence the term 'serving at the council's pleasure'.

- Compared to the UK the finance function was fragmented. In both cities there was a separate budget department which prepared the budget, monitored performance and undertook budget reviews. Phoenix also had an audit department which was responsible for probity, systems and performance audits and a finance department which was responsible for collecting taxes and other revenues and all payments. Seattle's finance function was even more fragmented. An elected treasurer was responsible for collecting taxes and revenues whilst an elected comptroller dealt with payments and internal audit. All of the finance functions were under the city manager's control in Phoenix. In Seattle the mayor controlled the budget department but the treasurer and comptroller were independent.

- The budget departments were not dominated by accountants. Neither of the two budget directors were qualified accountants.

- Staff, other than senior executives, were on civil service conditions and enjoyed considerable security of tenure. Appointments were made on merit through a pool system, coordinated by the personnel departments.

Lessons for the UK

Some features of US local government are interesting but could not be transferred easily because of differences in culture and tradition. Other features are both interesting and transferable.

Non-partisan politics

The great strength of non-partisan politics is that it highlights local as opposed to national issues and it brings in people who would otherwise not get involved in politics. But is non-partisan politics desirable? It is certainly strongly supported by the US public and probably would gain considerable support in the UK. However, it tends to promote the cult of personality and reduce discussion about ideas and policies. In any event it is difficult to see how non-partisan politics could be introduced in the UK. Party politics is deeply embedded in our culture. And in practical terms who would campaign and fund non-partisan candidates?

Public participation

Public hearings and citizen panels could be introduced immediately without any difficulty. No legislation would be required, unless citizen panels were given formal powers. There could be implications for the committee system and existing consultation arrangements in, for example, planning and education. There would be a financial cost, there would be more bureaucracy and decisions would take longer. However, the significant issues are:

● would it lead to genuine public involvement in local affairs?

● how would the arrangements be handled in a party political system?

It would not be far fetched to speculate that without safeguards nominations to citizen panels would be dominated by the majority party as has happened for governor appointments in some local authorities.

Referenda

The use of referenda would be the most radical development in public participation. Referenda work well in the USA - they act as a check on the system, are a source of democratic initiatives and give people real power. However, ballot forms can be extremely complex containing too many detailed and minor propositions. They also tend to result in more 'Nimbyism' and issues are often addressed in a piecemeal way rather than in the round. It must also be recognised that they have not improved electoral turn-outs in the USA. Overall, referenda add considerably to local democracy but clear criteria need to be established for their use. The UK government has suggested referenda could be required where a local authority is proposing to overspend. This seems unduly restrictive. Other possibilities are:

● the proposed budget irrespective of whether it is below or above the Standard Spending Assessment;

● major policy changes such as a proposal to privatise an entire service;

● proposed changes to the form of government.

It is also important that citizens have the right to place items on the ballot, but again clear criteria would be needed to keep voting simple and avoid emasculating government.

Fewer councillors

It would require a courageous secretary of state to reduce the number of councillors as there appear to be few political benefits. Fewer councillors would certainly produce a more business-like approach to decision making and would recognise the reality that councillors are not all equal. Many would be concerned that reducing the number of councillors would make local government more remote and would eliminate the councillor's role as local representative (Stewart, 1991). This would happen if no other mechanisms were developed to promote participatory rather than representative democracy. However, the councillor as local representative is something of a fiction; the Widdicombe research found that only 30% of people knew their local councillor and that the average councillor only spends 18% of his/her time as a local representative (Widdicombe, 1986). Perhaps the solution is to separate formally the role of policy makers and local representative as is the case at national level. This could involve developing a cabinet or mayoral system.

Elected department heads

The practice of having elected attorneys and treasurers is declining in the USA. In theory it provides a check on incompetence or corrupt officials. In practice the theory does not work. Ordinary people do not exercise any real choice in voting for such candidates - in the vast majority of cases they vote for the candidate with the official endorsement of the relevant professional groups. There are simpler and better ways of holding officials to account. Separately elected officials also tend to discourage a corporate approach.

Full-time paid councillors

US city mayors tend to be full-time and paid. In 1991 the mayor of New York received $140,000 (approximately £83,000) per annum compared to $90,000 (approximately £53,000) for Seattle's mayor. This may sound a lot but it does not compare favourably to the salaries of chief executives in large private organisations. Payment and conditions for council members is more variable. There would be no difficulties in paying UK councillors and many current leaders and committee chairs are already effectively full-time. The real issue is would full-time status and payment improve the calibre of councillors? The impression from the USA is that payment produced a small but detectable shift away from businessmen to community and neighbourhood activists. The council members were generally of high calibre and drawn from a predominantly professional background.

General managers

Encouraging more general managers could be pursued immediately and some authorities have already instituted small scale secondment initiatives. It would probably meet with resistance from the local authority professions. It does, however, promote a more rounded set of management skills and helps to challenge some of the traditional professional practices.

Reduced security of tenure for senior officers

Reducing the security of tenure for senior officers would run counter to the UK tradition, although some authorities have introduced fixed-term contracts. The UK system promotes stability and reinforces the political impartiality of officers. It can make it difficult to deal with a poorly performing chief officer or to change direction. The latter can be a significant drawback during times of rapid change. A shift to the US system might reduce the attractiveness of senior positions with consequential effects on calibre, however, and could lead to more political appointments. One way of improving flexibility without reducing job attractiveness for senior officers might be:

● no contracts but higher pay;

● termination packages;

● local authorities required to provide reasons for dismissal.

The strong mayor model

The strong mayor model would represent a radical departure from UK tradition in two respects:

● separating elections for the executive and the council;

● departing from the tradition that officials are politically neutral.

The mayor's relationship to political parties, the council and appointed officials would need to be considered carefully.

In the UK a mayor would have to be elected on a party political basis. Political parties are much more important in the UK than in the USA: they provide relatively clear, recognised and distinct packages of ideas on public policy. Party political preferences also have an important influence on voting behaviour. Finally, political parties would provide the manpower and money to conduct campaigns. With a separate election for the mayor and council there would always be the possibility of a 'hung authority' such as a Conservative mayor and a Labour dominated council. However, this is no different from the situation in a hung council and compromises would have to be worked out.

There are two critical issues in relation to the council: what should its role be and should the mayor be on the council? Clearly a range of relationships is possible with variations hinging on the strength of the mayor and any democratic safeguards. The best system would be a council with a weak policy role and a strong scrutiny role. The weak policy role would mean only the mayor could propose policy, but it would require the council's endorsement and the council would be entitled to propose amendments. This would recognise the political primacy of the mayor, would minimise the duplication of policy discussion which existed in Seattle and would reduce the possibility of the mayor being nothing more than an agent of the majority party. The scrutiny role would involve a series of panels designed to probe and evaluate the executive's performance. They could operate as select committees, properly staffed, and with powers where incompetence or illegal activities are identified. The latter could provide a much stronger check on the executive in terms of probity and performance than currently exists in UK local government.

The government consultation paper on *The internal management of local authorities in England* (Department of the Environment, 1991) lays great emphasis on the need to protect the political neutrality of officers. This is strange and misses the real issue in relation to executive government. Surely the most dynamic form of city government is a mayor with political vision combined with a like minded and managerially able chief administrative officer. A good chief executive or chief administrative officer requires passion, commitment and competence. The point should be to safeguard not neutrality but competence. One possible way of safeguarding competence would be to establish some sort of approved list of potential chief administrative officers. Such a system would need to be broadly based to avoid the worst aspects of narrow professionalism.

The council-manager model

Introducing the council-manager system in the UK would be a less radical change than creating a strong mayor system. This is because it retains the traditional distinction between politics and administration. The biggest changes would involve:

● eliminating the operational management role of councillors;

● barring councillors from officer appointments;

● chief officers reporting directly to the city manager/chief executive rather than to a committee.

The operational role of councillors is already declining because of local management in schools, competition and the move towards enabling. In some senses the council-manager model would deliver the recommendations of the Bains Committee (1972) because it would give the chief executive formal authority. Again this has already begun to happen in some authorities (eg where the chief executive appraises the performance of chief officers).   Issues which would need to be settled in establishing a council-manager system would include:

● should there be a mayor and how should he/she be elected?

● what should the size of the council be?

● should the city manager and other senior staff have contracts?

The council-manager system would bring a stronger performance based culture, greater emphasis on corporate policy and management and clearer officer accountability.   It could be a useful asset in authorities with a clear political orientation and established direction.   However, it is difficult to see how the system would work effectively in an authority riddled with political tension and without any political vision.

Encouraging innovation

The government consultation paper on *The internal management of local authorities in England* (Department of the Environment, 1991) suggests that local authorities should be encouraged to innovate in their form and structure.   This is worthy but the mechanism for encouraging innovation needs to be considered. Inevitably local authorities will have a vested interest in the matter and the interests of the various players - the leader, the majority group, backbenchers, the council, the chief executive, chief officers - will differ.   Which council is going to agree to a transfer of power to an appointed city manager?   Which majority group is going to support investing considerable formal power in the leader (as a strong mayor) rather than the group?   Which backbenchers are going to vote themselves out of existence?   Another problem is the lack of experience of other systems.   Finally, and most fundamentally, who should be involved in agreeing to change the form of government?   Is it a decision for central government, the local authority or should the wider public have a say?

One way to encourage innovation might be a government competition along the lines of City Challenge. Local authorities could be invited to submit innovative proposals on internal management aiming to speed up decision making, increase public participation, improve accountability and so forth.   The winners would receive a financial prize and agree to comply with a research project to monitor whether or not the intended benefits materialise. At the end of the experimental period citizens could be invited to give their views. An alternative approach might be to introduce innovative systems of internal management in the new, unitary authorities which emerge from the government's review of local government structures.

It should be recognised that the review of local government itself will discourage innovation in internal management. Not many local authorities are going to invest a great deal of time devising a new approach to internal management when they do not know which functions they will be responsible for, whether the authority will continue to exist and how it will be funded. The government needs to make it clear whether functions such as education and police are to remain part of local government. It should also give some guidance on which authorities will disappear and which ones will continue in business.

Conclusion

There is much greater diversity in US local government than in the UK. Whilst there are significant differences between the two major forms of local government (mayor and manager councils) it has become increasingly common for councils to have directly elected mayors. Mayors increase the accountability and visibility of local government. However, a mayor does not need formal power to be an effective leader.

Both the council-manager and strong mayor systems could be adapted to UK local government, although the mayor system would involve departing from the tradition of officer neutrality. Other features of US local government, especially the public participation mechanisms, could also be imported. It would not seem feasible to import non-partisan politics and elected department heads.

References

Bains Committee (1972) *The new local authorities: management and structure*, London: HMSO.

Barrett, K. and Greene, R. (1991) 'How well managed are the cities? A special report on America's thirty largest municipalities', *Financial World*, 19 February.

Department of the Environment (1991) *The internal management of local authorities in England: a consultation paper*, London: HMSO.

Lavery, K. and Hume, C. (1991) 'Blending planning and pragmatism: making strategic planning effective in the 1990s', *Public Money and Management*, Winter issue.

Stewart, J. (1991) *Local democracy - representation and elections*, Belgrave Papers, Luton: Local Government Management Board.

Tranter, R.A.F. (1991) 'Strong mayors and city managers', address to the Annual Conference of the Society of Local Authority Chief Executives, Northampton, England, 18 April 1991.

Widdicombe, D. QC (1986) *The conduct of local authority business*, Cmnd 9797, London: HMSO.

part two

WORKING ACROSS THE BOUNDARIES

five

FINANCING URBAN REGENERATION

Nicholas Falk

One way in which the USA has influenced urban policy in the UK has been in the field of finance for urban regeneration. Ideas like public-private partnerships and urban development grants, as well as specific techniques like the adaptive re-use of redundant buildings have all emerged from visits to the USA by British people over the years. With growing European integration, however, and the collapse of ventures like Canary Wharf, doubts are beginning to surface over whether the US model is appropriate, or what lessons should be drawn.

It is important to identify what has really worked in the USA, and to see how it could be applied in the very different UK institutional context. This chapter, therefore, starts by looking at some classic examples of public-private partnerships, then considers the funding of community initiatives, before reviewing the institutional context and the scope for transferring lessons to the UK. It draws not only on my two years at Stanford Business School but also subsequent visits to regeneration schemes in Baltimore, Lowell and Pittsburgh, and valuable discussions with the staff at organisations such as Partners for Liveable Places, the Waterfront Centre, and the National Main Street Centre, all in Washington, and the Local Initiatives Support Corporation in New York.

The US way

The current US situation is both negative and positive. On the negative side, as in the UK, there is a mood of pessimism, with

many developers in financial trouble, which makes it difficult to
raise finance for any further projects. The reason is the over-supply
of new property, which has led to falling property values. This in
turn can be blamed on the relaxation of controls on investors,
starting with the savings and loans associations (the equivalent of
building societies), but followed up by banks competing for
business. As a result developers were able to borrow large sums of
money more easily than the ordinary person could raise a mortgage
on a house, with non-recourse funding in which the increasing
value of the property provided the basic security, rather than the
developer's own assets. A similar situation probably applies to
many of the younger British developers, with an over-reliance on
short or medium-term finance, rather than the traditional
dependence on the more conservative pension funds and insurance
companies.

On the positive side, while large areas of US cities continue to
fall apart, they have succeeded in devising schemes for restoring
old buildings and attracting people back to the waterfronts, and in
some cases revitalising town centres. As a result a number of
mixed use schemes have brought new spending power into
previously run-down areas and done something to stall the flight to
the suburbs.

US cities which were once dead, like Baltimore, are now alive
with thronging people. Specialist shopping complexes, food halls
and imaginative city financed museums have given run-down cities
a new lease of life. Historic buildings have been adapted to new
commercial uses. Public space has been landscaped and populated
with public art. Essentially European ideas about what makes a
city attractive have been imported (and then exported back to the
UK) (Falk, 1992). The attractions of a cosmopolitan downtown
area have then stimulated gentrification of the surrounding
neighbourhoods, but have still left large areas of dereliction close
by. Many observers have attributed the underlying reasons for
success as the more positive attitudes of US banks, influenced by
factors such as the Community Reinvestment Act of 1977, designed
to stop 'red-lining' or discrimination. Of equal significance in my
view, however, is the way government has positively sought to
work with the private sector, through various forms of public-
private partnerships and through support for community initiatives.

Public-private partnerships

The benefits of public-private partnerships can be considerable. The public sector brings to bear access to low cost capital, its regulatory powers (sometimes made more accessible through a 'one stop shop') and its working relationships with other agencies. It may also own part of the land or be able to acquire it more advantageously. The private sector brings to bear access to private capital, a speed of decision making that the public sector can never emulate and that important ingredient, entrepreneurial motivation or flair, often described as a 'gut feeling' about projects.

An early Urban and Economic Development Group (URBED) report *Lessons from the US* back in 1980 highlighted the crucial importance of the idea of partnership between public agencies and local business interests (Urban and Economic Development Group, 1980). An influential model for urban regeneration which was subsequently studied is Lowell, a working class town near Boston, once the centre of the textile industry and still dominated by giant mills and canals, and this example provides a means of understanding how the US system can work (Falk, 1986).

The initial improvements to the main street were made under the Model Cities Programme in the 1970s. Pavements and shopfronts were beautified, with extensive tree planting, landscaped courtyards and car parks and period street lighting, while shopkeepers have taken up the theme by eliminating clumsy neon signs. A main street coordinator was appointed through the National Trust for Historic Preservation, pioneering a programme which is also being applied successfully in Canada.

However, the main innovation in Lowell was the designation of the town as the first National Urban Historical Park. The National Parks Service has played a leading role in stimulating interest in the town, with a government investment of over $40 million. The main facilities are provided in an interpretation centre on the ground floor of a mill, whose upper floors have been converted into apartments for the elderly. Attractive landscaping with sculpture, fountains and banners, a food hall, and artists galleries, provide a focal point for tourists. From there visitors can take tours run by rangers, who in the summer are supplemented by students, with trips in a replica trolley car, or a canal boat.

The 'historic park' was initiated by an unusual organisation called the Lowell Plan, which had been formed to help implement the development strategy for the town drawn up by consultants.

The first step had been to persuade local banks to subscribe 1/20th of 1% of deposits to a fund to be invested in improvements. At the time Lowell had been written off as an economic disaster area and so few expected a return on the initial £300,000. Further funds were secured when the Lowell Plan, through an associated company, persuaded the federal government to make it the agent for all urban development action grant in the city (a grant regime that was scrapped in 1988). This meant that public funds, instead of going to developers as grants, were used as low cost second loans to be repaid to the development corporation. This created a revolving fund worth over $13 million in 1986 and the city has been able to secure the active support of local property owners and business people, who might otherwise have been apathetic.

The Lowell success story was made possible by four distinctive factors in the US financial system. The first is competition among the banks. There are nearly 250 banks in the State of Massachusetts and over 1,200 in the State of Illinois, which makes them more involved with local affairs and more willing to take risks in order to attract new business.

The second factor is the tax system that encourages private investment in property in general. In both the USA and Canada the initial expenditure on developments, which are called the 'soft costs', such as architects and legal fees, landscaping and financing charges, can be written off against tax. The investment can then be depreciated, and this has encouraged the formation of 'limited partnerships' to invest in particular projects. Professional 'syndicators' draw together investments of typically $10,000 to $25,000 each from people like doctors and lawyers who are in a relatively high tax bracket. The appeal is not only the considerable tax write-offs, which can cut the effective cost by more than half, but also the satisfaction that comes from being involved in an innovative as well as a successful business venture. The satisfaction is likened to owning a share in a racehorse! This equity investment is then leveraged or multiplied by bank loans. Much lower interest rates made projects viable in 1990 at returns of over 13%, compared to 20% or more that developers commonly expect in the UK.

To these incentives has been added a third factor in the USA of tax write-offs for investment in historic properties. This measure is believed to account for a vast increase in the investment in refurbishment, which in turn has caused the price of historic properties to escalate. Before President Reagan cut it back, the tax write-off allowed an investor to reduce his or her tax bill by 20% of the expenditure provided that the building is on the National Register of Historic Properties, the work conforms to nationally laid down standards, and part of the restored property produces an income. It was therefore quite easy to pay no tax at all by becoming involved in restoration. The main effect has been to stimulate the 'mom and pop' developer, the professional couple, who may take on a historic house, living in part and operating a business from the remainder. In the UK the nearest equivalent is the Business Expansion Scheme but apart from rented housing this has not been used to assist urban regeneration.

The final incentive was the scope for developers to issue tax exempt bonds for projects that involve the restoration of historic buildings or work in specified districts that need investment. Because investors can recover tax on such investments, the effect was to make funds available at interest rates of as little as 6% which again made development a far more attractive proposition for the private investor.

The combined effect of these measures has been to reduce greatly the cost of development for a product which is itself becoming increasingly popular. Though tax incentives are inefficient in many ways, often increasing the profits on what would have happened anyway or raising land prices, they do have the great appeal of appearing not to cost anything and being simple to administer. As a result far more finance has been provided for historic restoration than would ever have been made available as grants for historic structures or needy areas. They have also broadened the range of developers and produced a new industry, instead of relying on the 'professionals' who still tend to see restoration as too problematic and risky to be worth bothering with.

One similarity with the UK is the growing involvement of insurance companies and pension funds - often British - in directly investing in new office blocks. Faced with this competition, US developers are turning to more complex and profitable projects. They see their role as devising imaginative schemes and assembling the finance, often playing a project management role in partnership with an institution. Mixed use schemes are thus far more usual, and it is quite common now to see buildings with shops on the ground floor and the top floors given over to housing in condominiums.

Some exciting regeneration projects have been undertaken in the most unpromising circumstances, of which the best known in addition to Lowell are probably Baltimore Inner Harbor and Pittsburgh. Almost every town and city, however, has some kind of scheme, though too many have tried to copy formulas that have then not worked. Thus the 'festival marketplace' concept promoted by the Rouse Corporation is becoming discredited, with financial failures in three of the four projects they have undertaken with the Enterprise Development Corporation following the success of the early commercial ventures in Baltimore and Boston.

One lesson from the failures is that successful places are those that build on their own particular resources, and bring together local interests in projects that are undertaken incrementally over many years. So it is extremely disturbing that instead of making the most of their own resources, UK authorities and developers are being seduced by pretty pictures and a belief that regeneration schemes can be implemented in one 'big bang' (Falk, 1992).

Some of the most impressive US developments are those that emphasise the provision of public space of different kinds, from high quality landscaping with fountains and public art, to ecological wetlands and interpretation programmes. The use of special purpose agencies, drawing together different types of funding, enables the front-end risks to be reduced, which often makes it easier to involve the private sector in undertaking specific projects within their particular field of competence, rather than acting as general developer. Public art has also been greatly encouraged by the requirement in many states for developers to allocate 1% of development costs to public art and this is inspiring similar initiatives in UK cities, like Birmingham. What in the UK we call 'planning gain' has also been greatly encouraged in the USA by the requirement made by many planning authorities, such as Boston, that developers of commercial projects should contribute to public objectives through what is called 'linkage'. Thus in Boston developers are required to pay $5 for housing and $1 dollar for job training for every square foot of floor space over 100,000 (Hambleton, 1990, p 20).

Community initiatives

While each area varies, there are certain elements in the way regeneration projects are put together which might usefully be applied in the UK. As well as the idea of public-private partnerships there has also been a greater involvement of local communities in regeneration than we in the UK are used to. The process typically starts with local people drawing attention to the potential of a historic building or waterfront, and putting pressure on the municipality to do something. Communities are often helped by the common practice of organising what might be called 'action planning' events in which some outside experts help to generate fresh ideas, in consultation with local interests. Perhaps the best know system is Regional and Urban Design Assistance Teams (RUDAT), which is run by the American Association of Architects, and three or four similar events have been held in the UK, called UDATS with the Urban Design Group acting as the enabler. A typical event will bring a diverse group together for three or so days, with plenty of background documentation, and is a good way of starting the regeneration process with limited funds.

In some cases the community group will promote a project itself, sometimes inspired by what are seen as irrelevant or harmful proposals emanating from a private developer. A classic example is in Providence, the state capital of Rhode Island, where a local architect, incensed by grandiose schemes for the downtown, promoted the idea of opening up the rivers which had been buried under concrete, and diverting both the rail tracks and the freeway to make this possible. An initial grant of £35,000 from the National Endowment for the Arts (which is something like the Arts Council) enabled the architect to undertake the necessary consultations and studies needed to win support. As there were substantial transport advantages, most of the capital came from government sources and this amazing project, which even involved changing the course of two rivers, was seen as a shot in the arm for the area's failing economy. Another fine model is Pittsburgh, where the Union Station renovation has been promoted by an individual taking advantage of tax incentive funding, and using a not-for-profit company as the overall developer.

Important sources of funds and expertise for community led projects are the Trust for Public Land and the Local Initiatives Support Corporation. The Trust for Public Land acts rather like the National Trust in helping to take land into public ownership, except that it usually acts through local trusts. Funding is raised through a combination of tax incentives to the owners and ingenious deals, for example through land swaps. The Trust has been responsible for some impressive achievements. A report by URBED for the Groundwork Foundation entitled *Putting waste land to good use* proposed that a UK equivalent might be set up through

Groundwork but so far this idea has not been taken further (Urban and Economic Development Group, 1986).

In looking for a way of helping community initiatives to get off the ground, considerable interest has been shown in the Local Initiatives Support Corporation (LISC). Based in New York, and with offices in many other cities, LISC has managed to establish a leading position as a kind of fringe bank, specialising in supporting community based initiatives in disadvantaged areas. LISC started with the support of the Ford Foundation, who 10 years ago put £10 million together with some support from a couple of major companies and financial institutions who were close allies. The idea was to use this risk capital to 'leverage' other sources of funds and to make them available on advantageous terms, together with technical assistance to groups with projects that had the prospect of being self-sustaining. LISC has gone on to manage over £250 million, which comes from a variety of sources. A small part is still effectively grants, but the majority comes from low cost finance provided by institutions who can claim tax credits, and from government sources.

LISC operates through a series of local advisory committees in some 23 'areas of concentration', which are states or cities. LISC's role includes:

- managing the National Equity Fund which channels corporate equity investments into low cost housing;

- managing a secondary market in community development loans, which are underwritten by LISC;

- packaging funds from other sources.

The impact of LISC can be seen from the fact that in 10 years it has assembled £300 million from 600 corporations and foundations. This has then been used to leverage over £1.3 billion of direct investment in over 600 community development corporations and countless public-private partnerships, which in turn have helped to create 21,500 units of affordable housing and 5.5 million square feet of affordable space. Their annual report, from which these figures are taken, stresses the "belief that locally-oriented physical change is a uniquely powerful tool for revitalising communities".

During this time LISC has become a highly professional organisation with some 100 staff, of whom about half work in New York. The board of directors comprises 19 leading individuals from a diversity of backgrounds including, interestingly, the president of National Westminster Bank in New York. While LISC would not want to suggest that it provides the answer to the problems of urban regeneration, undoubtedly a well resourced intermediary operating in the grey area between commercial and charitable objectives is invaluable in enabling local aspirations to be fulfilled at minimum risk or cost.

The institutional context

Whereas projects in the UK often proceed in a somewhat random and unpredictable way, for example depending on a politician's personal enthusiasm, in the USA there seems to be a well established procedure for taking ideas forward which we may be moving towards. Once the municipality is convinced by local pressure that a project is needed, it will seek to raise the funds for what is effectively a feasibility study from municipal, state or federal government. When the funds are made available, it means that there is an 'in principle' commitment to implement the project, subject to independent consultants' reports and popular support.

The next step is for the municipality to issue a Request for Proposal (RFP) which invites a number of firms to put forward tenders, and this typically proceeds in four stages. First, there is a market study to establish whether there is sufficient demand to justify the development. If the demand is there the next stage is to commission both an 'environmental impact assessment', which examines a number of alternatives, including doing nothing, and a construction study, looking at the design and financial implications. With these reports, the municipality is in a position to start raising funds for the public contribution to the project. Sometimes this used to be through an urban development action grant (on which our city grant is modelled), though this is not nearly as important as is often believed and was scrapped in 1988. Far more important typically is the local authority's role in helping to assemble the land, where it is in different ownerships, and in providing infrastructure or environmental improvements. In order to finance this, the local authority will typically issue a bond which is linked to the project. A bond pays a fixed interest and is backed up by the municipality's capacity to collect property and other taxes. Bonds have to be approved by a referendum, which enables the public to influence whether a major project goes ahead or not.

Other alternatives are available, including declaring a 'local improvement district', which enables a collective assessment to be made on property owners. This, however, can fail if there is any opposition, for example from a business who will be dislocated by the project. Other possibilities include 'revenue bonds' where income from the project is used to pay the interest and eventually retire the bond. 'Tax increment financing' ploughs back increases in property values arising from the project into retiring the bond, which requires a two-thirds majority in many states. Tax 'easements' are also used to encourage private developers, by deferring property and other taxes.

Other possibilities which can be used are loan guarantee powers (which come under the small business administration), enabling municipalities to underwrite part of the risk on what are seen as worthwhile projects without having to put up the finance. There are various forms of grant, including cost-sharing grants, for example for resource conservation and development, and outright grants, such as from the National Endowment for the Arts. There are also a number of what are known as 'formula grants' available from the different federal agencies, such as community development block grant (which works rather like the old UK rate support grant), and grants for coastal management, construction and access, community and economic development and historic preservation, most of which have their UK equivalents.

One often remarked advantage of the USA is the much greater importance of private foundations in funding innovative projects which are undertaken for the public benefit. Much of these funds goes into arts related projects, and are often concentrated in the places where the foundation's money was originally made. This has given Pittsburgh, for example, a particular advantage that an equivalent city like Sheffield does not have as it makes possible projects that would not normally pass through all the stringent tests that are laid down for public funding.

While there is an established process for taking forward regeneration projects it is still considered extremely difficult to set up mixed use waterfront projects, which are seen as something that require specialised expertise. The developer helps to provide the important pre-risk money needed to tie up the property and employ professionals on preparing preliminary plans, market studies and, most important of all, the business plan. This work can also be done by the municipality and in a difficult market it becomes almost essential to do this work first before inviting proposals from developers. The developer's vital role is then in raising the private money, and here key ingredients are a relevant track record, and knowing who has financed similar projects before. On major schemes, such as the redevelopment of historic waterfronts, a complex approach is needed, particularly as deals can take many years to put together. Given the popular myth that it is much easier to develop property in the USA, it was significant that developers I spoke to at the Waterfront Centre's Annual Conference in Washington in October 1990 were saying that the process was becoming virtually impossible, because of the long drawn out system of approvals, and also because of the difficulty of securing binding commitments on the part of local authorities. This could lead to a project being set up under one administration and then being turned down by a successor, and developers felt that the prospects no longer justified the exceptional efforts involved (compared with other simpler forms of development). I was told real estate development is a visceral thing, "everyone's hungry and everything's negotiable" and that the "idea of inter-agency collaboration is garbage".

The effective developer helps the process along by picking consultants that the regulatory agencies like, or using the local authority as a co-applicant. It has been found that agencies sometimes prefer to deal with the principal rather than a consultant. However, there are a number of professional firms who provide municipalities with help both in drawing up briefs for sites, attracting developer interest, and then negotiating the right terms, and this is particularly important for smaller communities who lack in-house expertise. It is significant that such firms tend to be economics or business based, as there is no direct equivalent to the UK surveyor.

An example of how the process can work is provided by the Philadelphia Marine Development, which is a mixed use project around a marina. Here the developer put up 10% by way of equity and the local authority raised funds through a bond issue, which was promoted and underwritten through the Philadelphia Economic Development Corporation. In this project the security was provided through the value of the property and a financial partner was brought in by the developer. This happened to be a property company subsidiary of the local telephone utility, Bell Atlantic, who provided a 'comfort letter' which said that the company would never reduce the asset value to levels that would cause foreclosure on the loan. Their motive incidentally, apart from the return on their equity, was providing a showcase for the parent company who wanted to become involved in the Philadelphia Waterfront. Other incentives for participation were provided by the favourable depreciation rates available on certain kinds of development that enable tax savings to be made.

The scope for innovation in the UK

A fundamental reassessment of how urban regeneration in the UK is organised and financed is urgently needed. The collapse of the property market means that neither developers or financial institutions are in a position to take a lead. Local authorities lack people and money. Community groups, for the most part, have little experience of playing a positive role. And development corporations, which should have provided the answer, are becoming increasingly discredited. The problems are symbolised in London's Docklands by Canary Wharf, which as a result of public subsidies, including tax incentives, has produced a vast amount of office space in a location that cannot handle it, while other major schemes around the London railway terminal stations grind to a halt. The subsequent collapse of the developers Olympic and York, and the need to inject still further public finance into propping up this part of Docklands might have been avoided if the more rigorous and planned approach used in the USA had been adopted.

Those involved in regeneration in the UK, including leading developers, now recognise the need for the public sector to take more of a lead, in particular as far as improving the environment and infrastructure in concerned. But this in turn depends on having an organisation controlling the land which can take a long-term view (Baltimore after all having taken over 30 years to turn around), and can also respond to short as well as long-term demands. I have likened the process to that of the theatrical producer or 'animateur', communicating a shared vision, setting the stage, mobilising the actors and attracting the audience. Projects that URBED has managed, such as the regeneration of the Little Germany quarter in Bradford, demonstrate that the process works.

Successes have been achieved within the current UK local government structure. For example, local authorities can commission master plans or development briefs that excite interest. But the visions can only be turned into results where there are mechanisms for funding the creation of an environment in which enterprise will flourish, and this is where the UK system currently falls down. So what needs to be done? Here are four practical suggestions for creating regeneration partnerships. First, we need to encourage 'city visions' by enabling community groups and other concerned interests to discuss and articulate what is needed. This means using conferences, exhibitions, public art and what we call 'action planning', that is the use of events to set new agendas. These could be assisted by the Arts Council, with their new interest in architecture, or by the Department of the Environment, through their Special Grants Programme for voluntary and environmental groups. Another possibility is the Training and Enterprise Councils who have a legitimate role in bringing the business community together. A good practical outlet will be the setting up of planning and architecture centres to provide a public focus in areas undergoing change.

Second, we need to create local agencies that can bring different interests together, and here the model of the 'development trust' seems to provide a good approach. These could be greatly helped by the Department of the Environment providing seed capital (perhaps through City Challenge or Task Forces), and through the use of targeted tax incentives to enable limited partnerships to be set up for innovative or catalytic projects. Perhaps the term community development corporation would be appropriate, though the important point is that each should be unique to the area and tasks it takes on.

Third, we need a process for funding the preliminary stages of development to support efforts to focus on areas that might otherwise be disregarded. It is important to be able to devise regeneration strategies and put development projects together without having to rely on private developers. Here the Welsh and Scottish Development Agencies provide a good precedent and the equivalent is needed for the main UK regions, focusing particularly on the former metropolitan counties. The Urban Regeneration Agency could provide the vehicle provided it acts in partnership with local communities and takes a much wider perspective than building business premises.

Finally, we need a UK LISC or what I call Local Initiatives Finance and Training (LIFT). An effective intermediary would not only be able to generate and evaluate good projects, but also have funds on tap for 'getting the ball rolling'. This can range from purchasing land or buildings in advance of having a scheme all worked out, to undertaking the necessary professional work to put development schemes together. Just as with LISC, the initial funds might come from a small number of organisations or individuals. Possibilities include charitable foundations, companies who are supporting regeneration projects and private individuals who have discretionary funds, for example as a result of selling their business. These might then be matched by organisations such as English Heritage, who are keen to find ways of making their grants go further, and the Department of the Environment. In addition, once LIFT was up and running, funds might be raised through imaginative means such as under the Business Expansion Scheme for rented housing with assured tenancies, and drawing on the Architectural Heritage Fund where projects and their promoters qualify (with LIFT providing the repayment guarantee). It may also be possible to tap institutional finance for projects in which community groups secure some 'planning gain' from major development schemes, as for example is happening in Spitalfields.

By setting up regeneration partnerships along the lines above, it will be possible to encourage development that is rooted in local needs and that applies resources more productively than has happened over the last decade.

References

Falk, N. (1986) 'Baltimore and Lowell: two American approaches', *Built Environment*, vol 12, no 3.

Falk, N. (1992) 'Turning the tide, British experience in regenerating urban docklands', in B.S. Hoyle and D.R. Pinder (eds) *European port cities in transition*, London: Belhaven.

Hambleton, R. (1990) *Urban government in the 1990s: lessons from the USA*, Bristol: SAUS Publications, School for Advanced Urban Studies, University of Bristol.

Urban and Economic Development Group (1980) *Local economic development: a guide to US experience*, London: URBED.

Urban and Economic Development Group (1986) *Putting wasteland to good use,* London: URBED.

six

VOCATIONAL TRAINING

The role of churches and religious groups

Sandra Newton

> Society must be so arranged as to give to every citizen the maximum opportunity for making deliberate choices and the best possible training for the use of that opportunity.
> (Temple, 1942, pp 18-19)

Introduction

The research on which this paper is based took place in the USA between August 1990 and January 1991 with prior studies in UK cities in the spring and summer of 1990. The aim was to see whether the churches (in the broadest sense of institutional religious organisations) could play a more active role in vocational training in areas of severe urban deprivation, and if so how. Although different in history and government structures, the UK and the USA have shared an increasingly similar pattern of planning and delivery of training, persistent urban decay and churches concerned to do something to help people break out of the welfare cycle. What were they doing in practical terms to make the best use of the available resources and to tackle their common problems? What more could be done or could it be done differently?

While most sharply focused on the deprived central or outer areas of cities, the challenges to and for churches in suburban or rural areas are variations on the same theme. Many of the examples of involvement and the problems they address are closely comparable to those faced by secular voluntary agencies in both countries. This chapter illustrates a much more general concern, challenge and opportunity for particular bodies and locations.

The policy concerns and background

One of the principal stimuli for this research was the mixed experience in both countries of the churches and other religious organisations[1] with government funded training programmes. With rising youth unemployment in the UK in the early 1970s, churches were encouraged to help deliver a range of training programmes for unemployed young people. Foundations laid at this time were built upon progressively until the early and mid 1980s, with the development of the Community Programme (CP) of temporary work for unemployed adults, of which churches had 6% (15,000) of the total places and around 16% of the charitable experimental places. With the move to the New Job Training Scheme (NJTS) in 1988, Employment Training (ET) in 1989 and the similar changes to Youth Training (YT) in the next year, funding and administration of public training programmes became much less attractive to churches. Unit costings, the beginnings of payments by results and for qualifications attained, and the shorter placements, preferably with private sector employers, made churches (and their main client groups) a less easy fit in the new provider jigsaw. The move in the USA to Private Industry Councils (PICs) to plan and deliver training locally, combined with budgetary reductions as unemployment fell, also had a detrimental effect on church providers - either on their own or more usually in collaboration with secular voluntary agencies.[2]

On both sides of the Atlantic, churches seemed better equipped to provide support before or around training rather than to manage the delivery of the training itself. With relatively low levels of unemployment in both countries towards the end of the 1980s and very early 1990s, the proportion of hard core unemployed in the total rose. Before many of the longer-term unemployed and others at a disadvantage in the workforce could even consider training, intensive psychological and practical preparation was often necessary with similar support that could be sustained through the training process. This ancillary help for trainees was not allowed for in training budgets.

This suggested the need for a very different and much broader view of church resources and potential than had been taken hitherto by churches themselves as prospective contractors, if they were to have a continuing role in training.

The *Faith in the city* report (Archbishop of Canterbury's Commission on Urban Priority Areas, 1985) challenged the church to play a more active role to reduce poverty in society. The report was critical of recent trends in government training and employment provision but, despite a plethora of negative reaction from the popular media, looked at what the church itself could do.

"The most practical and public sign of the concerns of the Church of England for the inner cities and outer housing estates of our community" (Grundy, 1990) was the Church Urban Fund (CUF). Established as a registered charity in 1987, CUF set out to raise £18 million in four years from all the dioceses. With additional funds from the Church Commissioners and corporate donations, CUF sought to achieve £80 million to spend over 20 years. Grants were and are made as matching funding to projects for capital and current expenditure over two to three years. Very few have gone directly to training but they have helped to open up provision in such skills as construction and caring as work gets underway.

The Jubilee Ministry in the USA offers a similar programme run by the Episcopal Church: "a ministry of joint discipleship with poor and oppressed people ... to meet basic human needs and to build a joint and peaceful global society" (quote taken from promotional literature). Although established in 1970 to "develop recommendations and strategies which will be of concrete assistance to the Church in metropolitan areas" (quote taken from a report of the General Convention of the Episcopal Church, 1970) much of the activity has in practice been recognising work already being done, giving very modest grants (averaging $20,000) to projects and encouraging 'cheap labour' internships for urban priority area (UPA) churches. Steps are now being taken to raise the quality and practical impact of the ministry but, like CUF, its impact on helping people to break out of the welfare cycle has been very small.

Churches and training in the USA

Involvement of churches in training in the USA ranged across the whole spectrum of possibilities: from praying for the unemployed to managing large scale general training programmes (see Figure 1). The spectrum was and is neutral in itself but churches taking their social responsibilities seriously had to find the right place for themselves and review whether and how they should change it over time.

Figure 1: The spectrum of church involvement in training

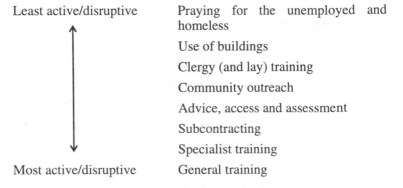

Least active/disruptive

Praying for the unemployed and homeless

Use of buildings

Clergy (and lay) training

Community outreach

Advice, access and assessment

Subcontracting

Specialist training

Most active/disruptive

General training

Underlying all the work done by churches was prayer and a great deal of voluntary activity. The two could be seen at work in St Luke's Episcopal Church in downtown Atlanta. Here homeless people were prepared for training by feeding, free medical attention, a PO Box service, a clothing store and confidence building through such activities as a choir. Recognition of value, and training for the participants, was given in an annual requiem mass held at the Episcopal Cathedral in Atlanta for homeless people who had died in the last year.

Moving further along the spectrum, the management and use of buildings had to become much more professional. Many churches had converted, let and shared buildings for the training activities of themselves or others. Rather fewer had crossed the threshold to economic rents! This posed a real problem to balance 'God and Mammon' in acceptable and effective ways. The move to charging economic rents often arose (as in Hyde Park, Chicago) from bad experiences with previous tenants and the need for increased investment in planned schemes. It could also come from the needs of an area. In the west side of Chicago, the presbytery was located in a converted garage that also housed two social/economic voluntary organisations. To a much greater extent than in the UK, clergy training courses had been adapted to include exposure to urban needs and conditions. Giving clergy the skills that they needed was a vital first step to their recognising and meeting the skill needs of others. Variants from short 'urban plunges' to full year courses and postings were found operating interdenominationally in Chicago and Atlanta. Student placements were much more general. Training for laity on church premises and through church intervention was also highly effective. Examples were, respectively, stonemasonry and arts management at the Cathedral Church of St John the Divine, New York, and the National Cathedral, Washington DC, and the consortium of black/Catholic churches in the Oakland Church and Community Organisation that led a cascaded training programme for community organisers.

The normal community outreach of churches can imply or prepare for skill training. Examples of such activities were providing clothes and bursaries for trainees in Indianapolis, literary tutoring led by volunteers in Washington, training in hostel management in New York and training in self-advocacy among homeless people in Atlanta.

Turning to involvement that imparted skills more directly, in the sense of the range of training and educational activities that explicitly help to prepare people for paid work, US churches were again contributing in a range of ways. Very often church representatives on PICs would provide valuable advice on the needs of 'their' communities and through bridging cultural and language barriers give effective access to training for groups of people otherwise distanced from public bureaucracies. Good examples of this could be seen among the Polish and Hispanic communities in Chicago, Hispanics in Washington and Chinese in Boston. Church representatives would also draw on opinions in their congregations about the perceptions and performance of programmes, publicise their availability, provide counselling for individuals and help to guide the selection of projects.

A relatively low risk way for churches to become directly involved with training is to subcontract for a 'part of the action' from another organisation. The Jewish Vocational Services branch in Atlanta had begun in 1990/91 a 10 place customised training subcontract for the local PIC as a pilot exercise. Although only a limited success so far, both sides wanted to repeat the experiment the next year.

Many churches were attracted particularly to helping people at most disadvantage in the labour market. Specialist training for particular groups or situations can be combined with subcontracting but can also be commissioned directly. Project WISH in Washington was created by black and Catholic churches to offer housing management training to residents of rented apartments and work towards owner-managed cooperatives for the apartment blocks. WISH also trained clergy in awareness of housing issues. In Indianapolis, Volunteers of America (a breakaway from the Salvation Army) specialised in residential rehabilitation of ex-offenders and has offered advice to the USSR on non-medical aspects of drug abuse.

Very few churches want or are able to take the significant further step of directly running general training programmes. Inherent in the shift is a larger scale and greater diversity of training offered. Churches that do move to this point actually need to 'secularise' their operation with professional managers and trainers, financial advisers, marketers and so on. Two very good examples of successful general trainers are Goodwill Industries in Indianapolis and the Neighbourhood Institute in Chicago.

Goodwill Industries is an international company, best known for its thrift shops. It was founded in Boston in the 1930s by a Methodist clergyman who wanted to create jobs for immigrants. In Indianapolis, the fourth largest unit in the USA, the financing and training opportunities of the thrift shop are combined with sheltered workshops and a career development centre majoring on skills at the forefront of demand.

The Neighbourhood Institute (TNI) began as a community organisation in a poor southern part of Chicago working with and through many local churches. From needs identified, and significant help from a local bank, TNI now trains in all major basic and clerical skills, rehabilitates buildings using the full range of construction grades, and provides starter units for small businesses and creative opportunities for local artists.

These examples along the spectrum of involvement show the practical possibilities for churches - and training funders - who can overcome inertia and inhibition. Their experience could be repeated in many other US cities. In assessing their performance, a number of points need to be borne in mind.

● *Direct funding*:

very few of the examples relied solely or mainly on public funds, drawing in preference on endowments, donations and private philanthropy.

● *Limited aims*:

very few of the US churches involved in training progressed to direct general training and even then (as in Chicago) their geographical area was usually limited. Churches were cautious to take on tasks they thought they could fulfil satisfactorily, sharing responsibilities where necessary with other sacred or secular bodies.

● *A stretching experience*:

training involvement had stretched church resources for money, space and people and challenged their own views of other players in the training field. By no means all experiences were positive and funding from outside was precarious from year to year.

● *Value of a supporting role*:

many churches had found that their best contribution to training was in fact not to train at all! It was, rather, to prepare people for and help them through the training process by housing, feeding, counselling, giving day care to dependents and offering volunteer tutoring.

Assessment

The first and very obvious thing to say about the US approach to the problems and potential of church involvement in training is its diversity. There are as many approaches as there are dioceses and churches, ranging from a decision that churches should save souls and then cities would follow to a very significant redirection of churches' ministry and organisation to achieve social goals.

It seemed to this author, however, that black churches had in common an ambivalence towards involvement in training. With a high proportion of black residents concentrated in the urban priority areas of both countries, churches of mainly black denominations might be expected to form a natural focus for economic regeneration: reskilling their people and area as they have often provided a political and educational focus. Difficulties encountered in the UK by Task Forces and the (former) British Council of Churches in securing a practical interest in training initiatives were found on a larger scale in the USA. These included a widespread pietistic approach to religion, majoring on the gospel of personal salvation rather than social assistance, widely travelling clergy without administrative support back at base and a frequent paralysis of decision between a priority for social action or social service in the church (but see also Morris, Chapter 12).

This latter difficulty is a long-standing one for all churches but is seen most sharply among black churches: whether to work to overthrow or improve the existing social system (see, for example, Parris, 1985; Johnson, 1980). Organisations such as Concerned Black Clergy and the Baptist Southern Leadership Conference took a great deal of time and energy across large geographical areas, protesting on important issues such as infant mortality and crime prevention. Locally, work to increase voter registration and polling, and lobbies on city policing took priority over training. Interestingly, a balance between social service and social action was seen to have been achieved most productively in Atlanta out of the six cities visited. Here the well established tradition of political activism was not threatened but rather complemented by support for training, counselling and education. Another example of blending educational, political and training activities was found in operation PUSH, based in Chicago but with a national network of groups. Except for Atlanta, most of the later points in this section refer to the activities of white (or predominantly white) churches.

As the research progressed it became clear that the dynamics of involvement differed between the UK and USA. In the UK public concern and funding had led to an early start by churches in training and, as policies became less attractive and lucrative, an increased interest could be seen in other social help, such as housing. From the identification of need and direction of (especially) federal funding in the USA, American churches often entered the welfare field in help for homeless people and have only very recently diversified into training to try to break the welfare cycle. In each case, at least the vestiges of the earlier interest remain as the new developments are added in but the emphases of provision are influenced very directly by the availability of private and public funding.

The white US churches have for many decades been filling gaps in the welfare system and generally find less moral difficulty with this than do their black US or white UK counterparts. The existence of significant endowments and often larger clusters of buildings than in the UK meant that churches of many denominations were able to exercise considerable independence in deciding where their intervention was best placed and how their labour should be divided.

However, a key barrier to US church involvement - more important than either principles or practice - was the constitutionally enshrined separation of church and state. Originally designed to protect the freedom of worship of the early settlers, the measure had become a frequent mental and political blockage. Churches were reluctant to take a high profile in joint ventures with secular voluntary bodies for fear of prejudicing funding and public officials would much rather support training in, for example, colleges than churches. Ironically, the required conditions of acceptable training in religious premises were hardly any different between the UK and the USA but the mystique around the US division was such that it had needed strong determination and more than usual common sense if the inhibition barrier was to be broken.

The most commonly heard description of what US churches were trying to do in the training field was to go 'beyond the Bandaid'. They wanted to create a permanent improvement in people's condition rather than temporarily stem their discomfort. The strong individualism in the USA was here a very positive force in encouraging churches to help people secure real choice, economic independence and personal fulfilment. Even with a large slice of American optimism, however, this was seen as a long-term objective. Bandaids of various shapes and sizes had to be applied meanwhile.

Policy setting: comparisons

While several of the points given above could apply equally to UK as to US churches there are a number of features of US society which offer distinctive stimuli to church involvement in training.

A very noticeable difference is in the level of church attendance and giving by congregations. According to a Gallup poll of 1989, over 40% of the US population attended church weekly and the US population rated God more highly in their lives than members of any other major country (see Wills, 1991). Compared with around 5% weekly attendance for the UK, the US situation gives a great deal more power to churches as institutions to consider involvement in training.

Church attenders are also large and better givers, in cash or in kind (see Wineburg, 1990). Most of the churches visited in the US were seeking a committed 5% income from their congregation whereas the average level of parish giving in the UK is around 2.5% per head. Pioneering work by the independent sector has shown the concern of congregations and their churches to give to humanitarian programmes as well as religious activities (see, for example, Wuthnow and Hodgkinson, 1990). Around 50% of expenditure given was used for other than religious activities with about 40% of this sum going on education and welfare - about $9 billion in 1986. Training is potentially well supported in intent and wherewithal among the US churches.

The particular commitment of US congregations is set against an already very active US culture of philanthropy where people give and are expected to give time and money to people less fortunate than themselves. It has been said that "one of God's purposes in creating poverty was to make charity possible" and that "one of God's purposes in creating US wealth ... must have been to make philanthropy possible" (quoted in Bremner, 1988). Without needing to agree, it is very clear that the contributions of Carnegie's libraries, Mellon's church endowments, Lilley's religious and social trusts and many more, laid the foundations for a real individual and corporate consciousness of the responsibility to give. The individual contribution to philanthropy is dramatic. From a total charitable giving of $104 billion in 1988, 90% came from individuals. The average annual contribution was $700 and one half of the population volunteered at least 3.5 hours of their time each week. Religiously affiliated organisations received around half of the total given (see Wuthnow and Hodgkinson, 1990; Newton, 1991).

Apparently cutting against these two positive forces is the separation between church and state mentioned earlier in the chapter. Although in perception often an inhibitor, however, there is no reason why US practice should differ from the UK's monitored declaration of independence of intent and methodology from proselytising and furthering the denomination. It could, in fact, be the case that the necessary demonstration of independence from specifically religious activities in the USA has produced an earlier and deeper shift to a professional management of church related training activities. Encouraging churches to work with and through secular groups, often in complementary skills and resources, a synergy has been created where there is at least the initial will to become involved.

Falling US unemployment until 1990 reduced public funding for training on a pre-arranged formula for allocating budgets to states. With direct parallels in the UK, US churches have in many cases lost their training contracts with the PICs and been forced to merge or move to other areas of support. In many cases, however, the cushion of funds from their own resources has softened this blow for churches in the USA and the culture of philanthropic collaboration has helped to provide alternative partners and/or clients.

The welfare system of the USA both gives churches a larger role to play in the gaps and points them to groups that receive least help from social security and other provisions. One example is the almost complete lack of income support for the unemployed, single and (often black) young man. Single mothers (but not all women) receive the major share of social security payments for non-pensioners, leaving a gaping hole for young, inner city men who are understandably attracted to crime and prostitution. Even in training, no income allowance is given to such people. Churches and other organisations have tried to bring practical support in counselling, welfare, training and business start up. The best route away from 'the endangered species' for young men is a job. Training for school drop-outs is a real way that churches can help.

Young black men are one example of people with special needs but, as has been said earlier, churches are also well placed to help other parts of the system that public funds find difficult to reach. In the US context, redeploying older workers and language and literary training for immigrants and under-achievers are very important economic as well as social tasks - church organisations are involved in both these fields with full-time and volunteer staff.

The local responsibility and accountability of the PIC offers further opportunities for church input and assistance. The whole spectrum of church involvement in training can help the PIC, directly and indirectly, to meet its training objectives. Despite - and often because of - recent funding cuts, churches and PICs continue to experiment with new ways of working together for particular projects, groups, areas or skills.

Possibilities of transfer

The cities for this study were selected deliberately to provide non-extreme examples that had parallels of scale, economic conditions and industries with major cities in the UK.   Pittsburgh and Sheffield, Chicago and Birmingham, Atlanta and Bristol or Swindon are certainly not identical but they and other possible pairings do share a number of characteristics that suggest the possibilities of transfer are worth looking at.

Another source of encouragement is the long history of trade in training programmes across the Atlantic.   In particular, youth training and help with business start up have attracted US interest, and the Boston Compact and the PIC concept has crossed to the UK in recent years.   Despite our increasing formal links with the European Community, the cultural sharing across the Atlantic tends to be as great if not greater in training than that across the Channel.

This high level of mutual awareness in the training field is reinforced by relatively close similarity in political and economic conditions and even institutions.   Despite what many Americans still think, the parallels between political views on the role of the state, the contributions of private/public funds to training, individual responsibility and working on financial incentives are very similar on both sides of the Atlantic. While almost everything in the USA is larger, urban deprivations and its persistence are a common problem. The persistence and visibility of churches in urban areas is also a shared feature and challenge.

While the two main positive advantages enjoyed by the USA - higher church attendance and giving and a supportive culture of philanthropy - cannot be quickly or easily replicated, there are a number of practical possibilities for churches and Training and Enterprise Councils (TECs) - the UK equivalent of PICs - to explore as described below.

A strategic approach

Only the Chicago diocese among the US cities visited took a deliberately strategic approach to church development and clergy postings to social ends.   With 13 charities supported by the Episcopal Church in the city, and a very large area of economically and racially mixed congregations, this was seen to be the only viable approach.

The well known independence of parish clergy can be a liberating feature, allowing new ideas to grow unchecked. However, when personnel and money are under pressure, there can only be a cost-effective use of people, positions and provision for training or anything else if strategic thought and planning are brought to bear.

Public and now PIC/TEC officials in each country generally lack a strategic view of how churches could contribute to achieving their goals. Churches in the UK are probably the largest 'company' represented on TECs and are often also used as proxies for voluntary sector representation on boards and advisory groups. It would benefit all parties, and certainly people needing training, if churches and PICs/TECs took time to think and talk together about possible ways ahead.

At the local level, the use of consultants to help parishes know what social roles they could best play is much more widespread in the USA than the UK. The lapsed programme of social audits, following *Faith in the city* could be usefully revived, using paid or volunteer help, to see what is the best form of involvement for a particular place and time.

A professional orientation

UK churches have depended for too long on the 'gifted amateur' and unpaid volunteers. With much less money and people power than their counterparts in the USA, churches in the UK must become much more professional in their approach to training (among other things). The 'chicken and egg' cycle of challenge and giving needs to be broken into and, within a strategic approach, plans laid down to attract support from in and outside the church itself.

Churches need to become more:

- *professional*: managing and delivering training is a professional skill - as is researching the market for the products a church has to offer. Churches must expect no special treatment but be judged by their delivery of goods in demand;

- *political*: why should church providers always be among the first to be cut out when times are hard? In Liverpool, the church training providers are untouchable because they have learned how to work the political network;

- *in partnership*: UK churches are far too shy of linking with secular organisations at all and certainly in seeking sponsorship. Churches in this country have little idea of what they have to sell to contractors. Is it therefore surprising that an increasing amount of their resources is under utilized?

- *pragmatic*: as well as going where the money is, churches should charge realistic rates for use of their premises and personnel. Churches should also make the best use of what they have in particular markets, be it a passive letting of space or an active part in training management.

Less direct delivery of training

With increasing emphasis rightly being placed by TECs on professional training deliverers, vocational qualifications and more comprehensive administrative systems, many churches may not want or be able to compete for training business.

Rather than treating involvement as 'all or nothing', UK churches would be well advised to examine the spectrum of involvement and especially two particular stages along it.

- *Support for training*: with increasing public support for example in relieving homelessness and care for children and older people, churches can often receive tangible resources to give help in these areas. They would thereby be allowing people to think about training and to survive what can otherwise be fatal domestic crises during the course of a training programme. The easy accessibility of churches in many urban priority areas and the implicit trust people often still have in the church as an institution are major advantages.

- *Subcontracting/specialising*: very few churches want or would be able to meet all the conditions of a general training programme. They could, however, major on particular skills (eg construction), or groups (eg the illiterate, redundant executives) to complement the facilities of other providers.

More practical training of clergy

If any or all of these explorations are to be conducted, training of clergy before and after ordination needs to have a much more practical emphasis on clergy responsibilities in UPA parishes. There are many US examples of ways in which courses can be adopted to enable a realistic exposure to urban needs and opportunities to be gained. Demand needs to come from clergy themselves for such better provision. It should also be registered by parishioners who experience and work with the problems daily.

In exploring these lessons from US experience, the church in the UK should also find itself exploring more deeply the economic and personal relevance of the faith it professes and the purposes of the God it worships in giving people the skills that they need.

Notes

1. The research focused especially, but not exclusively, on the involvement of episcopal churches in both countries. The word 'church' is used here as 'a gathering of people principally for the worship of God and the service of people'. This obviously embraces all Christian denominations, Jewish synagogues and a number of other religious organisations for whom the arguments and illustrations in the paper are equally relevant.

2. PICs were established under the Job Training Partnership Act, passed in 1983. They comprise a majority of senior private sector industrialists with community and education representatives. They receive devolved funds from the states to plan and deliver local training, enterprise and vocational education programmes.

References

Archbishop of Canterbury's Commission on Urban Priority Areas (1985) *Faith in the city*, London: Church House Publishing.

Bremner, R.H. (1988) *American philanthropy*, Chicago: University of Chicago Press.

Grundy, M. (1990) *Light in the city*, London: The Canterbury Press.

Johnson, O.S. (1980) 'The social welfare role of the black church', unpublished PhD thesis, Brandeis University.

Newton, S.C. (1991) *Bandaid and beyond: a study of church involvement in community outreach and vocational training in urban priority areas in Great Britain and the USA*, unpublished report for the Harkness Fellowships.

Parris, P.J. (1985) *The social teaching of black churches*, Pennsylvania: Fortress Press.

Temple, W. (1942) *Christianity and the social order*, Harmondsworth: Penguin.

Wills, G. (1991) *Under God: religion and American politics*, New York: Simon and Schuster.

Wineburg, R.J. (1990) 'The role of religious congregations in Greensborough, North Carolina', *Giving USA Update*, Spring.

Wuthnow, R. and Hodgkinson, V.A. (eds) (1990) *Faith and philanthropy in America*, San Francisco: Jossey-Bass.

seven

STRENGTHENING SCHOOLS THROUGH BUSINESS INVOLVEMENT

Richard Bolsin

Introduction

There has been a good deal of transfer of ideas between the UK and the USA in recent years about education. Cooperative learning approaches in US elementary schools[1] and the notion of a national curriculum are developments which originated here. The Compact, now a UK institution, was invented in Boston.[2] Some of the approaches to testing and assessment, including the acronym SAT (which refers to Scholastic Aptitude Test in the USA and Standard Attainment Target in the UK), are borrowed from US models. And the belief that more effective partnership between schools and the business community will improve public education was born in the USA long before it began to find advocates in the UK.[3]

Education is a complex framework of partnerships between national and local government, schools, children, parents and communities, including the business community. Parts of the framework are well developed in this country, but by comparison with the USA, the role of the business sector is less well understood. There is still a good deal of scepticism in the UK about collaboration between business and education. There is also suspicion about the underlying motives; from business takeover of the curriculum to meet short-term manpower demands on the one hand, to traditional resistance from the education establishment on the other. Alternatively, some see any talk of partnership as symptomatic of the problems caused by underfunding education in the UK. Evidence from the more successful US cities suggests that without the understanding, support and investment of the local business community, schools and education systems will fail their students and communities and worse, the cities in which they are located will themselves face serious decline.

Education in the USA

First, it is important to understand how education in the USA works and what its main differences are from the UK situation.

The US education system

Unlike the UK, education in the USA has always been a local responsibility. Until the Carter administration there was not even a US Department of Education. Responsibility is devolved to each of the 50 states, most of which delegate control to school districts. There are 16,000 of these in the USA, varying in size from New York City (with its 7,000 central education administrators whose annual overhead amounts to nearly $7,000 per student) to tiny rural communities with less than 15 total student enrollments.

Each district will usually elect its own school board, raise its own education tax and appoint its own superintendent. The board will be responsible for the district's education unless the state has cause to intervene (which it might do if standards become unacceptably low, or there is fiscal or other impropriety, or the district becomes bankrupt). The superintendent is accountable to the board and in turn the district's staff, including school principals, are accountable to the superintendent for all that they do. Other than as board members, parents and the community at large are not usually involved in what goes on, nor is the education system as much a part of the wider local government scene as it is in the UK.

Such fragmentation creates substantial obstacles. Unlike the UK, there is no federal stake in education policy or finance except for the odd programme, such as Headstart for pre-school children, which the US Department of Education provides. Neither president nor congress can legislate with executive power for school reform in the same way as UK governments have over the years.

Instead, influential alliances are formed to bring pressure to bear nationally and locally on schools and school districts to improve. Recent presidents, US secretaries of education and numerous umbrella organisations representing business and education interests, all have a good deal to say about what they would like to happen.[4] The president also relies heavily on the support and influence of the business sector. These alliances are also reproduced at local levels and, as I shall demonstrate later, can play a significant part in helping to improve schools.

Comparisons with the UK

The substantial autonomy of US school districts and the relative fragmentation of the education system by comparison with the UK contribute significantly to two factors which are closely related to the success of education/business partnership in the USA.

The first concerns the opportunity for influential leadership within the local education community. Take teacher salaries and conditions. Each district is responsible for negotiating union contracts for its staff, including teachers, within the budgets it has available through its tax base. In practice, the amount invariably reflects the relative economic prosperity of the city or community. For each school district only the more representative of the USA's two main teacher unions is given the right to bargain although the outcome applies to all the district's teaching staff. As a result there can be significant differences in salary and conditions between one school district and another, plenty of incentives for dynamic and imaginative union presidents and district superintendents to exercise leadership qualities and no shortage of local accountability on both sides. It is evident that leaders in the more successful school districts have used these opportunities to bring about very effective school reforms.

The second factor helps to explain why the business sector in the USA appears, by comparison with its UK counterpart, much more imaginative and ready to invest in public education. The explanation is cultural, economic and fiscal.

Culturally, the concept of 'volunteering' is embedded in the American psyche at both personal and corporate levels. This means it is much more common to find individuals, companies and communities volunteering their time, efforts and resources to the improvement of their localities.

Secondly, US cities are considerably more independent of state and federal government than our own. They therefore enjoy and suffer the consequences of their decisions without any cushioning, just like their school districts. Attractive cities attract a greater tax-base and get richer and vice versa. Once decline sets in it becomes very hard to arrest, as can be seen in the case of Detroit. Businesses, therefore, have a prime interest in helping to make their communities more 'livable'[5] and in return the cities themselves are much more directly accountable to their business communities through local taxation than here in the UK.

Finally, and maybe most importantly, companies are encouraged by US tax laws to invest in a tax-exempt sector (see Hambleton, 1991). This enables them to use their profits to establish or support foundations whose work is essentially seeking to improve the conditions in which people live, whether locally, regionally or nationally. Education meets those criteria and much of the partnership activity between public and private sectors in the USA involves non-profit organisations.

How partnerships work

There are nine features which determine whether partnerships will improve schools and school systems as described below.

Two strands

The more successful education systems reveal that partnerships have been part of a double-stranded strategy to improve public schools. One strand addresses the changes needed internally within schools and the school system; the other mobilises external support and resources. Paul Hill of the Rand Corporation observes that in many US cities the latter is more developed than the former. He adds that both strands need to be closely developed and well articulated if real and lasting improvements are to be achieved (Hill et al, 1989).

Louisville, Miami and Pittsburgh are examples of cities where the double-stranded approach is succeeding. On the one hand, this appears to result from a close understanding about the need to change on the part of administrators and teachers (under the leadership of influential superintendents and union presidents). On the other hand, a powerful and influential coalition of corporate business and community leaders has come together in each city to support and provide resources for the reforms.

As traditional communities and family structures have deteriorated, in many places schools have become the last rallying point left for a community (see Schlechty, 1990). This means asking teachers and schools to do much more than they are able to, especially where many of the problems facing students are created by factors outside the control of the education system. In some cities business and corporate leaders have begun to appreciate the economic consequences of a failing school system (inadequate high school graduates and an unattractive if not dangerous environment into which new employees will be reluctant to relocate). They see the very livelihood of their enterprise at risk unless they act to bring wider community and corporate resources to improve schools.

Pittsburgh provides a good case study. During the late 1970s the city went through an economic and educational depression. The accelerated decline of its manufacturing base was accompanied by a stressful desegregation process, sharp test score declines, open conflict between the school board and school administration, and teacher strikes and work stoppages. These parallel developments led to rapid middle class flight from the city.

By 1980, Pittsburgh's highly effective business and civic organisations had come to recognise the schools as a major liability and had pledged to improve them. The teachers' union leadership came to the same conclusion and abandoned its long tradition of confrontational bargaining in favour of collaboration with the school system. The new superintendent in 1982 was thereby able to create a district-wide strategy for school improvement by capitalising on these trends and developing both strands: internal change and external support. In Paul Hill's words:

> The public supports improvement because it understands that the failure of the education system could threaten the social and economic future of the community, not because it is offered a surefire curriculum or other educational panacea. Because public support is based on the importance of the problem, rather than on a promised easy solution, this support can be sustained through the inevitably long process of trial and error that big cities must undergo to improve schooling. (Hill et al, 1989)

No quick fix

There is no 'quick fix'. Partnerships will not provide quick or easy solutions, nor is there any evidence at all that such solutions lead to lasting education reform. Confidence, common understanding, trust, changes in attitudes and roles develop slowly; especially where there has been a previous history of trauma or unsettled relationships.

In the case of all three cities mentioned above, the process of school reform began up to a decade ago. Early in the 1980s the businesses of Louisville, Kentucky, were keen to improve the image of their city in order to attract more corporate investment and persuade major companies to relocate. They decided to take external advice, expecting the report to confirm their view that the city's airport was too small.

The work was duly completed, but its conclusion came as something of a surprise. It was true that improved airport facilities and better connections with other routes would be useful, but first the city should concentrate on seeing that its public services, especially education, lived up to the expectations of the ambitious, articulate and demanding corporate leaders whose business and employees it was trying to attract.

Louisville's superintendent of schools seized the opportunity to involve the business and wider communities in the city's education system. Within the decade, without any major revolution and by and large with the same personnel he inherited, he has implemented what many commentators regard as one of the most successful programmes of school reform in the USA (see David, 1990).

Schools in Jefferson County say in their mission statement that they believe that public education is best served through a spirit of community collaboration. Evidence of this includes parental involvement in school councils, school-business partnerships, and the utilisation and integration of both the school district's and the community's resources into schools.

The Gheens Academy, run by teachers of Jefferson County Public Schools to link staff development to school improvement, is an example of the strategic partnerships which have been forged in Louisville. Since its opening in 1983 and over two phases of the Academy's development, the Gheens Foundation has provided funding to enable high quality, professional staff development to become a feature of Jefferson County's public schools (see David, 1990).

Investment, not charity

Partnerships can assume an almost infinite variety of forms. They can range from the highly complex - multiple agencies interacting with entire city school systems - to relatively simple relationships between one partner (often a business) and one school. What they must all have in common is a goal or series of objectives shared by all partners and agreement about the action to follow.

'One on one' partnerships, where a single organisation and one school engage, may lead to an improved dialogue and better understanding for each partner of the issues facing the other. There may be other spin-offs for students, staff, employees and the business. Not only should such partnerships be encouraged and nurtured, but they may also form part of a system-wide improvement plan and are indeed strong features of the more successful US city education systems. They will not, however, alone lead to the wholesale, systematic and system-wide improvements evident in the more successful US cities.

Similarly, where businesses see schools as a potential commercial investment, as in the Apples for Students campaign (see Bolsin, 1990a) or the Classroom Channel initiative,[6] the partnership may be highly successful in commercial terms and attractive to schools. It will not alone achieve lasting reform, however, although it may act as a catalyst.

There are a wealth of examples of successful partnerships. They range from mentoring programmes, mini-grants, work-experience schemes, paid internships and in Miami particularly innovative and successful projects to establish 'satellite schools'[7] on employers' premises and to reward excellence.[8] What determines whether these partnerships succeed in improving schools, however, is not their generic nature but rather the levels of commitment and understanding the partners have about what precisely they are trying to achieve.

Education partnership needs to be an investment in education, not a charitable donation. As in any investment proper cost-benefit analysis is needed in advance before any successes can be evaluated.

Need for evaluation

Some education partnerships in the USA claim remarkable successes. However, there is little evidence of any systematic or objective evaluation of the contribution they have made to improve school performance in the USA. Some of those which I have observed and some of the evidence I have considered suggest that many are established for 'feel-good' reasons or as part of a general public relations strategy. That is not to question their quality or positive contribution, simply to make the point that more objective evaluation of partnerships is needed, whether in the USA or the UK.

Role of third parties

The incentives in the USA for business to invest in the non-profit sector (see Hambleton, 1991) mean that 'third-party' agencies, such as Public Education Funds play a valuable role in many US cities and some states by providing a point of focus between the education system and the diverse interests of the wider community. As well as promoting reform, they sometimes also take a lead in building inter-institutional links.[9]

In Pittsburgh, the Allegheny Conference on Community Development, a loose alliance of business and civic elites which was instrumental in establishing the platform from which the Pittsburgh reforms were implemented, became the model for other education funds. With support from the Ford Foundation, 53 such bodies have now been established in cities across the USA.[10]

Role of school districts

If school improvement is to become systematic rather than an unrelated series of idiosyncratic or fortuitous occurrences, there must be a single agency responsible for identifying, promoting, developing, extending and evaluating good practice. In both the Rand study and in the samples I have considered successful, this agency has been the school district. Where school districts are small and fragmented, third party organisations have played a significant coordinating role which sometimes extends across other local government service boundaries as well.

Teachers

In the successful cases one of the main devices for promoting and developing within the school system a climate which is conducive to change has been a strong emphasis on the professional development of teachers backed by attractive salary and conditions packages.

The Gheens Academy in Louisville, award-winning Teacher Centers in Pittsburgh and enhanced opportunities for professional development for teachers in Miami have all played an important part in each city's successful education reforms. Confidence in the teaching force in Pittsburgh and Miami is also borne out by recent salary increases.[11]

Leadership

The leadership and vision of the superintendent and teacher union president in each city is critical. Each has the power to prevent progress. The recognition by each in Miami and Pittsburgh that the system in which they operate has to change internally if reform is to be achieved has created the climate for the external strand of the partnership to develop. In Pittsburgh, the union leadership recognised in 1985 that if it were to wait until the expiry of the teachers' contract in 1986 before it got round the table, much valuable time would be lost dealing with the economic issues before discussion moved to much needed professional development. The contract negotiation was therefore opened a year early; the negotiating teams settled the money matters; and the main discussion was able to focus on professionalising teaching and improving education (Fondy, 1987).

There is a similar story of mutual concessions and waivers between district and union in Miami to meet the target of introducing site-based management to schools.

Role of universities

The university sector in the USA is much involved in public education issues. Teachers and administrators rely on post-graduate study for career advancement and salary becomes considerably more attractive for teachers with higher degrees. Yet the practical involvement of the higher education sector in improving schools in the USA stems not from an ivory tower but by partnership and collaboration.

In Chicago, for instance, which recently implemented a radical restructuring of the country's third largest school system, representatives of the city's universities have taken the lead in establishing the Consortium on Chicago School Research (Community Renewal Society, 1991) to support and evaluate the reforms. Another of the city's universities has for the last 13 years run the only teachers' centre in Chicago, not from a university campus but on the top floor of one of the city's high schools. The head of the centre, whose office is in the school, is also deputy to the university's dean of education.

In summary, typical features of the US cities where the more successful education reforms have been introduced are:

● previous conflict or distress, often dating from issues which arose in the 1970s, such as civil rights;

● up to a decade of stable leadership by both superintendents and teachers' union presidents;

● increased taxes for education reflecting widespread community support and confidence;

● external resources and investment in education reflecting corporate confidence;

● 'inside' and 'outside' strands to the improvement strategy;

● support and involvement of major universities.

The context of partnership in the UK

The major differences in education in the UK and the USA which have been explained earlier mean that what works in the USA will not necessarily be replicable in the UK. Also, the UK starts from a position of relative advantage if we begin to consider some of the broader aspects of education partnership.

UK schools and school systems already have potentially powerful partnerships with governing bodies involving parents, teachers and school communities. These are considerably more developed and sophisticated than any comparable bodies in the USA. Training and Enterprise Councils have the potential to engage the corporate sector in partnership with education authorities and local government. The national curriculum, local management and parental choice add a strategic framework to education missing from the USA. There is also nothing in the USA which matches systematically the technical and vocational strands of the UK curriculum, however imperfect they may be.

On the other hand, there are also some potential obstacles in the UK to the development of strategies for school improvement and partnership. Nationally led negotiations with teacher unions have never traditionally incorporated the sort of localised reform-minded conditions and waivers evident in some US cities. Resources available to Local Education Authorities (LEAs) to promote the sort of imaginative teacher development schemes evident in the better US cities are also limited. And the increasing numbers of grant maintained schools and city technology colleges are currently independent of any LEA plans.

Also in the UK the degree of national taxation paid by business (including the unified business rate which is set nationally) reduces the scope, incentive and opportunity for imaginative collaboration between the business sector and local government.

Systematic, district-wide improvement strategies will, therefore, be harder to plan and implement in the UK, yet it is important that the UK learns from the USA about the substantial obstacles to improving a fragmented education system.

What are the messages for the UK?

It is clear that there are elements of the US approach to successful education partnership which could work successfully here in the UK without eroding further the framework which so characterises UK public education by comparison with the USA. In the right policy environment the following seven components derived from successful US approaches could be adapted to work to the UK's advantage. I have listed them as far as possible in an order of priority.

Incentives to collaborate

It is difficult to see how similar private sector responses to public sector issues will be generated in this country unless businesses and the communities in which they are located are offered tax incentives to collaborate. Such tax reforms might, for instance, be used to encourage the development of Public Education Funds which operate so effectively in this sector in the USA. Third parties such as these could play an equally important role here in drawing potential partners together around common issues, especially if the local government framework is to be radically reconstructed.

In addition, the evidence from successful US cities suggests that the scope for local initiatives would increase if communities were able to offer tax incentives to stimulate local economic development. In other words, the ability of cities and communities to raise local taxes is an important feature of effective private sector partnership and means that the business community has a more direct stake in public education.

Local leadership

Local leadership which is both stable and of high quality is indispensable. This means there must be a wider vision of education in each locality than just the schools' and yet a more localised one than that of the government or its regional agency. The US evidence points strongly to the need for education to remain a local service. Schools in this country are increasingly being encouraged to see their future in the grant maintained sector outside any local framework. The strength of this approach will need careful balancing against disadvantages caused by fragmentation and competition between institutions. Many businesses and most universities will see little benefit from investing in just a single school, or even a series of them separately.

Role of teacher unions

In the USA localised pay bargaining certainly leads to some imaginative outcomes. It also provides a powerful platform locally for the union president and school superintendent to demonstrate their leadership qualities even if occasionally their antagonism leads to damaging breakdown and strikes. At the same time the scene is free for the national union presidents to hold centre stage on matters of reform and improvement: in other words to enhance the debate about quality rather than remuneration. This is a very different picture from the UK where national teacher union politics are overwhelmed (with some justification, perhaps) by the issues of salary and conditions, the nature of which stifle any scope for the imaginative, local waivers and agreements which characterise some US cities. The time may be right in the UK to try a different, more localised approach and there are places which would relish the challenge of establishing such a partnership with their teacher unions. Such partnership could be even more effective if in the UK the most popular union had the right to represent *all* teachers within its locality. Professional leadership of teachers would also surely be enhanced.

Status of teachers

The quality of education depends principally on the quality of teachers. There are two concerns: first, that the profession attracts and retains the right people; and second, that those it does attract are able throughout their career to develop skills, knowledge and expertise to meet shifting demands and develop state of the art techniques.

The first concern is essentially one of teacher salary and status. Recently the UK has been able neither to attract the right calibre of teachers into the profession, but worse, not even keep those it has. There is evidence from the USA that teacher salary and pupil performance may be more closely linked than is thought (Bolsin, 1990b).

The second concerns professional development. Conditions for this in the UK and investment in it are paltry by comparison with the way other parts of the public or private sector treat similarly qualified staff. They are also poor by US comparison. Much could be improved by partnership in this country, as it was in Louisville with the Gheens Academy, or by establishing the Teacher Centers in Pittsburgh. The growing trend in this country to see schools as self-governing islands, often competing rather than collaborating with their neighbouring education institutions, is not conducive to such a strategic approach.

Role of higher education

Universities, polytechnics and colleges in the UK need to collaborate with schools and public education generally from a position of much closer practical involvement and support. Research and evaluation on the one hand, and partnership with schools and school districts to implement reform initiatives on the other, are both areas where US universities excel in partnership with schools and where the higher education sector in the UK could work more closely alongside schools.

Time

There is simply no quick fix, unless improvement is to be superficial and short-term. Investment in education reform must evaluate benefits over decades rather than for re-elections. Dismantling systems and attitudes and installing new visions and methods takes time. So does establishing trust and confidence among the people who are going to make it work. This is not just a lesson from the USA. Our own experience with successful education reform, through the Technical and Vocational Education Initiative (TVEI) offers the same message (and also confirms the value of investing in staff development).

Investment and evaluation

These are concepts little understood or practised in partnerships either in the USA or the UK. However, where the partnership has developed around a need to invest in schools (as in Pittsburgh or Louisville in the examples I refer to in this chapter) there is good evidence that goals and objectives are more clearly stated and understood. As a result investment decisions (eg in the Gheens Academy or the need to establish magnet schools in Pittsburgh) are better informed. Schools have much to offer business and communities in return, both in the short and long term, and need to undertake their own self-appraisal before expecting business to invest in them.

Evaluation of partnership also becomes easier if it has developed from investment rather than charity.

Conclusion

The problems facing education in the USA are awesome and I have deliberately concentrated on one area, of education partnership, where the UK can learn in a number of small, practical ways how to improve its own public education system. The faltering steps currently being taken here reflect a degree of scepticism and a good deal of ignorance about how the concept of partnership or, more accurately, investment in education actually works.

Similarly, there are aspects of education in this country which we take for granted, like the role of school governing bodies and parental choice, which education reformers in the USA can conceptualise but have great difficulty in translating into successful practical solutions. The gulf between concept and pragmatism is one which education has traditionally found hard to bridge.

I am certain it would be excellent value to immerse groups of UK educators, business representatives, community leaders and parents in the practice, rather than the policy of the US approach through short, sharply focused exchanges or study visits. Opportunities for professionals to engage in international dialogue of this sort continue to exist, while the other equally important players in the education team are rarely involved in such comparative studies. It is time we recognised that to make education reform really successful we must involve more than the professionals, important though they are.

Notes

1. There are various universities involved in cooperative learning initiatives, one of the leading examples being the Center for Research on Elementary and Middle Schools at John Hopkins University, 3505 North Charles Street, Baltimore.

2. The Compact was developed in 1982 as a vehicle for promoting education business collaborations to improve the public schools and provide better job and college-going opportunities for Boston youngsters.

3. The National Association for Partners in Education claims that in 1956 organised efforts to recruit, place and train volunteers to work in classrooms were taking place in New York. 1983/84 was declared the Year of Partnerships in Education by the then President, Ronald Reagan.

4. See note 3 for evidence of Ronald Reagan's part. At least two of the six national goals for education set in 1990 under George Bush's presidency specify responsibilities for business and his Education 2000 programme, launched in April 1991 earmarked $150 million from business, together with other

contributions to skills clinics. Umbrella business organisations such as the National Alliance for Business (NAB) and the Business Round Table (BRT) publish advice and were consulted on the strategy.

5. Places Rated Almanac, Rand McNally, Fortune Magazine, the National Civic League and many other organisations and publications regularly list the most 'livable' cities from various perspectives.

6. The Classroom Channel is a service of Pacific Mountain Network, PO Box 280369, Lakewood CO 80228, 1/303/980-1411. Funding is provided by Whittle Communications L.P. Participating schools receive free telecommunication hardware in return for transmitting to students satellite news broadcasts produced by the Pacific Mountain Network. The costs are recovered through advertising which appears during the broadcast. The Pacific Mountain Network is solely responsible for the selection and acquisition of material transmitted on the Classroom Channel. All programmes are intended for use at the discretion of and under the direction of school officials who are required to broadcast a minimum number of programmes annually to remain in the scheme.

7. Miami has three 'Satellite' schools, one at Miami International Airport, another at the Miami-Dade Community College and a third at the headquarters of a large insurance group. More are planned; the Florida State Government has encouraged the initiative by offering tax incentives to companies to participate; and the evaluation of the initiative suggests remarkable benefits to employers, students and the school district.

8. The Dade County Teacher of the Year Award is sponsored by a local dairy, one of whose competitors does the same for the Principal of the Year Award.

9. As in the case of the Mon Valley Education Consortium, a local education fund operating in the greater Pittsburgh area which works with 20 school districts in four counties.

10. The Public Education Fund is a national non-profit organisation founded in 1983 to provide technical assistance and developmental grant support to the 53 Local Education Funds (LEFs) it spawned. LEFs are third party, non-profit

entities which develop supportive community and private sector relationships with a public school system. They provide limited private sector support to launch initiatives and broker relationships aimed at school improvement.

11. From September 1991 teachers in Pittsburgh can earn over $52,000; in Miami at least $47,000.

References

Bolsin, R. (1990a) 'A free byte of the apple', *Education*, 14 December.

Bolsin, R. (1990b) 'No pitfalls in Pittsburgh', *Education*, 16 November.

Community Renewal Society (1991) 'Business pitches in - is it enough?', *Catalyst: voices of Chicago school reform*, vol II, no 6, Chicago: Community Renewal Society.

David, J.L. (1990) 'Restructuring in progress: lessons from pioneering districts', in R.F. Elmore et al, *Restructuring schools: the new generation of educational reform*, San Francisco: Jossey-Bass.

Fondy, A. (1987) *The future of public education and the teaching profession in Pennsylvania*, Pittsburgh Federation of Teachers/American Federation of Teachers.

Hambleton, R. (1991) 'American dreams, urban realities', *The Planner*, vol 77, no 23.

Hill, P.T., Wise, A.E. and Shapiro, L. (1989) *Educational progress: cities mobilise to improve their schools*, Santa Monica, California: The Rand Corporation.

Schlechty, P.C. (1990) *Schools for the 21st century: leadership imperatives for education reform*, San Francisco: Jossey-Bass.

part three

CRIME AND POLICING

eight

YOUTH CRIME PREVENTION AND SOCIAL POLICY

Jon Bright

Introduction

There is some disagreement in the UK over which policy area the prevention of youth crime falls into. Some say it is mainly the province of criminal justice policy. Others argue that it is largely a matter for 'mainstream' social policies, in particular, education, employment and those targeted at the family. Yet others suggest a new policy area - children and youth - to ensure that prevention is incorporated into services for children and young people rather than marginalised in policy areas which already have crowded agendas. It is the rapidly changing definition of 'crime prevention' that accounts for this uncertainty. In the last two decades, policy has moved from a preoccupation with preventing offending through the criminal justice system to an emphasis on reducing opportunities for crime to the current interest in social crime prevention or the prevention of criminality.

Youth crime has always been a subject of public concern. It has recently been raised higher on the political agenda in the UK for a number of reasons. First, there is increasing awareness of the limitations of traditional approaches to controlling crime. Second, one-third of young people have a criminal record by the age of 31 (Home Office, *Criminal Statistics in England and Wales*). Third, the recorded crime rate in the UK has been rising at a rate of 6% per annum since 1945 with some of the highest increases taking place in 1989-1990 (Home Office, *Statistical Bulletin* no 7/85).

Fourth, crime has a significant impact on the quality of urban life and can jeopardise regeneration policies which depend on retaining the skilled working and middle classes in large cities. Finally the costs of crime are considerable, estimated in the UK at £5 billion per annum.

In the USA, the same reasons for public concern apply, only more so. First, the costs are enormous and unsustainable. Second, persistent offending by young people is associated with poor school attendance and sharply reduced employment prospects. This has serious implications for an economy desperate for skilled, literate personnel. Third, high crime rates have accelerated the decline of many cities, generating considerable costs for businesses and the public sector agencies responsible for managing conurbations whose economic stability has been damaged and social controls eroded. Finally, the association of high violent crime rates with the hyper-segregation and poverty in some inner cities has obvious consequences for political stability.

In both countries and in the West generally, there is little doubt that crime prevention and community safety will continue to have a high political profile. In addition to the reasons listed above, the de-industrialisation of domestic economies may be accompanied by persistently high levels of unemployment. Increased migration from economically depressed or war-torn countries (particularly into the USA and some European countries) increases inequality and the sense of relative deprivation, both of which are associated with crime and social unrest. Concentrations of unemployed or under-employed youth in public housing developments create the potential for outbursts of violent disorder which are exacerbated by racial tension. The riots of 1991 and 1992 in both countries provide ample illustration of this. These are clearly matters that are causing great concern in both countries at present. It should be clear to all that they are beyond the scope of the criminal justice system to address.

As a result, there is increasing interest in the capacity of agencies *outside* the criminal justice agencies to prevent crime and a slowly emerging understanding that the prevention of crime and criminal behaviour is not a 'stand alone' policy area but one that should be seen as integral to mainstream, 'macro' social policy. At a local level, it can be addressed by a comprehensive approach to prevention targeted at the family, school and community, incorporating the following themes:

● early childhood development;

● opportunities for young people;

● safer neighbourhoods.

This chapter will examine the extent to which the US experience can contribute to the development of this framework in a UK setting.

The US approach to policy

There are significant differences in the scale and nature of youth crime between the UK and USA. In the USA, serious youth crime is associated with the poverty and joblessness of the US ghetto which generates a level of violence far greater than that seen in any European country. This is currently linked strongly with drugs. In the UK, on the other hand, the overwhelming majority of offences committed by young people are non-violent, property crimes, many of which involve motor vehicles. Nevertheless, almost one-third of young people have criminal convictions by early adulthood, about one-half of all recorded crime is committed by juveniles, and, as in the USA, a high proportion of recorded crime is committed by a small number of persistent offenders (see Wolfgang et al, 1972; Rutter, 1980; Farrington and West, 1981).

Many theories have been submitted to account for the involvement of such large numbers of young men in crime. The dominant perspective underpinning US crime policy is derived from conservative criminology. It seeks to explain crime by reference to the breakdown of authority in the home and school and to the 'dysfunctional character of ghetto families' (Wilson, 1975). This results in a strong policy emphasis on deterrence, law enforcement and the restoration of authority.

But does the USA really have a crime policy? The term 'policy' has been defined as 'a course of action adopted in *governmental* affairs' and implies a degree of uniformity which does not exist in the USA (Pocket Oxford Dictionary, 5th edition). The USA has a crime policy in so far as there is a dominant perspective on crime which is shared by most levels of government and reflected in legislation. However, there is a great deal of local variation and experimentation in approaches to law enforcement, the treatment of offenders and prevention which influence the crime policies of individual states.

It is, therefore, possible to identify four main features of crime policy in the USA:

- an emphasis on deterrence through the operation of the criminal justice system, in particular through the use of imprisonment, mandatory sentences and vigorous supply-side drug prevention;

- an encouragement of community self-help, through schemes such as Neighbourhood Watch;

- an interest in developing demonstration projects focused on the family and young people with the aim of disseminating successful practice into mainstream services;

- an emerging, though by no means national, interest in addressing the problems that generate high levels of neighbourhood crime through 'problem-oriented' community policing.

It is unquestionably the emphasis on deterrence and the criminal justice agencies which characterises US crime policy. Conservatives argue for tougher legal sanctions, believing to increase the 'cost of crime' to the offender will reduce its incidence (Wilson, 1975). Indeed, it is reasonable to assume that perceptions of cost might have some weight in influencing people's behaviour. But as we will see below, the evidence that deterrent custodial sentences prevent crime and recidivism is not strong and substantially increased expenditure on the criminal justice agencies over the past two decades has failed to reduce the very high levels of crime currently found in the USA. In fact, the cost of this policy is unsustainable and even vigorous advocates of law and order are starting to look to prevention and alternatives to custody (*Criminal Justice Newsletter*, 1991).

Many attribute the US failure to invest more in prevention to a lack of federal leadership in domestic policy over the past two decades. This explanation, however, is incomplete; the real causes lie deep within the US political system. Ethnic heterogeneity, individualism, political decentralisation and fragmentation, belief in limited government, scepticism about the effectiveness of social programmes and the sheer intransigence of social problems are the principal reasons for the lack of political vigour in tackling domestic problems. Prevailing wisdom holds that the Great Society programmes of the Kennedy/Johnson era failed and that social intervention does not work, in spite of the evidence to the contrary (Marmor et al, 1990).

In addition, times have changed considerably since the late 1960s. The dramatic economic and social transformations of the cities have occurred only in the last 15 years, since the 1970s recession and oil crisis precipitated the rapid decline of traditional manufacturing industries. The consequences have been widespread and devastating. When Europeans ask why Americans do not seek inspiration from the policies of those developed countries with less crime, Americans reply that since European countries have not had to contend with such serious problems, they cannot know that their policies would be effective in the USA. Europeans argue that their problems are less serious partly because of their policies. And so on. The debate quickly becomes circuitous.

So in spite of the severity of the US predicament, there is much less government emphasis on prevention than there is in the UK and still a heavy reliance on the police, the criminal justice system and the capacity of local communities to protect themselves.

An evaluation of US policy

In this section, we will examine the effectiveness of the four elements of US preventive policy listed above.

The criminal justice agencies

As already noted, the evidence for the success of policies based on the concept of deterrence through the operation of the criminal justice agencies is not strong. The formal processes of the criminal justice system - apprehending, prosecuting, sentencing, punishing and rehabilitating offenders - have been shown to have only a limited effect in controlling crime (Graham, 1990). There is little evidence that people are deterred from crime by the prospect of being caught and sentenced or that detection and conviction deters them from future offending (Steinmetz, 1982). Increases in police manpower do not necessarily lead to reduced crime (Clarke and Hough, 1984). Rates of recidivism following release from prison remain very high and therapeutic treatment is relatively ineffective (Graham, 1990). Only about one-quarter of crime is reported to the police of which only about one-third, on average, is cleared up (Mayhew et al, 1988; see also Home Office *Criminal statistics*, published annually). It is true that the huge increase in imprisonment has probably kept the crime rate slightly lower than it would have been but its impact has been small, relative to the investment (Currie, 1985).

Moreover, the criminal justice agencies in many jurisdictions are absolutely overwhelmed by the amount of crime they are required to process. In one major city, plea bargaining for serious felonies and a lack of prison space means that serious offenders are receiving unduly short sentences. Many misdemeanours are simply ignored. Three-quarters of the adults who are on probation are not supervised by probation officers. One-half of the adults on probation who are supposed to be periodically tested for illegal drugs are not tested. Offenders on probation who commit robbery or burglary are not charged with those crimes but only with violating the terms of their probation in order to ease jail overcrowding and reduce court caseloads. If more than 5% of cases go to trial, gridlock sets in. The same people are being repeatedly processed through the system. Any deterrent effect that may have been created by the certainty of swift and sure punishment has been eroded by a system that can no longer cope. Convicted offenders are not receiving appropriate sentences, or being rehabilitated, community safety is being compromised and crime is certainly not being prevented (see articles in *Los Angeles Times*, 17-22 December 1990). These problems are probably mirrored to a greater or lesser extent in most of the country's 10 largest cities.

This is not to argue that the police, and to a much lesser extent the other criminal justice agencies, have no part to play in crime prevention. The police hold the information about crime and offenders, have much experience in crime opportunity reduction and are the only agency trained, equipped and authorised to confront most crime problems. Community crime prevention initiatives are unlikely to work unless there is an appropriate police input and in many cases this may be a precondition for community mobilisation and activity by other agencies. A number of community policing programmes have been demonstrably successful and there is a need for much more commitment to this area of police work. If the community policing revolution is successful, the police contribution to crime prevention will increase significantly.

There is a tendency to overstate the role of the police, however, particularly when they are expected to act alone. Most of the effort of most police forces is still reactive rather than preventive. They do not have the resources and authority to intervene in many of the circumstances which lead to crime being committed. As one UK author has put it:

> The police are not for the main part the prime movers, the initiators of the processes that control deviant behaviour. On the contrary, they work at the margins where the usual processes of control have broken down ... they act as a continuation of ... more general efforts by the mass of people and institutions to maintain order, control and coherence. In other words, they are a small but extremely important element within a much larger complex of interrelated systems of control. (Smith, 1983)

Understanding the limits of policing - as well as its potential - is essential if crime prevention initiatives are to achieve long-term success.

Community crime prevention

US politicians and community activists argue that communities can be a principal force for preventing crime. However, it is important to be clear about what different types of communities can realistically be expected to achieve. Skogan's (1990) review of evaluations of community crime prevention reaches a number of discouraging conclusions.

He found that anti-crime community activities are least common and least successful in the areas in which they are most needed, namely poor, minority, high crime neighbourhoods. They are more common and successful in moderately cohesive, homogeneous, middle and working-class areas. Where they do exist in high crime areas, active participants are more likely to take protective measures and are more prepared to intervene. However, levels of participation are modest at best and there is no 'rub off' effect on non-participants. Attempting to set up new anti-crime organisations in high crime areas is extremely difficult. Participation is low even when substantial efforts are made to organise people and rather than uniting communities in outrage or common purpose, crime can undermine the capacity of communities to organise in high crime areas and can divide rather than unite people.

Almost every study of community crime prevention activity charts a decline in participants' interest and enthusiasm over time. Local organisations that are set up for the sole purpose of tackling crime do not persist. Participation is highest when existing successful community organisations add crime prevention to their agendas. People participate because they are already members of a group that pursues multiple goals. Programmes organised on the assumption that people join groups because of crime rarely last. Rigorous evaluations of community crime prevention initiatives in the USA have by and large failed to find clear cut evidence of success. Only one showed positive results and here the fear of crime went up and the positive effects had disappeared after 18 months. Furthermore, all the signs point toward declining levels of voluntary participation in urban organisations in the future.

None of these conclusions bode well for a community crime prevention policy that relies heavily upon voluntary participation. They also suggest that the theory upon which community crime prevention is based may be flawed, or at best applicable only in certain circumstances. This holds that crime and disorder will incite people to collective action and thereby stimulate the informal social controls which will lead to a reduction in crime and disorder. This theory is not supported by the evaluations that have so far been undertaken. Not only has there been no impact on crime but programmes to date have failed to activate the processes in the community through which reductions in crime and disorder were to have been achieved (Rosenbaum, 1988; Skogan, 1990; Schorr, 1988).

Although they have vital roles to play, too much has been expected of both policing and community organisations. The police have been expected to compensate for the breakdown of other networks of control and order. Community organisations have been expected to address problems that they have neither the resources nor the authority to resolve.

Demonstration programmes: families, children and young people

The purpose of preventive demonstration projects is to identify the elements of successful practice so that they can be translated into national or state policy and thereby local services. Unfortunately, there is no effective means for disseminating good practice and even when there is consensus, there is rarely sufficient money to implement successful approaches widely. For example, there is wide agreement on the benefits of the Headstart pre-school programme which was designed to provide disadvantaged children with enriched pre-school education. The aim was to give them a 'headstart' so they would be better able to compete with their more privileged peers. Yet, over 25 years after its inception, only 20% of eligible (poor) children are enrolled. Nevertheless, there is much to be learned from the following evaluations of US programmes targeted at families, children and young people.

Teenage pregnancy prevention

These programmes aim to prevent teenage child-bearing, maternal school failure (and in consequence, reduced lifetime earnings) and dependence on public assistance. The children of teenage mothers are at greater risk of school failure, poor cognitive, social and emotional development, delinquency and unemployment. The first step in social prevention is, therefore, to prevent school age child-bearing. The programmes which have been most successful have been those which have been confidential, accessible, free and staffed by caring professionals. For example, a school-based clinic in St Paul, Minnesota, serving four high schools led to a 50% reduction in school age child-bearing. Fewer than 2% of students had second pregnancies and 90% of those who did become pregnant were able to finish high school (Schorr, 1988).

Parental and family support

Pervasive family chaos and discord are associated with anti-social behaviour and delinquency. The main problem is family stress which can have a number of causes. Whatever the cause of the stress, families need immediate support.

If support is not forthcoming to families which are both socially isolated and multi-stressed, serious consequences can follow. Unsupported young mothers may reject their children, particularly if they are unemployed and uneducated. Socially isolated families are associated with very high levels of abuse, neglect and later delinquency. Children raised by a socially isolated mother living alone are more likely to fail school, truant from school, fight in school, drop out of school and become delinquent (Schorr, 1988). Family support programmes seek to prevent family breakdown and out of home care. The first was the Tacoma Homebuilders, a not-for-profit independent initiative. They now exist in many states, often as part of the social services department, and provide a variety of services - goods, information, support, advice - and help cushion families against the harmful effects of stress. They differ from traditional family services in a number of important ways: they emphasise early and continuing support; have strong ties to neighbourhoods and a commitment to empowering families; involve parents as partners; and stress the importance of meeting family needs before crises occur, thereby preventing the persistent and chronic family breakdown that triggers public agency interventions. In order to be effective, specially trained social workers have two or three cases and they offer whatever assistance is necessary to sustain the family as a viable unit.

Ideally, family support programmes are intensive, comprehensive, flexible, personalised and community-based. Successful programmes in the USA claim to achieve substantial reductions in foster care and other out of home placements. They have helped to improve family functioning, children's school performance and parental employment; to increase parental self-esteem; and to reduce child abuse and neglect, family size and help families make better use of service and facilities. They can be cost effective, saving $5 for every $1 invested (Schorr, 1988). The direct impact of family support programmes on the future delinquency of children has yet to be demonstrated by longitudinal studies. However, since we know that delinquency is associated with family discord and breakdown, strengthening families and reducing out of home placements might reasonably be expected to influence children's later offending patterns.

Pre-school education

Although the initial objective of pre-school education is to prevent school failure, the best pre-school programmes address the educational, social and health development of children and have many long-term benefits.

The frequently cited High/Scope Perry Pre-school Programme in the USA is one of the very few to have looked at the link between pre-school education and delinquency. This programme strikingly demonstrates the potential benefits of high quality early childhood programmes for disadvantaged children. It shows convincingly that pre-school participation can increase the proportion of young people who at the age of 19 are literate, employed and enrolled in post-secondary education, and can reduce the proportion who dropped out of school, were labelled mentally retarded, had been arrested or were on welfare (Schweinhart, 1987; Ontario Ministry of Community and Social Services, 1990). In order to achieve these outcomes, the following conditions are necessary:

● a curriculum based on child-initiated learning;

● teachers trained in early childhood development;

● classes with two adults and fewer than 20 children;

● systematic efforts to involve parents as partners;

● continuity with infant and primary programmes.

An economic cost-benefit analysis of the Perry Pre-school Programme and its long-term effects revealed that such a programme can be an excellent investment, returning $6 for every $1 invested in a one year programme and $3 for every $1 invested in a two year programme. However, it is important to stress that these positive effects were found only for good pre-school programmes.

Schooling

School effectiveness research in both the UK and USA has demonstrated that even when catchment area and intake are taken into account, schools can have markedly different rates of delinquency. This has led to the conclusion that schools can have a much greater *independent* effect on pupil outcomes than was previously thought (Graham, 1990). More recent research has sought to identify precisely why some schools are able to inhibit delinquency amongst their pupils while others fail to.

To date, the most popular school-based approaches to reducing delinquency have been police-school liaison schemes, substance abuse prevention programmes and personal responsibility sessions on the school curriculum. However, there is little evidence that, on their own, these approaches are effective (see Bangert-Downs, 1988). Less attention has been given to strategies which improve the management, ethos and climate of schools so that they are better able to meet the needs of those students who bring with them problems that interfere with their capacity to learn. Until recently, it was widely thought that schools could do little about students who fail or behave disruptively or truant, and that these problems were largely due to the individual student and his/her family background. In fact, research now suggests that schools can exercise significant influence over these outcomes (Graham, 1990).

Schools which are able to offer students a sense of achievement regardless of ability and are able to motivate and integrate them are likely to reduce the incidence of negative outcomes. Similarly, schools which are likely to have high rates of delinquency among pupils are those which segregate pupils according to academic ability, concentrate on academic success at the expense of practical and social skills, categorise pupils as deviants, inadequates and failures and refer responsibility for the behaviour and welfare of their pupils to outside agencies and institutions (Graham, 1990).

For example, the Yale/New Haven School Development Programme focuses on changing the way schools are managed and ensuring that their management is informed by the principles of child development. It considers the child's behaviour within the wider context of the school as a social system. The most important feature of the programme model is *a planning and management team*. It is directed by the school principal and consists of teachers, teachers aides, parents and a mental health professional. Its task is to interrupt the forces of confusion and conflict and to establish an orderly effective process of education in the school. The purpose of the team is to consider opportunities and problems in (a) the school climate and social environment and (b) academic curriculum and staff development.

The results show that its impact can be quite remarkable. In 1969, the students in the first targeted school were 18-19 months behind grade level in reading and mathematics, and there were serious behaviour and attendance problems. Since 1976 that school has been among the top five schools in the city in attendance and has not had a serious behaviour problem in a decade. By 1979, students were approximately at grade level in reading and mathematics. Staff attendance is among the best in the city and staff turnover is among the lowest. Parent participation has been responsible and enthusiastic. Attendance at school events remarkably improved. In general, the results of this project are extremely encouraging (see Ontario Ministry of Community and Social Services, 1990; Cauce et al, 1987; Comer, 1980a, 1980b).

Youth work

There is a widespread belief that social and recreation programmes for young people will divert their energies into more constructive activities and, as a result, they will be less likely to drift into offending. In fact, there is not very much research evidence to support this view, either in the UK or the USA (Graham, 1990). For example, research into programmes ostensibly aimed at reducing gang related crime found that they were unfocused in aim and had no clear goals. Not only did they not reduce gang related crime but they sometimes made matters worse. At best, their impact was negligible (Spergel, 1990).

In a review of 143 US adolescent drug prevention programmes, those found to have a measurable effect were (a) those school-based programmes which focused on teaching youth refusal, social or life skills directly related to drug usage, and (b) community-based programmes which did not necessarily address the issues of drugs directly but which offered a range of activities aimed at achieving multiple positive outcomes (Tobler, 1986). Successful programmes were involved with young people, used youth-peer mentor leadership strategies, worked with families and operated in the community. As we have seen, school-based programmes which focus only on informing young people about the consequences of drug taking or which seek to enhance their social and personal growth have had little impact. Yet in spite of these negative findings, more attention has been given to such school-based programmes than to more broadly conceived, community based approaches (Botvin, 1985).

In connection with anti-gang strategies, Spergel (1990) argues that anti-gang programmes should be planned by city wide, multi-agency coordinating groups whose task would be to develop a comprehensive strategy for the parts of the city where gang activity was a problem or likely to become one. This strategy should include youth outreach workers, remedial education, training and employment opportunities, deterrence, increased supervision, community policing and gang suppression. The most promising results would involve targeting 10-15 year olds on the fringes of gang activities. Similarly, the Eisenhower Foundation has identified model inner city youth empowerment programmes which aim to address the multiple problems faced by inner city youth. The key elements are extended family type support, remedial education, peer group support and activities, employment training and creation and job placement (Eisenhower Foundation, 1990).

Training

The relationship between crime and unemployment is a complex one but research suggests that young people who are unemployed or under-employed are at greater risk of offending than those who are not. Those most at risk of being unemployed often lack exposure to work and access to the informal networks necessary to find jobs. They need help if they are to have a chance of succeeding in the future. In the USA, there are three types of youth employment initiatives which provide remedial education, vocational training, and/or paid work experience for young people: school-to-work transition programmes, out-of-school remedial education, and conservation and service corps programmes (Children's Defense Fund, 1989).

Although some of the effects of the relationship between unemployment and crime can be alleviated by public policy and community support, employment and training programmes set up with a main objective of reducing crime have been few and far between and have rarely been successful (McGahey, 1986). Programmes providing vocational help alone have had least effect on criminal behaviour. Those which focus on providing long-term, quality employment are more likely to be effective than those which simply try to change behaviour or only provide short-term employment (Currie, 1985).

Programmes which seriously address the depth and complexity of high risk populations can make a difference. In the USA, Job Corps involved six month residential settings and a tough programme of education, skill training and health care and worked for a substantial number of participants. Graduates got better jobs, earned higher incomes and were less dependent on welfare. Every $1 invested in Job Corps returned $1.45 to the US taxpayer (Eisenhower Foundation, 1990). Supported work programmes offer advice, counselling, training, real jobs and a working environment and are often necessary because high risk people need to be levered into the job market slowly and with support.

Summarising the US experience of employment programmes, Currie (1985) concludes that there are often substantial benefits while in programme but they peter out steadily afterwards. Even the most intensive work programmes are undermined by the limitations of the market in which graduates eventually find themselves. He argues for a national employment policy and national and local planning agencies which would set priorities for economic growth in ways which stabilise communities, create training and employment opportunities and aim to achieve "community full employment".

Community policing

Earlier, it was argued that most police resources were committed to responding to crime after the event and that the police had less of a crime preventive effect than is traditionally thought. However, it is probable that the police contribution to crime prevention and community safety has not yet been realised. Perhaps one of the most important revolutions in public service over the past decade - and one with major implications for community safety - has been the emergence of 'problem oriented', community policing.

The key elements of this form of policing are partnership with the community, involving the community in setting police priorities and assigning officers to permanent neighbourhood beats. Officers use a 'problem solving' approach to address the root causes of crime and disorder problems (rather than reacting to isolated incidents) and coordinate strategies for addressing community problems with other public and private agencies and the community itself. This approach involves decentralising decision making and making police management more participative. Most importantly, it requires officers to address not just crime but the wide range of incivilities and disorders that disfigure neighbourhoods and which are themselves associated with crime and fear of crime (Skogan, 1990).

Most evaluations of community policing to date show that it can be effective in reducing fear of crime and improving police-community relations, but not, as yet, actual crime (Tronjanowicz and Bucqueroux, 1990). The new models being developed in some US cities, however, show great promise, particularly when developed as one element of a multi-faceted approach to prevention. To date, much of what has been called community policing has lacked purpose and direction and has not been effective because insufficient thought has been given to the role and functions of community police officers. This is why the term 'problem oriented' is so important because it implies the systematic analysis of crime related problems and the planned implementation of agreed solutions.

Weaknesses and strengths of US policy

Generally, there is little evidence of national or state crime *prevention* policies or strategies, and no clear mechanisms for disseminating and implanting the principles of good practice. There is a heavy imbalance in favour of reacting to crime rather than preventing it. In fact, this reliance on reacting to crime after the event may be causing the criminal justice system to collapse in some areas, as we saw earlier. It could, therefore, be argued that the policy is failing on its own terms. Not only is imprisonment not controlling crime but the system used to deliver that policy is itself collapsing under the increasingly heavy demands that have been placed on it.

On the other hand, there is plenty of scope for local decision making and an avoidance of uniform and, therefore, possibly inappropriate solutions. There is an impressive emphasis on evaluating initiatives and a willingness by the federal government and private foundations to fund demonstration projects. This is a strength from which the UK has much to learn. As a result of this experimentation, a number of successful approaches have been developed and their critical elements identified. Some of the demonstration projects have had a measurable benefit for participants and also for local communities (Eisenhower Foundation, 1990).

This brief evaluation of the elements of US crime prevention policy suggests that there is much that may be of value to the UK. To what extent can the lessons of successful practice in the USA be incorporated into UK policy?

Policy setting and policy transfer

The successful preventive elements of US policies that might be transferable to the UK are (a) programmes and services targeted at families, children and young people in disadvantaged areas and (b) community policing. In this section, we will consider their policy context and the extent to which this may influence their transferability.

Many of the demonstration programmes in the areas of family support, teenage pregnancy prevention, pre-school education, schooling and youth work have been undertaken in settings that are very different to those found in the UK. The incidence, severity and concentration of child poverty in US ghettos, the level of inner city joblessness, the ethnic heterogeneity, the drugs problem, the availability of guns, the fragmentation of the political system and the prejudices against proactive policy making create a very different social and political environment to that found in the UK.

At the same time, many successful initiatives have been undertaken with disadvantaged populations in settings in which the problems are worse than those found in the UK. If they work in such areas, it seems logical to assume that, with appropriate adaptation, they may work in the worst parts of the UK where preventive initiatives have so far achieved limited success.

Yet if they do work in UK cities, will they work as successfully? There has been more investment in mainstream health, social and community services in the UK. It is possible that a higher proportion of families that fall through this safety net and come to the attention of UK authorities have more intractable problems and may be more resistant to the interventions described here. We do not know.

There are institutional differences between the two countries in the way that social, youth and educational services are provided and this will influence the way in which new approaches are taken forward. Within the UK, there will be party political differences over the targeting of these initiatives, whether they should be universally provided or targeted at those households defined as 'at risk'. Initiatives focused on the family have to be presented carefully to avoid stigmatising the poor, or appearing to blame the victim. Similarly, approaches concentrating on reducing problems by improving the management of schools or housing estates have to be balanced with an awareness that in some cases, more investment is also necessary.

Let us now turn to community policing. More attention is paid to this form of policing in the USA than in the UK. This may be due to differences in systems of accountability and to the incentive created by more severe crime problems. However, the reasons for its appeal in the USA apply equally in the UK. Achieving the required shift in emphasis within police forces may require guidance and persuasion from the Home Office, adjustments to the structure of police accountability, carefully designed demonstration projects and dissemination of their findings.

The dramatic deterioration of some US cities and their high crime rates are a result of rapid economic change, concentrations of poverty, suburbanisation and over-ambitious urban renewal projects which damaged the fragile urban ecology. This was exacerbated by an absence of planning regulations (which might have been designed to reinvigorate central cities at the expense of suburban cities) and an inadequate policy response to the economic changes of the 1970s. The UK has more planning regulation and more government intervention in the economy. Nevertheless, the US experience is a salutary reminder that the health of cities (and consequently their crime rates) is to a large extent dependent on (a) the willingness of governments (through planning policy) to encourage the middle and skilled working-classes to remain in the cities and (b) training and employment policies to compensate for the permanent loss of manufacturing jobs from central cities.

What will work in the UK?

To what extent can the US experience contribute to the UK preventive model described in the introduction?

Early childhood development

Teenage pregnancy prevention

The programmes which have been most successful in the USA have been those which have been confidential, accessible, free and staffed by caring professionals. There is no reason to suppose that such programmes would not be effective if developed in areas where there are high levels of teenage (or unwanted) pregnancy. Perhaps the 1991 Children Act may provide an opening here.

Family support programmes

These should be developed with the aim of reducing family stress and discord and reducing the incidence of receptions into care (Schorr, 1988). The US model exemplified by Tacoma Homebuilders in Washington State and Families First in Michigan could be adapted for use in the UK. The 1991 Children Act could be the incentive for this. Extra resources will be required initially for social service departments or the major children's charities to develop intensive preventive services which, if successful, will lead to savings elsewhere in the system.

Pre-school education

This should be available to all 3-5 year olds in disadvantaged neighbourhoods. It should also be available to disadvantaged children who do not live in disadvantaged neighbourhoods. Curricula should reflect the practice of successful evaluated programmes. Again, the 1991 Children Act could provide the legislative impetus for increasing provision to levels found in many European countries. The widespread interest in pre-school programmes in the USA and the UK can be attributed to their multiple benefits. They are good for families as well as children. They have short-term as well as long-term benefits. They result in less school failure and fewer arrests by the age of 19. They are even good for the economy.

We do not know whether the more structured curricula of some pre-school provision in the UK have the same effect as that of the successful demonstration programmes in the USA because there have been so few rigorous evaluations. We do know that pre-school provision in the UK varies widely and that the children who are most at risk do not, by and large, attend the facilities that are likely to offer them the best advantages. In our judgement, it is now possible to argue with some confidence that:

- educationally-oriented pre-school programmes can prevent cognitive and behavioural problems later in life;

- the children in the UK who are most at risk of behavioural and intellectual problems do not attend day nursery provision;

- there is, therefore, an urgent need to improve educational provision in day nurseries if the life chances of so many disadvantaged children are to be improved.

(Sylva, 1989)

Opportunities for young people

School effectiveness

The principles of school effectiveness are applicable to both primary and secondary schools in the UK. The emphasis is on changing the ethos, organisation and management of schools so they are better able to motivate the disaffected. In the USA, over half the school districts have developed school improvement programmes in which the lessons learned from research are translated into practice. This has not occurred in the UK. Guidance has been issued but insufficient help has been made available to schools to implement it.

UK schools need to be managed in such a way that a much higher proportion of pupils succeed at something. At present, 30-40% derive little from school and a much higher proportion than in the USA leave at the first opportunity (Mortimore, 1991). The authors of a UK study argue that if all schools were improved only within the current range of performance of urban comprehensive schools, the standards of secondary education would be transformed (Smith and Tomlinson, 1989). This would impact on delinquency rates because of the links between school failure, truancy and offending.

Youth work

In the UK, youth programmes may be less structured than some in the USA which have more serious problems to confront and require more commitment and intensive participation from young people if they are to succeed. Nevertheless, the emphasis on detached and multi-focused youth work addressing the multiple problems faced by those disadvantaged young people who are most at risk of offending is certainly applicable to the UK situation. UK youth agencies could play a bigger role in the prevention of delinquency without compromising the principles of youth work by targeting their resources in high crime areas. One of their aims would be to reduce the harm that young people do to the community as well as themselves. The Youth Service's ambivalence about its role in delinquency prevention would be inexplicable to the US community based youth programmes referred to earlier.

Training

Quality training programmes should be provided for all 16-19 year olds as part of an employment policy designed to attract employment to the regions that most need it. Particular attention should be given to training and job placement and support for those young people most at risk of drifting into persistent offending. On housing estates, efforts should be made to persuade firms to employ local labour for local contracts, young people should be helped to set up community businesses and priority should be given to employing local people to provide community services such as youth work.

Generally, family and youth policies should be strengthened and the *preventive capacity* of social services departments, education and youth services developed in the light of what can be learned from the US experience. The government should fund demonstration projects to identify what works in what circumstances. Furthermore, the policy shift in the UK towards an emphasis on the preventive role of the non-criminal justice agencies should be completed and these agencies adequately advised, and where necessary, resourced to fulfil their new role.

Safer neighbourhoods

There is much to learn from the rigorous, systematic, 'problem oriented' approaches to community policing being developed in the USA. There is an urgent need to undertake demonstration programmes in medium to high crime areas in order to be clearer about the different crimes and incivilities that community policing might be expected to impact upon and to be more precise about the role other agencies should play.

This chapter deals with what the UK can learn from the USA. It should not go unsaid, however, that in terms of strategic planning, multi-agency action and the safety and security of the built environment, there is much that the USA can learn from the UK. These issues are critical to the development of a policy that seeks to make a significant and sustained impact on crime and create safer neighbourhoods.

We can also learn from what has not worked in the USA. Preventive strategies need to take account of the political economy of crime and note the effect on crime and disorder when communities are afflicted by high levels of joblessness and poverty, when private investment and the middle and working-classes leave the cities for the suburbs, when cities are allowed to become places where only the poor live. The limits of voluntarism or self-help approaches to crime prevention in high crime areas should also be acknowledged.

Finally, high crime neighbourhoods have multiple problems which must be addressed by strategies involving multiple solutions. The prevention of crime will not be achieved by a crime policy alone; prevention must be incorporated within mainstream social policies. Crime is not a 'single solution' problem.

Conclusion

We cannot really talk about a US crime prevention policy but only about approaches to the prevention of crime that are being developed in different parts of the USA. In this chapter, I have considered and evaluated these approaches, assessed the extent to which their policy setting influences success and failure and identified those which may be transferable to the UK.

References

Bangert-Downs, R.C. (1988) 'The effects of school-based substance abuse education: a meta-analysis', *Journal of Drug Education*, vol 18, pp 243-264.

Botvin, G.J. (1985) 'The life skills training programme as a health promotion strategy: theoretical issues and empirical findings', *Special Services in the Schools*, vol 1, no 3.

Cauce, A.M., Comer, J.P., and Schwartz, D. (1987) 'Long-term efforts of a systems-oriented school prevention programme', *American Journal of Orthopsychiatry*, vol 57, pp 127-131.

Children's Defense Fund (1989) *Tackling the youth employment problem*, Washington DC: Children's Defense Fund.

Clarke, R. and Hough, J. (1984) *Crime and police effectiveness*, Home Office Study no 79, London: HMSO.

Comer, J.P (1980a) *School power: implications of an intervention project*, New York: Free Press.

Comer, J.P. (1980b) 'Improving the quality and continuity of relationships in the inner city schools', *Journal of the American Academy of Child Psychiatry*, vol 15, pp 535-545.

Criminal Justice Newsletter (1991) vol 21, no 18, Washington DC: PACE Publications.

Currie, E. (1985) *Confronting crime: an American challenge*, New York: Pantheon.

Eisenhower Foundation (1990) *Youth investment and community reconstruction: street lessons on drugs and crime for the 1990s*, Washington: Eisenhower Foundation.

Farrington, D. and West, D (1981) *The Cambridge study in delinquent development, (UK) in prospective longitudinal research*, Cambridge: Cambridge University Press.

Graham, J. (1990) *Crime prevention strategies in Europe and North America*, Helsinki: The Helsinki Institute for Crime Prevention and Conference.

Marmor, T. Mashaw, J.L. and Harvey, P.L. (1990) *America's misunderstood welfare state*, New York: Basic Books.

Mayhew, P., Elliot, N., and Dowds, L. (1988) *The 1988 British crime survey*, Home Office Research Study no 111, London: HMSO.

McGahey, R.M. (1986) 'Economic conditions, neighbourhood organisation and urban crime' in M. Tonry and N. Morris (eds) *Crime and Justice*, Chicago: University of Chicago Press.

Mortimore, P. (1991) 'Bucking the trends: promoting successful urban education', *Times Educational Supplement*.

Ontario Ministry of Community and Social Services (1990) *Better Beginnings, Better Futures*, Ontario: Queens Printer.

Rosenbaum, D. (1988) 'Community crime prevention: a review and synthesis of the literature, *Justice Quarterly*, vol 5, no 3.

Rutter, M. (1980) *Changing youth in a changing society*, Cambridge: Harvard University Press.

Schorr, L. (1988) *Within our reach*, New York: Doubleday.

Schweinhart, L. (1987) 'Can pre-school programmes help prevent delinquency?' in J.Q. Wilson and G.C. Loury (eds) *From children to citizens*, vol III, New York: Springer Verlag.

Skogan, W. (1990) *Decline and disorder in American cities*, New York: Free Press.

Smith, D.J. (1983) *Police and policing in London*, London: Policy Studies Institute.

Smith, D.J. and Tomlinson, S. (1989) *School effect*, London: Policy Studies Institute.

Spergel, I. (1990) 'Youth gangs: continuity and change' in M. Tonry and N. Morris (eds) *Crime and justice: a review of research*, vol 12, Chicago: University of Chicago Press.

Steinmetz, C. (1982) 'A first step towards victimological risk analysis: a conceptual model for the prevention of 'petty' crime', in E. Knehthorn and B. Svensson (eds) *Crime Prevention*, Stockholm: The National Swedish Committee for Crime Prevention.

Sylva, K. (1989) 'Does early intervention work?', *Archives of Disease in Childhood*, vol 64, pp 1103-1104.

Tobler, N.S. (1986) 'Meta-analysis of 143 adolescent drug prevention programmes: quantatitive outcome results of programme participants compared to control or comparison group', *Journal of Drug Issues*, vol 16, pp 537- 568.

Trojanowicz, R. and Bucqueroux, B. (1990) *Community policing*, Cincinnatti: Anderson.

Wilson, J.Q. (1975) *Thinking about crime*, New York: Basic Books.

Wolfgang, M., Figlo, R., and Stellin, T. (1972) *Delinquency in a birth cohort*, Chicago: University of Chicago Press.

nine

THE COMMUNITY AND THE POLICE

Karamjit Singh [1]

Introduction

The acquittal of four Los Angeles police officers in April 1992 after charges of assault involving a black citizen had been filed against them resulted in three days of urban disorder, culminating in 42 deaths. In the summer of 1992 there were small scale disturbances in the UK on specific inner city estates resulting in major damage to property.

Such events focus attention dramatically on the relationships between the police organisations and their local communities (particularly those in large urban conurbations). This paper initially discusses the wider context in which relationships between the community and the police should be considered and the historical development of US policing. It then focuses on the civilian oversight dimension - its definition and relevance, historical development and evaluation - whilst identifying new challenges for the policing function. In conclusion the possibilities for policy transfer between the USA and the UK are discussed within the framework of current debates about the nature of policing and citizen participation.

The wider context

Any discussion about the nature of policing as the 21st century approaches needs to take account of the following aspects of the present situation.

- Police organisations like other public sector institutions in the modern urban setting have to face the challenge: how do they make themselves receptive, responsive and representative towards their local communities?

- Policing itself has to be viewed as a service which needs information, public cooperation and support (against a backdrop of changing assumptions and debate internally and externally about the nature and form that relationships between the community and the police should take). The terms client, consumers, citizens and customers which are used frequently all imply different relationships with the organisations providing services, as does the concept of them as individuals or collectively.

- The relationships between police and community are part of a complex, sometimes sensitive, and changing social mosaic. Perceptions are often as important as the reality, if not more so.

- Police organisations face the internal challenges of debates focusing on the nature of organisational transparency versus opaqueness. This subsumes the question of how an organisational orientation looking outwards towards the community can be achieved.

- Like other public services, police organisations have to deal with increasing expectations of service delivery within fiscal constraints and a continually changing customer base.

- Community involvement in the policing process has to be conceived in broader terms than the commitment to reduce crime. The effectiveness of the policing function is directly related to the issue of public confidence.

Police organisations are not unitary institutions. They contain within them a diverse range of attitudes and responses towards their external environments. Because one of the major social influences in the development of the USA has been immigration, the concept of 'community' within the major urban areas has never denoted homogeneity. The heterogeneous populations of these large metropolitan areas cannot accurately be defined by geographical boundaries alone but increasingly by other variables such as language, ethnicity and race. In the same way that linguistic and other parameters can mean that the concept of community is a relatively narrow one for some individuals, police organisations, like many other public sector institutions, traditionally provided services and conducted themselves as if the social reality they were facing was homogeneity rather than diversity. Continually changing assumptions about the relationships between police and community (which themselves are a product of rapid social change) have posed major challenges to police organisations, although their significance has sometimes not been recognised.

Historically, the response of the public sector more generally has been to focus inwards on organisational definitions of parameters and expertise as the appropriate manner in which to manage such external issues. One effect has been to hinder the willingness of institutions and individuals to accept the need for cooperation and to recognise that multiple problems require multiple solutions which no single agency or process is able to provide. This pattern of problem resolution and innovation may increasingly become more prevalent in the public sector. It can be argued that the key components of such relationships are likely to be: an ongoing commitment to develop them; the acceptance of a shared contribution; and recognition of mutual needs and benefits. The acceptance or otherwise of the concept of collaborative joint action to solve a problem is perhaps at its most stark when considering the question of accountability both for individuals and institutions. These general points are as applicable to public services in the UK during the 1990s as they are to the USA.

The historical context of US policing

At the present time there are an estimated 20,000 police departments ranging from one person sheriff's departments in the rural areas of South Carolina to New York City Police Department with nearly 30,000 police officers. One result is that no uniform organisational model or practice has emerged. The constitutional development of the USA has resulted in a policing function which is considerably diverse. The division of constitutional powers, the concept of federalism and emergence of strong local self-government (in some areas) has been responsible for this trend.

The political development of the large urban centres, particularly those on or near the eastern seaboard, during the early part of this century and previously, had profound implications for the nature of policing and particularly the web of relationships between police departments, city governments and local communities. The rise of political machines and emergence of strong mayors with processes incorporating direct personal accountability on the part of police chiefs to them, often led to external perceptions that corruption existed within police departments. A series of public scandals did little to challenge this view. This contributed in part to the development of a 'professional model' of policing from the 1920s onwards which sought to provide models of good organisational practice in order to achieve law enforcement goals.

One of the features of this professional model was that it emphasised the distance between police departments and their elected officials. This was usually achieved through the creation of police commissions and similar structures (with varying terms of reference) whose membership invariably consisted of political appointees. The focus on organisational rules and emphasis on internal management had the effect - anticipated or not - that police departments did not integrate the concept of community partnerships or external assessments into the process of developing effective law enforcement strategies. The historical pattern of policing - with some sections of the community being (to all intents and purposes) invisible in terms of employment practices and services provided - was reinforced by these internal practices.

The definitions and relevance of civilian oversight

Civilian oversight has been defined by one observer as:

> In the management of citizens' complaints against police officers, a government entity is constituted through a legislative or administrative act which mandates citizens' participation in the processing of these complaints through to the disposition of complaints. (Patterson, 1991, p 269)

Such definitions of civilian oversight which focus on the review of complaints made by members of the public relate to only one aspect of the broader question of generating public confidence in the police. In practice this particular definition differs little from the term civilian review which is an after the event evaluation of individual police officer conduct. Such definitions underline the importance that grievances, whether expressed individually or collectively, have played in shaping the emergence of institutional arrangements governing relationships between the community and the police. The same observer also suggests:

> Another approach in defining the role of civilian oversight would be to broaden the frame of reference, its disciplinary responsibilities would not be diminished, but it would exist within a larger context ... where citizens and police officers debate the ends and means of policing in relation to specific circumstances raised by a complaint. ... Such an approach to civilian oversight would offer the opportunity for conciliating differences between police and citizens and for clarifying the community's moral consensus as to what is the appropriate police response to crime and disorder. The results would minimise the ambiguities faced by police officers as they are called upon to serve in our culturally diverse communities. (Patterson, 1991, p 273)

Expanding the definition of civilian oversight in this way has relevance for policing patterns and for the organisation of the policing function.

Civilian oversight has a major role in the complex web of relationships which police organisations and citizen groups need to manage effectively if policing services that are perceived to have equity and integrity are to be provided in cities. The nature of civilian oversight itself also highlights the relationship between police organisations and their communities as one in which a broader question is raised: how does effective citizen participation in the policing process occur? A distinction could be made between genuine citizen power sharing (citizen control, delegated power and partnership) as opposed to token power sharing (for example, placation, consultation and informing). Another dimension is the question of empowerment, that is, the extent to which a community is able to communicate about and influence policing services which are being delivered.

Most police contacts with citizens are unsupervised and this has implications for individual citizens, citizen groups and their representatives, and for individual officers, their managers and police departments. When combined with powers of discretion, the actions of individual police officers can have a disproportionate impact upon community perceptions about police organisations, for better or worse. The civilian oversight process is relevant not only because it captures individual recollections and organisational responses towards these incidents, but also because it can focus attention on the broader context in which policing within urban areas occurs.   Other forms of police-community initiatives have traditionally run the risk of being processes in which the police are perceived to have a dominant role and because of this have encountered problems of legitimacy.

Civilian oversight : past and present experiences

The diversity already noted in the size and nature of police organisations in the USA is matched on a smaller scale by a corresponding mix in city-based civilian oversight structures. Differences in systems mask the fact that the philosophical assumptions underpinning them are often similar.   In perspective, a 1987 survey found that less than 20% of the largest 100 police departments had any form of external civilian involvement in the processes for dealing with complaints from individual citizens or groups (West, 1987).   The external structures reviewing complaints have been defined by a number of commentators as falling into the following broad categories:

●   those where the external agency has the power and resources to record, investigate, adjudicate and recommend discipline to police management (two examples are the Ombudsman in Flint, Michigan, and the Office of Citizen Complaints, San Francisco);

●   those where the external agency might have similar functions as described above but where responsibility for the investigations rests with police departments (the New York Civilian Complaint Review Board is one example);

●   those where the external agency might function as described in both categories above, but where the city's chief administrator acts as an arbitrator/mediator of disciplinary disputes between the oversight agency and the police executive (Cleveland and Cincinnati, Ohio, are both examples of this particular category);

●   those where the external agency monitors the complaints process and can intervene either by recommending further investigative work or debating the merits of a complaint with police management before a final decision is undertaken (one

example of this is the role of the Police Services Committee of
Evanston City Council, Illinois);

● those where the external agency audits the complaints process.
This is a narrower remit than the category above because the
function of such agencies is to comment upon the fairness and
thoroughness of the internal complaints procedure undertaken
rather than consider individual cases (one example is the Police
Internal Investigations Auditing Committee in Portland,
Oregon).

Clearly each of these broad categories incorporates a number of
more subtle variations in procedures and powers. The level of
resources allocated is dependent upon a number of factors
including the demands of the process and the requirements of
differing urban communities. One further category merits
attention: those processes where the police organisation directly
employs civilian employees. The Office of Professional Standards
within the Chicago Police Department is an example of this
incorporation of civilians into an essentially internal system.

The primary questions asked about civilian oversight have
centred on aspects such as:

● who should receive the complaint?

● who should determine the allegation?

● who should investigate?

● who should adjudicate or mediate?

● who should impose sanctions?

Debate has traditionally focused on the processes rather than on
what outcomes are expected from them. The arguments about
using police or civilian investigators have been central to such
debates. A range of systems using civilian investigators
exclusively (for example San Francisco and Chicago), joint teams
of police and civilian investigators (New York and Detroit) and
police investigators only (several systems) have emerged. No
system currently exists which has an overriding or exclusive
civilian input in all the five main stages identified above.

Civilian review initiatives which emerged during the 1960s
implicitly reflected a stream of allegations centred on police
brutality and improper conduct, particularly towards racial

minorities. A series of national commissions examining urban disorder in the 1960s mentioned the lack of effective methods in dealing with complaints as one contributory factor in the police-community alienation which had occurred. The national emphasis on civil rights issues also helped to focus attention on concerns about perceived inequities in policing, both in form and practice.

Early initiatives, such as those in New York and Philadelphia, failed because of a combination of such factors as resource constraints, shifting political commitment, heightened community expectations about the potential impact of these processes and hostile police comment. One reality in all systems is that no matter who is investigating individual police officers, their collective bargaining representatives do not like the process. In the USA this opposition has manifested itself through legal challenges, political lobbying, campaigning in referendums and industrial action.

Historically, there has been a pattern of mutual mistrust which police departments and their communities bring into the dialogue following a specific incident triggering disproportionately serious consequences for police-community relationships. These perceptions are often added to by a sense of injustice which is felt by both sides. Two issues consistently having this dramatic impact have been the use of deadly force and large-scale public order policing; race and/or historical perceptions of inequitable policing have usually been major factors in the saga of subsequent events. As one commentator aptly put it "police shooting incidents or violent confrontations ... [have] been a lightning rod in police community relations and the point at which the depth of alienation is revealed" (Patterson, 1991, p 263).

Civilian oversight mechanisms in the USA have had a number of common experiences, regardless of the extent and nature of police participation in the process, and these are relevant to any discussions about such processes in the UK. All regulatory processes face the challenge of internalising, consciously or unconsciously, the perceptions and definitions of police organisations towards matters raised during the civilian oversight process. One illustration of this is the way the annual reports published by some agencies indicating the numbers of complaints as a percentage (often declining) of the numbers of service calls made by the police departments' personnel are used. Not only may the sensitivities and tensions surrounding a relatively small number of incidents contribute towards the impetus for change, but the polarisation that occurs during this period can have an impact on the subsequent effectiveness and performance of an agency. The initial experiences of civilian review boards in New York and Philadelphia during the 1960s and 1970s are examples of this. There is considerable evidence to demonstrate the diversity of opinion and conflict between differing interests such as the civilian oversight agency, community groups, the media, senior police managers, police unions, administrators and legislators. One common source of conflict is illustrated by the need to preserve confidentiality versus wider access to information in the public interest. An example of how restrictive the former could be is illustrated by the successful legal action of a police union in preventing a San Francisco agency from publishing aggregate statistics of public complaints. When evaluating the performance and impact of civilian oversight processes, the focus has traditionally been on statistical measures but this raises further questions about the use of statistics and their interpretation. One police department stated that its interpretation of falling trends in complaints statistics indicated increasing satisfaction with policing patterns but some community perceptions were more critical.

Debates have occurred around the representative nature (or otherwise) of agencies, whether the processes should be independent in function or form, and what level of resources are considered appropriate. The experiences of civilian oversight agencies with their government structures in local communities bear more than a passing resemblance to various aspects of statutory/non-statutory relationships within the UK urban context. The experiences of the New York Civilian Review Board and other agencies has been that large-scale public order incidents created an expectation that immediate action will follow. A large number of lengthy investigations with seemingly few criminal or disciplinary conclusions led in turn to critical comment which highlights the mismatch between performance and expectations. Media focus on such issues as corruption can lead to misconceptions about roles, since agencies may not in practice have the remit to deal with this aspect of police misconduct. The impact of judicial decisions and media coverage upon police practices has been dramatic. This reflected not only the wider role of the law in the USA in shaping public policy but also the importance of decisions defining the status of individual police officers and the liability of their employing organisations. In one mid-west city the media played a major role in facilitating the creation of an agency by undertaking a series of exposes about various aspects of unreported and uncorrected misconduct by police officers.

Only a small number of civilian oversight agencies had terms of reference which enabled them to focus on issues wider than on the actions of individual police officers. The Rodney King assault in Los Angeles and its consequences demonstrated that it is also necessary to have adequate resources to meet policy challenges and monitor the resource allocation processes. The success or otherwise of the agency or process in dealing with the large proportion of cases consisting of differing accounts of the same incident by citizens and police officers (with no independent witnesses) regardless of the burden of proof or who is undertaking the investigations, has a direct impact upon perceptions about its relative effectiveness. The level of resources allocated, the potential pool of personnel and their investigative skills together with the possible range of subpoena and other legal powers are also significant factors. Whatever the degree of police participation in the process or the nature of the organisational arrangements, at some point the agencies and processes themselves become the target for critical comment. Perhaps this is inevitable where there is a perception that existing systems are not operating effectively. Such experiences in turn are often sparked by a small number of high profile incidents which focus general attention on existing patterns of law enforcement. The Los Angeles riots referred to earlier are an illustration of this. Few civilian oversight systems in the USA have avoided this cycle.

Objectives and evaluation

Despite the structural differences, it can be argued that all civilian oversight agencies and processes in the USA and elsewhere, could be assessed against three primary criteria:

1.   how accessible and credible as grievance mechanisms are the processes perceived to be, given the variety of different standpoints both in the wider community and the police?

2.   to what extent does civilian oversight make a meaningful contribution to strengthening the relationship between the police and the community?

3. what is the impact upon reducing the extent of police misconduct towards citizens?

In order to meet these criteria each agency needs successfully to:

● develop the participation of citizens and police officers in the complaints process;

● reduce complainant abuse of the process by sensitive and credible filtering mechanisms;

● create a balance of authority which is widely perceived to be a suitable compromise between strongly held differing opinions on such process issues as who should investigate and discipline;

● deal with the frustration engendered by police unresponsiveness (perceived and real);

● develop performance indicators which go well beyond relatively narrow statistical assessments that are based on casework.

All civilian oversight processes experience debates about the extent of police participation. In addition, agencies within relatively formal systems have to counter the various pressures of promoting awareness of the system, increasing its use by citizens, the forbidding formality of the process and dealing with the suspicion that it is not truly independent. How do such bureaucracies become more responsive to community evaluation? Critical self-evaluation has not traditionally been perceived as a major strength in the public sector generally. In a current environment stressing quality of service and citizens rights, the relative 'transparency' of organisations (within the police service or otherwise) provides another dimension to the concept of accountability.

The experience of different cities and systems in the USA has shown that this is not an easy task and is prone to dynamics which are usually created by fast moving events that are external to the civilian oversight agency or process. The development of alternative dispute resolution processes which are conciliation based such as those in Metro Dade County, Florida - needing, as they do, changes in skills and perceptions on the part of individuals and institutions - provides another vehicle to deal with citizen concerns. The potential significance of such processes in both the UK and USA is that they provide a model separating public complaints from police discipline processes and could link complaints to broader issues such as the quality of service.

The challenges for policing

The development of civilian oversight during the last three decades has also witnessed new external challenges for and internal changes within the policing function in the USA. Whatever mayoral and city manager forms of government have emerged in many large US cities, one constant political reality facing city governments has been the multiplicity of powerful and very often single interest groups. This trend is likely to continue. In practice this means that a kaleidoscope of ever changing political realities confront police chiefs, directors of public safety, civilian oversight agencies, elected and appointed officials, and community representatives. This has obvious implications for the development of civilian oversight and the relative importance it enjoys at any given time.

There has been an increasingly enthusiastic response towards 'community orientated policing' by police departments throughout the USA. In broad terms this could be defined as a series of policing principles emphasising the practical implementation of an external orientation towards the community and away from the 'professional model'. The result has been a variety of initiatives most notably in relation to issues such as drugs education programmes, crime prevention and the consistent deployment of beat officers in local areas. Police departments are now beginning to consider the implications of applying these concepts to matters such as citizen complaints, police discipline and civilian oversight structures. Because these issues have traditionally been addressed internally, it is not surprising that opponents of civilian oversight have emphasised that police organisations need only look inwards for their solutions. Such resistance inside and outside police organisations has conceived of policing in terms of law enforcement activity, minimising any form of community involvement and includes a failure to recognise the alienation which can occur in police community relationships.

Another challenge facing police agencies who are seeking to apply community-based policing concepts is that police discipline systems do not necessarily have the same objectives as those of individual citizens or communities. What relationship, if any, should there be between individual citizen complaints (however defined), wider community concerns, and police discipline structures? Does a general organisational orientation to look outwards to the community for possible solutions require new definitions of non-technical management problems? Traditionally, police departments have been hierarchical, paramilitary in nature and with highly formalized procedures governing organisational activity. This is the antithesis of the leaner, flatter and outward looking organisations with fewer rules that are espoused by the advocates of community oriented policing and new management styles more generally. Advocating greater delegation and use of discretion by individuals creates its own tensions when viewed in the context of traditional organisational cultures emphasising adherence to internal directives in sanctioning acceptable actions.

The police themselves have tended to see civilian oversight processes as actually limiting the effectiveness of individual police officers and their departments in law enforcement terms. Today the current scale and nature of drugs related activity in the USA poses new challenges. The relationship between individual civil liberties and use of police powers in this area is likely to give rise to an ongoing debate. Another potential flashpoint is being added to a traditional source of police-community polarisation: the use of deadly force. It can be argued that the conflict is an artificial and unconnected dichotomy - civil rights should pose no threat to the proper and authorised use of police powers.

The experiences of a Maryland police department which saw calls for service rise by some 33% during the same period that the personnel increased by 0.3% is not untypical. The use of performance measures, such as response times, fiscal constraints combined with heightened community awareness and calls for an external civilian oversight process following a series of shooting incidents produced a combination of internal and external pressures. Managing such pressures is an increasingly common pattern facing police departments.

Police organisations depend on their effective assimilation of information and its translation into intelligence. Historically the importance attached to criminal intelligence has not been matched by other information flows, for example in the areas of community relations and complaints. In the USA, it could be argued that few police departments have utilised the full potential of the information contained within these two functions. Traditionally, community relations has been viewed as a functional area of activity that suddenly acquires a disproportionate importance in organisational terms when critical situations emerge.

Another relevant issue here is that complaints systems are usually modelled on casework processes which have not traditionally been an effective conduit for organisational learning or creativity.

Law enforcement agencies will increasingly recognise the impact of new technology. One illustration was shown by the repeated television showing of the Rodney King assault in Los Angeles in 1992 which had been recorded visually. Such incidents have considerable implications for institutional/individual accountability and the traditional assumption that the investigation process (and sometimes the adjudication) is not public. In Dallas and Los Angeles, for example, community groups were reported as monitoring the actions of police officers with the extensive use of camcorders. This particular confluence of new technology, administrative processes and legal considerations is still relatively uncharted territory in terms of the implications for evidence and processes heavily dependent upon written statements rather than video tapes.

The possibilities for policy transfer to the UK

Observers have pointed out elsewhere the importance of understanding the broader context before discussing the possibilities of transatlantic policy transfers. This chapter has previously referred to the fragmented nature of law enforcement in the USA and to the historical, constitutional, legal and administrative reasons for its development in local communities. Allied to this is the relative financial independence of local governments within the USA within a much looser statutory framework of central-local relations. The Constitution, for example, does not even mention local government. Another important distinction in legislative terms can be drawn between municipal ordinances, administrative regulations and parliamentary statutes.

The question 'will it work in the UK?' contains assumptions about the nature of successful transnational policy transfers. Successful policy transfer needs to examine successes and failures, the latter not only to understand why initiatives fail in one institutional setting but also how they may flourish in different settings. The question might be posed as: 'can the experience of the civilian oversight process in the USA provide insights which would be helpful within a UK context?'

Given that there are many similarities in the economic, social and environmental problems facing urban communities in the two countries and in the nature of citizen expectations and interaction with governmental structures, it is assumed that this is indeed the case. One observation directly relevant to the policing function and relationships with individuals and communities in the USA and the UK highlights this:

> Many people in inner cities would be more appropriately described as recipients of services rather than consumers, in that they lack choice. Because of poverty or lack of mobility they have little or no choice over the services they use. Indeed the fact that they use particular services demonstrates their lack of choice. Such service recipients, who do not have the 'exit' option, need to be able to influence services through ... 'voice'. (see Hambleton and Taylor, Chapter 1 in this volume)

Although the UK police service and the role of the citizen constable have evolved differently, the definition and presentation of policing problems have contained many similarities notwithstanding the differences between the two societies. The nature and boundaries of policing will inevitably change in both countries. In the USA there are already an estimated 3,000,000 security guards visible in areas such as shopping malls and housing estates, against some 600,000 police officers. This trend will clearly intensify here with an increasing identification of non-core business roles currently undertaken by the police and the growth of private security industry. The relationships between police chiefs and the elected leadership of local communities have increasingly come under scrutiny and sometimes given rise to greater scepticism about the limits of local accountability. One result of the Rodney King assault and the eventual acquittal of the police officers was that it focused attention on the inability of the Los Angeles Police Commission to dismiss the chief of police. Within the UK the future role and function of police authorities is becoming the subject of a polarised debate.

Highly publicised miscarriages of justice, various forms of public criticism and successful litigation by individual police officers are some of the factors which have combined to duplicate pressures similar to those described earlier. Changes such as: the relative use and deployment of civilian personnel; greater devolution of resource allocation and decision making to police sub-divisions; further abolition of middle management tiers; the use of opinion surveys; and greater consultation with local communities in determining priorities all have implications for the definition of policing today. These changes have also touched on the nature of supervision by senior officers and the employment status of individual officers. At the present time there is considerable discussion about the Citizens Charter and its application to public services such as policing, with an accompanying emphasis on performance indicators and quality control models. The success or otherwise of such initiatives is directly related to the demonstrable ability of public institutions to provide receptive and responsive services to increasingly diverse communities.

Three views which are emerging about the police discipline system and have implications for public complaints processes in the UK are:

- the argument that little or no change is necessary and those advocating change do not recognise the strengths of the present system;

- calls for the development of a two tier system differentiating between the nature of allegations, the level of police management with devolved responsibility and the level of proof necessary to substantiate allegations;

- suggestions that the police discipline system needs root and branch reform with replacement by a wider code of ethics.

Each of these suggestions has provoked strong responses within the police service. Little, if any, discussion has incorporated the implications of these options for local communities.

The relevance of the US experience for the UK in terms of civilian oversight is that it can contribute to the debate raised by the following questions.

- Are changes needed in the police discipline system?

- Can alternatives be put forward to the basic assumption underpinning appropriate sections of the three previous statutes that have been concerned with public complaints - that there should be an irrevocable link with the police discipline system? Should allegations, whistle blowing or grievances expressed by serving police officers continue to be differentiated from public complaints?

- Do existing processes of community participation meet the objectives of effective communication for police organisations, enhancing public confidence and providing empowerment for local communities?

- How can the factors pushing for the evolution of the policing function into larger administrative and economic units be balanced against the need to provide a local service to meet local needs?

- What implications do emerging priorities such as quality of service have for the policing function internally, its relationships with local communities and the complaints system?

- What unanticipated consequences internally and externally do emerging changes in police organisational structures, training and the employment status of individual police officers have?

- Can any part of the public complaints process be devolved geographically and/or administratively?

- What are the implications for existing legislation?

- How should civilian oversight be defined in the UK context?

- How can all these questions and others be debated within a non-polarised context?

The Royal Commission on Criminal Justice will inevitably touch on some of these issues, directly or indirectly. The concept of civilian oversight will be directly affected by the Royal Commission's deliberations about matters such as the scrutiny of police criminal investigations, the evidential assessment and utilisation of resources.

Whilst the US experience of civilian oversight has seen an explosion of institutional forms, this clouds the common experiences previously discussed and their contribution to debates within the UK.

Within the UK, comment about the nature of civilian oversight has often focused on complaints processes and specifically who should undertake the investigations.   Such debates have mirrored those in the USA with little emphasis on the relative opportunity costs of the various options suggested.   The experience of the USA suggests that there is no dearth of institutional mechanisms which could be duplicated, but for successful transatlantic policy transfer a more wide-ranging debate needs to take place linking relationships between police and community to policing outcomes.

Conclusions

This paper has considered civilian oversight in the USA within the broader framework of relationships between the community and the police.   Previous policy discussions have in the main been crisis driven and focused on processes rather than outcomes.   If the goals are sensitive law enforcement, a fair allocation of resources and provision of services, what role does the community have in setting and implementing these?   Civilian oversight can provide one opportunity for reviewing and improving the policing services provided to communities.   In the USA this has resulted in the emergence of a multiplicity of civilian oversight processes and models which have been based around specific urban communities. Police organisations are increasingly interacting with ever more heterogeneous communities and this in turn generates new demands on institutions and individuals.

During the 1990s there will be continued discussion about relationships between police organisations and the communities to which they provide services.   Institutions or individuals cannot automatically be assumed to have the sensitivity or resolve to undertake critical self-evaluation or indeed to advocate major changes.   Previous comments about the relevance of the US experience of civilian oversight have tended to focus on process issues such as who undertakes the investigation.   A policy orientated approach needs to consider a number of issues before seeking to identify prescriptive models for civilian oversight in the UK.

Finally, effective policing requires the meaningful participation of those who are being policed as well as those who are undertaking the policing.

Notes

1. This paper was written on the basis of observations made by the writer during a nine month period as a Harkness Fellow in the USA (1990/91). The author wishes to express his appreciation to the Commonwealth Fund, New York and the Home Office for financial assistance during this period. Any views expressed are personal and do not reflect those of the Police Complaints Authority.

References

Patterson, W.E. (1991) 'Police accountability and civilian oversight of policing', in A.J. Goldsmith (ed) *Complaints against the police*, Oxford: Oxford University Press.

West, P. (1987) *Police Executive Research Forum Investigation of complaints against the police survey*, Washington DC: Police Executive Research Forum.

part four

COMMUNITY RENEWAL AND EMPOWERMENT

ten

COMMUNITY DEVELOPMENT IN THE INNER CITY

Alex Norman

Introduction

The UK and the USA have borrowed policies and programmes from each other in an attempt to address problems of community development in economically deprived inner city areas. This chapter explores and analyses approaches used by government, business and major foundations in the development of a national policy of public and private partnerships to combat the urban blight and feelings of alienation among inner city residents that often lead to social unrest in the form of rebellions, revolts and riots. The preferred foundation approach is described in a case study of the United Neighborhood Council (UNC) which is used to highlight issues to be considered by non-profit neighbourhood development organisations (also called community development corporations) as they organise to engage in housing development, economic development and employment and training. The chapter dramatises how a fragmented and unclear policy can create situations whereby local politics can frustrate even the most well planned efforts by community development corporations to engage in community capacity building and citizen participation.

The UK, under the conservative government of Margaret Thatcher, and the USA, under the equally conservative administration of Ronald Reagan, have strongly advocated free economic market (or supply side) strategies and private sector management as a means of addressing issues related to community development and urban blight. Their approaches call for public funds to be used to leverage private investment through public and private sector partnerships. In the USA much of this effort has occurred through non-profit, non-governmental structures called community development corporations (CDCs): community based, self-help organisations engaged in the development of some segment of that community's economy (ie housing development and rehabilitation, employment and work training) with the help of external funding sources.

The passage of the Local Government, Planning, Land and Finance Act of 1980 in the UK created funding for enterprise zones and, therefore, a framework for urban development and new towns. In contrast, the USA has not been able to enact national legislation to either designate enterprise zones nor create the framework for public/private partnerships. The one exception is the Job Training Partnership Act of 1980 which established Private Industry Councils (PICs), comprised of representatives from business, education and social service, as policy-making bodies to share in the oversight of public sector employment and training programmes. Despite introducing six bills to congress and extensive lobbying during the Reagan presidency, no federal enterprise zone legislation was passed. A limited version which allowed the designation of zones was included in the Housing and Community Development Act of 1987. Thus no overarching national policy guides the development of these important public/private partnerships at state and local levels.

Nevertheless 37 states have enacted legislation designating more than 1,500 public/private oriented enterprise zones of which more than 500 are actively engaged in some forms of community development (Guskind, 1989). This has resulted in a melange of zones, ranging from small designated urban areas to whole counties, in an effort to attract business enterprise.

Enterprise zones are blighted, economically distressed areas that are designated by governmental authority for preferential treatment in order to promote private investment and job creation by businesses through the use of investment incentives and tax subsidies. Although originally conceptualised by Peter Hall (Guskind, 1989) as a strategy to spur investments in Asian free ports like Hong Kong, enterprise zones have been used in the UK and the USA to encourage private initiatives and ventures in economically depressed neighbourhoods. Theoretically, the basis for their success is the degree to which public and private sectors cooperate to rebuild sagging economies in low income communities, create jobs for unemployed and underemployed workers and foster economic growth for the general community. An assumption in this approach is that urban blight is related to lack of economic opportunities. In the USA it is also believed that this strategy will bring government to residents at its most local level and prevent the kind of riotous aftermath to social and economic injustice witnessed in the recent uprisings in south central Los Angeles, following the acquittal of the police officers charged with the beating of motorist Rodney King. This explains the inclusion of enterprise zone appropriations in the Urban Aid legislation that was developed in response to the 1992 'spring uprising' in Los Angeles, a somewhat unrealistic expectation when one considers that the root causes of such civil disorders are not due simply to lack of economic opportunities but due to deeply ingrained Euro-American racism and classism.

The experience of these zones in both the UK and the USA is mixed and fraught with controversy. One major reason is because enterprise zones as currently funded do not engage residents in a capacity-building, empowering process of participative decision-making relationship with the planners and policy makers. Other reasons have to do with the recency of enterprise zones as an urban strategy and the lack of enough sites for comparable evaluations. Despite their shortcomings they do encourage public and private sector cooperation.

Public and private partnerships are further encouraged by the Urban Institutions Program - a Ford Foundation and American Can Foundation funded programme to stimulate community revitalisation by creating partnerships between large institutions and their surrounding communities. The Structured Employment/Economic Development Corporation (SEEDCO), a non-profit tax-exempt organisation with the support of the two foundations, has the major objective of forging new relationships between community organisations and educational institutions and medical centres that will improve economic and physical development in low income areas. SEEDCO provides limited financial and technical support for activities in housing development, economic development and employment and training to 25 selected demonstration projects nationwide. Although the programme areas funded correspond to federal programmes in housing and urban development (urban development action grant), economic development (enterprise zones) and employment and training (Joint Partnership Training Act) there is no built-in coordination with local programme efforts.

This paper describes the development of one SEEDCO funded project to increase the capacity of non-profit CDCs, as centres of gravity, to attract funding from local government, foundations and businesses that will benefit lower income populations. Critical issues involving community initiative, community organisation development and representative governance at the neighbourhood level are presented, particularly for multicultural urban communities.

The paradox of community development corporations in the USA

"The business of America is business" said Calvin Coolidge, the thirteenth president of the USA, in a speech before the American Newspaper Editors at Chicago in 1925. This attitude has permeated government and the private/business sector and the result has more often been the exploitation of the poor in search of profits. With the exception of the New Deal Programmes of the Roosevelt era and the Great Society Programmes of the Johnson administration, little has changed as government reinforces its commitment to create private wealth with 'trickle down' theories and 'supply side' economics. Owing to the limited role of government in social welfare in the USA, there is a long and honoured tradition of non-profit, non-public organisations providing social welfare services. Similarly there is also a tradition of financial support to those organisations by the private foundation structure in the USA which is made up of national as well as local networks. It is within this context that the voluntary association infrastructure developed as a natural, fertile ground for developing organisations to respond to community needs.

Thus CDCs emerged in the USA, particularly in the 1960s and 1970s, as a community, self-help response to the need for social services and economic development. Supported mainly by funding from national and local governments as well as a few private foundations, CDCs play a major role in the fabric of community development in the inner cities where blighted and substandard conditions exist. In contrast this type of structure is rare in the UK, where neither the plurality of funding sources nor the specific intermediary roles played by voluntary organisations in the USA are easily replicated.

One other distinction should be mentioned and that is the tradition of advocacy and citizen activism that results in social legislation to support community economic development. As an example, civil rights activism by African Americans during the 1960s provided the groundswell by which Americans in general became more active in affairs of national and local government. One result of that activism was the Community Reinvestment Act of 1977, which was designed to combat racial discrimination and red-lining against African Americans and others in low income neighbourhoods and to require banks to make loans to residents (Bullard and Teagin, 1991). More recently the Home Mortgage Disclosure Act of 1986 required banks to disclose their loans to communities by census tracts in an effort to discourage banks to circumvent the legislation by using loopholes such as denial of loans that are not 'safe and secure', a loosely defined requirement (for example see Twist, 1987; Yang and Anderson, 1988). Additionally there are private grant-funded organisations like Local Initiatives Support Coalition which serve the 'watchdog' function of providing seed money to non-profit organisations and CDCs engaged in community economic development. Consequently the financial climate to support and expand community development is a contributing factor to the success of CDCs in the USA.

Despite these structural, infrastructural and climatic supports all is not smooth sailing for community development in the inner city areas of the USA. As Twelvetrees (1989) has noted in his comparative study of CDCs in the USA, the reliance of CDCs on substantial funding from government with its numerous regulations and from private investment from profit and non-profit sources, dilutes their self-help efforts by making them dependent upon the very sources from which CDCs hope to be emancipated. It further creates a paradox with dimensions that are paraphrased below (Twelvetrees, 1989, pp 188-93):

● CDCs must rely on substantial outside funding from government which has failed to deliver previously and which has a stronger commitment to create wealth through the private sector;

● CDCs need community controlled decision making in order to be successful, yet quick action on complex decisions demands a structure counter to local control;

- CDCs need to remain small to be effective yet must deal with problems requiring massive investment and a larger scale similar to that of the same developers who have historically competed against CDCs and exploited them;

- although public/private partnerships have historically run roughshod over local communities and their representatives, as the grass roots part of the relationship CDCs are necessary to the partnership.

With a history of limited, reactive support for community development it is small wonder that a US government which has failed to deliver programmes in housing, economic development and employment and training would also fail to develop coherent policy and programmes to assist CDCs. Thus the fragmented policy that exists to date has a plausible if not acceptable explanation. However it remains a fact that revitalisation of urban communities will require partnerships between the public, private and voluntary sectors. Consequently certain historical and sectoral conflicts between the private sector as part of a 'business culture' focussed on profits and the public sector as part of a 'civic culture' concerned with participative democracy in decision making must be resolved or managed through the structure of the CDC and through the process of interactions between organisations and people who are vital to those relationships. Robert Reich, a chief economic advisor to President Clinton, discusses this conflict at length in terms of the different perceptions of reality held by the sectors. The civic sector sees the common good being addressed through community and citizen participation while the business sector supports market-driven individual freedom as a means of addressing the common good (Reich, 1983). The case example that follows is one attempt to recognise and to overcome those obstacles.

Community initiative of the United Neighborhood Council

The initiative that resulted in the formation of a neighbourhood council was begun by the University of Southern California (USC) in April 1986 through its Office of Civic and Community Relations (OCCR). The University, located in the heart of an urban multicultural community, was acting out of self interests that included developing the blighted areas adjacent to its campus and creating housing for its faculty and students. At the same time USC realised that in order to accomplish these goals it would be necessary to create a partnership with the community in an exchange relationship. The University set forth a plan to take several initiatives:

● to expand the USC campus through a joint partnership with the City's Community Redevelopment Agency (CRA);

● to commit its resources to cooperative ventures with local public schools;

● to create a role for participation in community upgrading and economic development;

● to work constructively with community organisations, agencies, and residents.

The community initiative began with OCCR staff identifying and interviewing 136 community residents, service providers and people in leadership positions to learn about the community's most critical needs and concerns. Some of the people were already known to the university due to their participation on an advisory council. Others were identified through key informant interviews and by word-of-mouth. The group was representative of the community in that all racial, ethnic, gender, class and age groups participated in the initiative. A needs assessment was conducted in which 742 concerns were expressed with university/community programmes being of primary interest, followed by economic development, crime and safety, housing, public and social services, cultural environment, recreation, education and health services. These concerns were compiled into a report and served as the basis for a two and a half day off-site planning session three months later, with 20 people who represented a multicultural and intergenerational cross-section of the 136 interviewees.

Three actions resulted from the planning session. One was a further narrowing of priority concerns into seven areas which were crime, economic development, education, health/environment, housing, social services and community relations. A second outcome was the idea of developing a 'neighbourhood council' to engage in self-governance and to help the community determine its own destiny. The third was the establishment of a 'neighborhood council study group' composed of seven people selected from the planning group and six from an existing University Community Advisory Council, chosen because of their activism in community and university affairs. The group was representative of ethnic, gender, community, business, university and human service interests and had a broad agenda of determining the best approach to the creation of a neighbourhood council.

In November the study group deliberated its charge and elected as its chair a local, respected businessman who was also an alumnus of the university. Staff support for the group was provided by the director of OCCR who was also a member of the study group, and his assistant who was a graduate social worker. They had contacted the author about providing consultation on the process of developing the council. We met jointly with the chair of the study group and agreed that the author would meet with both OCCR staff and separately with the study group, to develop the model for the neighbourhood council. With the help of a planning grant from SEEDCO in December, I was hired to provide technical assistance to OCCR staff and to facilitate the study group's deliberations in developing the council concept into reality.

Developing the model

The study group met 13 times during an eight month period with an emphasis on creating an inclusive process by which all facets of the community would be encouraged to participate in the planning process. Thus the model was one that combined elements of the traditional community development approach, in which emphasis is placed on leadership development and empowering participants, with that of a social planning model, in which emphasis is placed on developing programmes to meet community needs. This mixing or phasing of approaches was deliberately undertaken in order to give equal importance to tasks (or programme outcomes) and process (the form that decision making takes). A fuller treatment of this issue is given by Rothman (1979, pp 3-26). One result of this sensitivity to process was that all large meetings were held on Saturdays to encourage participation and weekly meetings were held after the workday, with dinner provided, in order to assure maximum attendance.

During this period the study group selected a three square mile boundary which was divided into five districts which would elect their own representatives to the council. An area-wide sociodemographic analysis was conducted to determine the percentage of the population by major ethnic groups, gender, age, and income in order to categorise residential membership. Further analysis of business organisations and service providers was conducted to determine non-residential membership. These analyses provided OCCR with a breakdown of the percentages of different ethnic and cultural groups and types of organisations in the selected geographical area. They also provided a minimum percentage for participant representation in future activities. The study group also developed a mission statement, a set of goals based on the concerns identified during the community assessment/planning session and discussed the means of transferring responsibility once the council had been installed. At all steps along this process, care was taken to ensure that broad participation of the community guided the planning. For example, the study group members were themselves representative of all interests in the designated area and were charged with reporting the events to their respective communities and constituents.

A ratio of 60% residents to 40% non-residents was approved to make up the council and all other programme bodies emanating from the council. In this manner it was assured that residents would always have a numerical advantage. The method of selection was to be by a formal election process arrived at through a series of neighbourhood conferences, held on a day convenient to community residents. In April 1987 the study group mailed letters requesting an endorsement of their ideas to local politicians, community and business organisations, service institutions and community leaders with the president of the university and the mayor of the city as signatories to the letter and as principal sponsors of the proposed conferences. A total of 32 individual and organisational endorsements representing all segments of the community were received. In May more than 500 'letters of participation' were mailed inviting participants to the conference with 230 responding positively. The respondents' percentages approximated the percentages of the demographic analysis conducted by OCCR. This was considered quite a stroke of luck since this meant that we met our own minimum participation requirements. All ethnic, racial, age and income groups were included and this held true for the entire process that followed.

Forming the United Neighborhood Council

The First Neighborhood Council Conference was held on 13 June
with the university president and the mayor of the city presiding
and with more than 175 persons attending. The conference was
simultaneously conducted in English and Spanish with some
Korean interpreters at participant tables by request. Faculty
members from the two schools of social work served as conveners
at each table and facilitated discussion. Child care and
transportation services were provided and people with physical
limitations were accommodated. The author facilitated the
conference decision-making process by which delegates debated
and accepted the 'council concept', reviewed and discussed the
mission statement and goals prepared by the study group and
elected representatives from each table to meet as a task force until
a council could be formally installed. The task force was charged
with refining the mission statement, determining an appropriate
organisational structure and detailing strategies for reaching out to
include more ethnically diverse residents. A second conference
was scheduled to consider their findings.

The Second Neighborhood Council Conference was held on
22 August with approximately 125 persons attending. The task
force recommendations on the mission statement, organisational
structure, goals and outreach strategies were discussed and adopted.
The task force was given the additional charge for determining
geographical boundaries, composition of the board of directors and
criteria for selection processes of the membership. A third
conference was scheduled for this report amidst much discussion of
the merits of going slow so as to build accountability between those
taking on leadership roles and the general conference members.
Consensus was that these procedures should be followed even after
the council was formally installed.

The Third Neighborhood Council Conference was held on
24 October with 100 persons in attendance. The delegates adopted
the final versions of the mission statement, goals and objectives,
organisational structure, boundaries, districts for the election
process, board of directors composition and strategies for
publicising past and future events. Based on the task force's
suggestion of a 60%:40% ratio of residents to non-residents, the
conference appointed a steering committee of 10 residents and 5
business and institutions representatives to make all appropriate
decisions until a board could be formally installed.

The steering committee met over the next four months to design a geographically representative governance process which included an establishment of criteria for elective office, an election calendar, processes for district meetings, voting eligibility, terms of office and an installation date. To do this they organised into three subcommittees by function and selected a convener for each; (i) organisational structure, (ii) the election process and (iii) publicity and community outreach. Seventy five persons and two student organisations volunteered to design and monitor the election process which was held on 12 March 1988 with more than 2,000 people casting votes in the 5 districts.

The board of directors of the United Neighborhood Council (UNC) was formally installed on 26 March amid the presence of the elected officials of the Los Angeles city council districts included in the geographic boundaries of the council. Five resident directors from each district and three non-resident directors from each of five groups (large businesses, small businesses, churches, institutions and community organisations) were officially handed the responsibility for guiding this new organisation's policy development and operations. A total of 40 directors were installed which included 25 residents (5 from each district) and 15 non-residents from businesses and institutions (3 each from large businesses, small businesses, churches, social institutions and community organisations). Its membership was multiracial and multicultural and included representation from all socioeconomic levels in the community. The board continued to meet monthly through the summer in order to become oriented to the purpose of the UNC and to negotiate relationships with each other. The author facilitated their first team building session on 2-3 December to help the board decide how they would work together to address the priority problem areas identified in the earlier assessment of their community. Over a two day period seven subcommittees engaged in goal setting and team building relationships and, at the end of the day, had a more definitive direction for the organisation and some idea of what would be required for them to operate as a team.

It should be noted that the building of affiliative relationships between business sector representatives and civic sector representatives, between community residents and professional service providers, and between representatives of various ethnic and gender groups reduces the possibility of culture clashes based on in-group differences. This is not to suggest that conflicts will not arise but when they do (as they inevitably will) the representatives will have a positive relationship from which to resolve or manage whatever develops. At the time of this writing, I am not aware of any major, cultural clashes that have developed.

Current history of the organisation

My contact with the UNC board ended at that point as an executive director was hired to provide staff assistance and I spent 6 months of a sabbatical year in the UK. Since that time the UNC has secured additional funding of approximately $100,000 from the Ford Foundation, SEEDCO and the Irvine Foundation to develop a strategic plan and a feasibility study for economic development. From those studies UNC has received an additional seed grant of $25,000 to develop an employment related project. Currently UNC and USC have entered into a partnership to develop a university/community child development centre, a partnership with Los Angeles County for job placement for conservation corps trainees and a separate contract of $60,000 to develop an information resource centre. In the final analysis there is a representative communitybased organisation in place to respond to community needs and to create a vision of community in a multiracial, multiethnic context. Can it be possible that this is not enough?

  The UNC recently experienced a source of frustration when the City of Los Angeles received a three year $2.7 million grant from the US Department of Labor to develop and operate a youth centre in a small geographic area with a high poverty rate. The demonstration project was the Department of Labor's attempt to support public/private partnerships cited earlier through the use of discretionary funding available to the secretary. It represented a collaborative effort between the PIC and the city's community development department which operates the JTPA programs. A group of directors and staff of UNC met with community development officials in a futile attempt to persuade them to select their geographical area for the demonstration. Despite the fact that the UNC community had an existing infrastructure and qualified as a high poverty area, another three square mile site in which there was neither infrastructure nor momentum was selected instead. The second UNC proposal, that its infrastructure be used instead of creating a new one also was rejected. Consequently an organisation will be built from the ground, using many of the financial and human resources that could have been applied to solve some of the problems faced by inner city youth. The deciding factor, we were to learn during a premature reception of the opening of the centre (the board has yet to be selected), was that the outgoing elected official wanted to "leave a legacy for our community" (his words). It mattered little that it took him 17 years to leave this legacy or that there was another needy population in his district that could have benefited.

At the time of the initial writing of this chapter, the centre was in its fourth month of limited programme operation even though no organisation had been created to run it and the executive with no board of directors had been fired. It was a prime example of operating outside the traditional planning rubric. With no oversight legislation, the pressure of local politics and business expediency resulted in snap decisions that proved to be more costly than a planned strategy.

An ending anecdote

There is a sad ending to the attempt at a public/private partnership described in brief in the above scenario. After the executive was fired the author was asked to assist the City Department of Community Development (CDD) and the Private Industry Council (PIC) in the development of a community-based organisation to operate the proposed Youth Employment Centre (YOU) as part of a university consortium (University of Southern California, California State University, Los Angeles and University of California, Los Angeles). Specifically the consortium was charged with creating a community-based board of directors for the organisation and provide university resources in programme areas of alternative education for youth, employment training, community outreach and provide executive leadership until a new executive director could be hired, all under contract with the CDD and the PIC.

During a four month period the consortium assisted in the development of a programme plan and the training of YOU programme staff, increasing the visibility and credibility of the organisation in the process. However all attempts of the consortium to develop a community-based organisation were resisted, initially by the PIC and later by the CDD as well. The PIC representative felt that the process of developing a community based board would take too long and that the community could be brought in at a later date.   The CDD representative felt that individuals selected from the community did not have the capacity to direct an organisation of this type, despite the fact that evidence to the contrary existed in the UNC example as well as others.   Any attempts on the part of the consortium to meet the stipulation of the contract to develop a community-based board met with threats from the CDD to fire any YOU staff who supported this idea and threats to withdraw the contract from the consortium.

A stalemate existed which required a Department of Labor official visit to mediate the dispute.   However when it became clear that the consortium was within its charge as stipulated by the contract, the CDD and the PIC representatives declared that their understanding of a community-based organisation was really a "traditional board of directors" and not one made up of people from the community.   At this point the author, as lead consultant to develop the board, withdrew from the consortium and refused to create a traditional board in place of a community-based board. The stalemate reached the newly elected city councilman's desk and a compromise was reached with the CDD and the PIC to delay further action until a new executive director was in place. Meanwhile the CDD would organise a board made up of representatives of elected officials and representatives from traditional educational and youth serving organisations city-wide.

A new executive director was hired but, before a plan for creating a board could be put in place, two key consortium members resigned and shortly afterwards the city was in the throes of the spring uprising.   Since the YOU centre was in the heart of the riot-torn area, several buildings were looted and burned but the centre was spared. Even the councilman's newly opened service centre adjacent to YOU was burned. At this time the status of the YOU project is unknown.

Conclusions

Similar circumstances in the UK and the USA have resulted in information and technology transfer between the two countries. Conservative approaches in government and subscription to a free market system have led a significant portion of leadership in the UK and the USA to endorse partnerships between the public and private sectors in an effort to solve problems of urban blight and economic development. This partnership strategy brings two cultures together with distinct differences in the way they view the world and how they solve problems: the business culture with its market-oriented 'bottom line' objectives and the civic culture with its emphasis on involvement and participation. This is graphically illustrated in the conflict between the CDD/PIC and the university consortium over the development of a community-based organisation. In this case, the consortium represented the civic culture while the CDD/PIC alliance represented a business approach that eschews planning in favour of short-term action.

Such an obviously conflicting situation demands some mechanism either to provide guidance to avoid clashes or to assist in their resolution when they occur, particularly since the community development approach involves empowering the community to engage in self-reliant activities. Failure to do so can result in a loss of momentum, a waste of funds and resources, and an increase in alienation and frustration of inner city residents, especially those who have been disappointed previously. Such failures make it difficult to re-energise community residents to collaborate with municipal departments who are not perceived to have the community's interest at heart.

Based on the experiences of the UNC and other CDCs in the USA, capacity building is a time-consuming yet time-saving activity requiring the patience and skills of seasoned facilitators. And because empowerment cannot be given or donated, an environment must be created in which people learn to develop and use effective self-help techniques. Simply stated, this means that the pace of development must be dictated by the community and not the businesses, the PIC, bureaucrats or the politics of funding as in the YOU example. The UNC stands in stark contrast as a preferred approach to the sad ending of the CDD/PIC experience.

Unlike the UK, the USA does not have legislation at the national level to give guidance for local initiatives, which results in a hodgepodge of efforts by government, business and national foundations to fund public/private approaches to solve urban problems. In such an environment, politics inevitably play an unwanted though necessary role. And while legislative oversight does not guarantee success when accompanied by a studied approach to community development, it increases chances immeasurably.

While in the USA the Joint Training and Partnership Act has served as the model for public and private sector collaboration it is the enterprise zone concept that has served as the driving force, albeit without adequate resources to accomplish the task. Those embracing this concept have tended to shun traditional planning rubrics in favour of business-oriented-free-market decisions, with its emphasis on 'bottom line' rather than 'process' results. In the meantime, sociodemographic shifts have so diversified urban communities by race, ethnicity, culture, gender and lifestyle that 'bottom line' results are no more important than the 'process' by which they were attained. Therefore, community and economic are intertwined in the development process. While the UK multicultural issues might be different, it bodes well to consider this approach in anticipation of demographic changes taking place.

The case study of the Ford Foundation sponsored UNC strongly supports the contention that journey (process) and destination (outcome) are inseparable. It is also a reminder that even though initiative exists at the community level to identify problems and marshal support to address them, it is the mysterious mix of local politics that represents the crucial variable to success. The UNC represents this author's best example of grass-roots community organisation development to date, yet the best plans without strong, consistent social policy as a guide can be foiled. By the same token, the CDD/PIC encounter represents business and bureaucracy at its worst. And in the absence of a defined social policy, the CDD/PIC example is likely to be repeated.

On the other hand, whether successful or not, the community is in a much stronger position as a result of the organisation of the UNC and its attempts to advocate for its economic development. Thus preparation is not lost simply because of lack of success in securing the YOU project. The intermediary role played by the non-profit sector CDCs in the USA can serve as a model for developing an intermediary role in the UK within the voluntary sector. The third sector is important because neither the private sector nor the public sector need give up on their respective roles or infrastructures, but by buying into a different kind of social responsibility, create a role that is compatible with community and economic development.

Many lessons can be learned from this experiment in urban living. Among them are that even in diversity there can be unity so long as the people feel they are represented. Another is that public and private partnerships require commitment, effort and a considerable amount of time. However as is evident in the youth centre fiasco, the saddest lesson is in the need to continue to pressure local government officials, who have their own set of agendas, that an important goal of community development is capacity building, without which empowerment is impossible. As a final note, despite the difficulties involved in the implementation of public and private collaborative initiatives in both countries they are likely to continue. Regardless of whether approaches have been evaluated to determine which is best, there will be an escalation in public/private partnerships. UNCs and organisations like them will be needed to bring governance to local levels due to the selfish political agendas of both national and local elected officials. Judgement of the community development process can not be based solely on the numbers of jobs created or the numbers of housing units built but also on the level of difficulty in the development of a community infrastructure. When one considers the success of the UNC as an experiment subjected to the whims of self-serving politicians and bureaucratic alliances with business myopia, the frustration of inner city residents is understandable. And when one considers that despite the disappointment of the residents in the community of the YOU project in the face of high expectations the marvel, then, is not in how well the bear dances but that she dances at all.

References

Bullard, R. and Teagin, J. (1991) 'Racism and the city', in M. Gottdiener and C. Pickvance (eds) *Urban life in transition*, Newbury Park: Sage.

Guskind, R. (1989) 'Round two for enterprise zones', *Planning*, September, pp 4-8.

Reich, R.B. (1983) *The next American frontier*, New York: Times Books.

Rothman, J. (1979) 'Models of community organisation and macro practice perspectives: their mixing and phasing', in F.M. Cox (ed), *Strategies of community organisation*, Itasca, US: F.E. Peacock Publishers.

Twelvetrees, A. (1989) *Organising for neighborhood development: a comparative study of community development corporations and citizen power organisations*, Hants: Gower Publishing Company Ltd.

Twist, D. (1987) 'Leaning on banks to lend to the poor', *Business Week,* 2 March, p 76.

Yang, C. and Anderson, R. (1988) 'The black aid: making banks better neighbors', *Business Week*, 15 August, p 101.

eleven

NEIGHBOURHOOD HOUSING RENEWAL

Philip Leather and Sheila Mackintosh

Introduction

During the 1980s there were a number of attempts to introduce urban regeneration initiatives from the USA into the UK. Experimental approaches to the regeneration of downtown and older housing areas in the USA such as the urban development action grant had been developed in the late 1970s with a strong role for private sector organisations (Hambleton, 1990). The Conservative government which came to power in the UK in 1979 was committed to increasing the role of the private sector in urban renewal and not surprisingly there was considerable interest in the US experience. But there are many difficulties inherent in the transfer of any policy initiative from one context to another. This chapter looks in detail at the attempt to transplant the US Neighborhood Housing Services (NHS) approach to the renewal of older housing areas into the UK. This programme, known in the UK as Neighbourhood Revitalisation Services (NRS), began in the early 1980s but ended in 1991 having made little long-term impact on the neighbourhoods in which projects were based or on the direction of housing renewal policy in the UK. As well as exploring the reasons why this initiative did not succeed in the UK and the lessons to be learned from this, the chapter also assesses the prospects for the introduction of a more effective NHS-type programme in the UK in the 1990s.

Context

By the beginning of the 1980s the private housing stock in most UK inner city areas was predominantly owner-occupied. More than three million dwellings had been transferred from the private rented sector between 1953 and 1980 as a result of favourable subsidy arrangements for home owners and legislation which made it unattractive to invest in housing for rent in comparison with other investment opportunities. However, many older inner city dwellings were in poor condition. The problem stemmed in part from the age of the stock but also because of under-investment in repair and maintenance by private landlords, combined with the inability of the subsequent purchasers, particularly older people, to afford to invest in their homes. In total there were more than 1.2 million owner-occupied dwellings in poor condition in urban areas in 1986 (Department of the Environment, 1988). Almost two-thirds of these were built before 1919.

Local authorities have traditionally played a major role in renewal policies for the private sector stock in the UK. During the 1960s and the early 1970s, there was an emphasis on large-scale compulsory acquisition and demolition of poor condition properties, which reached its peak in 1971 when 78,000 properties were demolished or closed. But government enthusiasm for demolition programmes waned, in part because of the high cost, but also because of increasing opposition from home owners to the loss of their properties and to rehousing in unpopular public housing projects. The 1969 and 1974 Housing Acts shifted the emphasis of policy away from demolition towards the refurbishment of the stock. However, local authorities continued to play the leading role in the implementation of renovation policies through their powers to initiate area-based renovation programmes such as housing action areas or general improvement areas, and to provide grants to home owners or landlords to assist them to improve their houses. Although at the outset it was intended that renovation programmes would stimulate home owners to invest their own resources in improving their housing, local authority and other publicly-funded investment by housing associations in the direct acquisition and improvement of privately-owned housing became increasingly more important in ensuring the success of area improvement initiatives as implementation progressed (Thomas, 1986). Furthermore, some four out of every five grants provided to private owners were for properties outside improvement areas, scattered throughout the older housing stock. Private sector financial institutions became only reluctantly involved in housing renewal in the late 1970s after the exposure of informal 'red-lining' policies which prohibited lending in some inner city areas.

The housing policies of the Conservative government which came to power in 1979 centred on the extension of home ownership through the large-scale disposal of publicly-owned housing to sitting tenants, the reduction of public expenditure on housing, and a shift in the role of local authorities in housing from large-scale providers to enablers. In all these elements there was strong emphasis on expanding the role of the private sector in financing and implementing housing policy. For some time the main emphasis was on the transfer of public sector stock into private ownership, but riots in some inner city areas in 1981 brought the problems of older housing to the top of the political agenda. A group formed from representatives of major financial institutions and senior civil servants (the Financial Institutions Group) began to look for ways in which private sector involvement in urban regeneration could be encouraged and building societies became involved in a number of housing renewal projects (Building Societies Association, 1985). In 1982 the group visited the USA to look for ideas which could be transplanted to a UK setting.

The Neighbourhood Housing Services (NHS) concept

One of the most promising initiatives identified by the Financial Institutions Group was the NHS network which in 1980 consisted of more than 120 neighbourhood-based projects in cities and towns throughout the USA that aimed to rejuvenate run-down neighbourhoods. Interest in the NHS initiative had first been stimulated in 1980 by the report of the Tri-national Inner Cities Project (Huntley, 1980) which compared approaches to urban renewal in the UK, Germany and the USA. On the basis of visits to the Neighbourhood Reinvestment Corporation in Washington, which provided developmental support, training, and financial services to individual NHS projects, and to the local projects in Chicago, Boston and Ithica, the study concluded that UK inner cities policy, which was based on a partnership between central and local government, largely excluded private sector organisations and local residents. It was felt that there was potential for the introduction of the NHS approach in general improvement areas and housing action areas in the UK.

The NHS initiative began in the central north side of Pittsburgh in 1968 when a group of residents joined with local financial institutions, businesses and government to promote housing regeneration in the area. Unlike the UK, grants to home owners did not form a major element of the policy. Work was funded by persuading financial institutions to make commercial loans available while a local charitable foundation provided $750,000 to capitalise a revolving loan fund at lower interest rates for those who could not afford conventional loans or who could not obtain them because they were thought to represent a bad risk.

Two years later the Pittsburgh project was picked up by the Federal Home Loan Bank Board which was concerned to stimulate lending in inner city areas by savings and loan institutions in the USA. The Bank Board had started a training programme for savings and loan staff and this was used to promote the Pittsburgh model in other areas. By 1972 there were four more NHS projects but the initiative took off on a major scale when it gained the support of the Federal Department of Housing and Urban Development which was seeking new housing initiatives following severe cuts in existing programmes imposed by the Nixon administration in 1973. This department, in partnership with the Federal Home Loan Bank Board, established the Urban Reinvestment Task Force (URTF) to promote and develop additional NHS projects and Neighborhood Housing Services of America (NHSA) to operate a secondary market for revolving loan funds. By purchasing these loans from individual projects NHSA would replenish the funds and enable projects to make additional loans. By 1976 there were NHS projects in 45 cities.

Other developments also encouraged the growth of NHS projects. In 1974, the introduction of the community development block grant to replace a range of federal programmes provided city and state governments with new opportunities for funding independent projects such as NHS. There was wide local discretion about how the community development block grant was used and in a number of areas NHS projects were able to obtain funds from this source to develop or expand their revolving loan funds. However the initiative finally came of age in 1978 with the Neighborhood Reinvestment Corporation Act which transformed the URTF into a congress-chartered non-profit organisation with public funding to support its activities in developing and supporting

NHS projects. In the same year NHSA began to raise private funding to increase the rate at which it could purchase revolving loan fund portfolios from individual NHS projects, supported by federal subsidy to bridge the shortfall between revolving loan and commercial rates. By 1980, there were 121 NHS projects, with a substantial amount of the expansion taking place in cities where NHS was already active. There were four projects in Chicago, for example, and two projects in Baltimore.

It was this successful initiative which UK observers visited in the early 1980s. By that time, the NHS model was well-established. The Neighborhood Reinvestment Corporation (NRC) served as an umbrella organisation with a role in developing new projects and supporting them for a year or so at the outset. It also acted as the channel for the revolving loan fund and provided ongoing training for project staff and others involved at local level. The NHSA liaised with the larger private sector financial institutions involved in supporting NHS and operated the secondary market for revolving loan funds. After the setting up period, individual NHS projects became autonomous bodies, managed by a local board, containing representatives of local financial institutions, businesses, and government, but with a majority of local residents. NRC had no direct authority over local projects, although various financial sanctions were available if necessary. Typically each project employed an executive director, a financial adviser, a rehabilitation specialist, and an administrative assistant, whose costs were met by contributions from private, charitable and government sources.

The role of the NHS project was to stimulate residents to revitalise their houses. This was achieved in a number of ways. First, projects aimed to increase community awareness and commitment to the future of each neighbourhood so that individuals were more likely to be willing to invest in their houses. Second, the project provided technical advice on what needed doing and how it could be funded. In some cases limited grant aid was available but most work was funded either by conventional loans from financial institutions or by special loans from the project's own loan fund at lower interest rates. Third, the project aimed to encourage local government to invest in the neighbourhood through environmental improvements and to persuade local businesses to contribute by upgrading or by making contributions to neighbourhood projects or activities.

NHS areas were chosen carefully. They were not the areas of poorest condition housing, which in most USA cities consisted predominantly of rented accommodation. The housing stock in project areas was to be basically sound, but showing early signs of deterioration. Chosen areas were required to have a high rate of home ownership (more than 50%), with evidence that residents were committed to revitalisation such as a strong residents' association. Local incomes were to be below the city average but not so low that residents could not support loans. The size of area (usually between 1,000-2,000 properties) was such as to show early visible success. These requirements had drawn the criticism that NHS success stemmed from its avoidance of more difficult neighbourhoods, but this was countered by the reliance of NHS projects for the most part on private funding sources. It was also argued that NHS projects were preventive, saving future public spending by attracting private investment. NRC were interested in working in poorer neighbourhoods but they took the view that in order to do so different policy instruments would be required.

There were also a number of broader requirements. The local authority was required to implement a code enforcement programme to ensure a high rate of participation by residents. This involved taking whatever steps were possible under local legislation to ensure that properties were brought into a state of good repair. At the same time the local authority had to undertake expenditure on environmental improvements in the area, and to contribute to NHS project running costs. Second, a group of local financial institutions were required to be willing to provide loan finance on reasonable terms to a majority of local residents. Third, there should be a source of finance for the establishment of a revolving loan fund to provide low interest or high risk loans.

The key features of NHS projects were thus their local autonomy and strong resident involvement, the involvement of local financial institutions and businesses in partnership with residents and local government, the use of private loan finance to fund the majority of work, and the careful selection of areas where this approach was likely to succeed. These features were carefully noted by UK visitors who saw the NHS initiative in what was, with hindsight, its heyday, at least in this form. Paradoxically the years after 1980 were difficult ones for NHS projects (Neighborhood Housing Services of America, 1990). Recession, declining public funding, and a scarcity of private funding made it difficult to keep even the existing projects afloat, and with many financial institutions in crisis (especially the savings and loan movement), it became more difficult to finance revitalisation work. As the 1990s approached, the initiative, renamed the NeighborWorks network, broadened its emphasis to incorporate affordable housing initiatives and to work in areas with more rental housing by developing mutual housing associations or by itself becoming a landlord. In part this reflected pressures from the federal government in response to changing national housing priorities. Whether this shift has led to a change in the type of area which NHS projects tackle or whether existing areas have changed as a result of recession and other social forces is not fully clear, but by 1990 over 50% of the housing in NeighborWorks areas was rental housing and a self-evaluation of progress concluded that there were:

> rapidly escalating social problems throughout urban neighbourhoods during the late 1980s. Unemployment, homelessness, at-risk youth, foreclosures, drugs and related crime became harsh realities that impeded local partnerships' efforts to rebuild healthy neighbourhoods. (Neighborhood Housing Services of America, 1990, p 30)

Despite these emerging problems, and although the projects have not focused on the areas with the most serious social problems, the NHS initiative has undoubtedly made a contribution to urban regeneration in the US context over an extended period. It has shown the capacity to evolve in response to changing problems and governmental policy initiatives, and it has drawn substantial commitment from both local residents and the private business and financial sectors to urban regeneration. We now turn to examine how the initiative operated when it was transplanted to the UK.

Neighbourhood Revitalisation Services (NRS)

Despite the publication of the Tri-national Inner Cities report and the Financial Institutions Group visit to the USA to examine the operation of NHS projects, practical progress with the introduction of an NHS-type initiative in the UK was slow. If the USA parallel had been followed, the first step would have been the establishment of a government-funded UK Neighbourhood Reinvestment Corporation to set up local projects, but instead, an existing organisation called the National Home Improvement Council

(NHIC) proposed to set up a small number of pilot projects following the NHS model.

The NHIC was a private organisation with membership drawn from trade associations, professional institutes, financial institutions, building materials manufacturers, builders merchants, and the fuel industries. It was established in 1975 to represent the interests of these organisations by lobbying government and by encouraging home owners to carry out home improvement and maintenance. The organisation was most well known for its promotional events, including National Home Improvement Week, and for the production of leaflets and publicity material for home owners.

The council formed a steering committee to develop more detailed proposals for setting up NHS-type projects in the UK and this reported in July 1983 (National Home Improvement Council, 1983). At the same time the council launched a special appeal for funds in order to finance the experiment and appointed a national coordinator with responsibility for the development and management of projects. Four pilot NRS projects were established in the cities of Sheffield, Bedford, Oldham, and Gloucester between October 1984 and December 1985 with a proposed life of two years.

The progress of the pilot NRS projects was monitored for the NHIC by Gibson and Groves (1986) and an independent evaluation of the Sheffield pilot project was also carried out by Kintrea (1987). An initial finding was that the planned two-year lifespan for each project was too short. An aggregate total of only 72 dwellings had been improved in the four areas by October 1986 (Gibson and Groves, 1986), and in the overwhelming majority of cases the bulk of the work had been funded by a renovation grant from a local authority with the owner contributing only the residue of the costs. Since NHS in the USA had already concluded that its projects took at least six years to 'turn a neighbourhood around', the two-year project life was completely unrealistic.

Despite these problems, the government was sufficiently attracted by the NRS concept to lend its support to a major expansion in the number of projects. From the experience with the pilot projects, however, it was clear that this would require a substantial input of public funding. The pilot NRS phase was originally to have been funded by contributions from NRS members, but less than one-third of the £1 million which was required was raised in this way (Kintrea, 1987). The substantial cash support from local foundations, businesses and financial institutions which met a large proportion of project running costs in the USA was not forthcoming. At the end of 1986, the government agreed to a programme of 25 new projects for which it would fund 50% of the running costs, with the balance to be raised by the NHIC from private sector sources. Initially funding was made available for two years, but this was eventually extended for a further two years until March 1991.

The subsequent performance of the expanded programme of NRS projects was examined by the present authors (Leather and Mackintosh, 1990). Table 1 shows that the new projects were again slow to start and less than 250 properties were renovated in the first two years. In the following two years, performance was very mixed, with a group of seven projects completing more than 100 property renovations in 1990, while at the other extreme nine projects completed less than 50 jobs.

It also proved difficult for projects to attract private funding either to fund building work for clients or for project running costs. In 1990 only a quarter of the costs of building work carried out with the help of NRS projects was funded from private sources such as loans, clients' own income and savings, charitable contributions or insurance claims. As Figure 1 shows, the majority of the costs of jobs were funded by grants from local authorities. More than nine out of ten renovations were grant-aided. In addition, the major part of the running costs for projects and for the central NRS management organisation were likewise provided from public sector sources, as shown in Table 2. Only 37% of project running costs and 30% of central running costs were met by the private sector. The main private sector input was from a major building society which provided resources for the purchase of project offices.

At the end of the experimental period the government introduced new funding arrangements for projects like NRS. Direct funding to the NHIC was withdrawn and instead local authorities were invited to bid for government funding to meet 50% of the running costs of any projects which they wished to support. Only 15 authorities submitted bids for the continuation of existing NRS projects and only seven of these were approved. One further project continued under independent local arrangements and eventually received government funding in 1992/93. The three remaining pilot projects were closed or merged with other projects in 1990. With the loss of government funding for the central NRS management organisation, the NHIC closed down the NRS initiative and dismissed both central and project staff. Those projects which continued did so under new local arrangements which usually involved the formation of an independent charitable organisation with strong local authority representation. In their subsequent activities these projects have continued to use local authority grants to finance the majority of building work.

Table 1: Performance of NRS projects 1987-90

	1987 and 88 a	1987 and 88 b	1989 a	1989 b	1990 a	1990 b
Buxton	89	272	125	552	121	446
Hastings	3	23	38	314	51	533
Coalville	13	41	27	110	1	5
Gresley	13	67	55	178	105	528
East Accrington	111	31	20	105	150	1030
Lowestoft	1	2	56	47	74	106
Nelson			23	58	50	317
Stockport			20	196	17	172
Wolverhampton	3	5	157	384	17	87
Bexley	1	6	131	476	48	232
Bedford					79	52
Oldham			3	7	117	393
Sheffield			54	303	61	400
Newham			13	10	3	16
Bristol 1			6	54	13	109
Bristol 2	1	0	39	53	18	177
Trafford	2	8	14	18	21	64
Lancaster	1	0	113	374	265	1589
Morecambe			48	382	73	644
Coventry	8	28	183	854	104	524
Maryport	1	0	29	68	92	428
Cleethorpes	3	7	106	215	43	112
Stoke			94	656	159	1737
	248	482	1249	5200	1652	10003

Notes: a = Number of jobs completed
b = Total cost of work (£000)

Source: Leather and Mackintosh (1992)

Figure 1: Amount of work and sources of funding

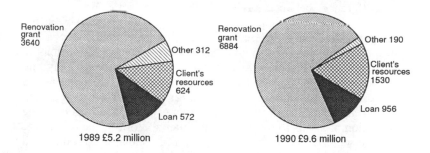

1989 £5.2 million   1990 £9.6 million

Source: Leather and Mackintosh (1992)

Table 2:   Sources of income for NRS running costs 1990/91

	Project running costs	Central running costs
Department of the Environment	58%	70%
Local authorities	4%	
Private sector	37%	30%
Other	1%	
Total (£000)	1355	562

Source: Leather and Mackintosh (1992)

Evaluation

In comparison with the progress of NHS projects in the USA, the UK NRS initiative was a disappointing failure. It is important to understand the reasons why NRS did not succeed. Were the problems experienced in the UK an inevitable consequence of differences in the context of housing renewal between the two countries? How far did the problems stem from the way in which NRS was managed and the comparative weakness of local community and business input? Were the areas chosen inappropriate for private sector solutions? And finally, could a similar form of initiative work in the UK in the changed circumstances of the 1990s when grant aid from local authorities is only available to those on lowest incomes? Differences between NHS and NRS projects are summarised in Table 3. First, the context for housing renewal in the UK in the early 1980s clearly differed substantially from that in the USA, despite the government's intention to involve the private sector. In the UK local authorities were the major agents for developing and implementing housing renewal policies through the declaration and management of area-based renewal projects known as housing action areas and general improvement areas and through the provision of grants to owners and private landlords. The role of the private sector was extremely limited, and financial institutions such as the building societies were only concerned with house purchase costs and played little part in the organisation of housing renewal.

From 1979 when a new Conservative government came to power, attempts were made to involve the private sector more actively in housing renewal. But new initiatives such as NRS had great difficulty in operating independently of local authorities, because of their dependence upon the powers local authorities possessed to declare improvement areas and provide grants. In many cases they also found it difficult to operate in partnership with local authorities because staff were concerned about the threat to their jobs posed by any initiative which could be interpreted as privatisation. The private sector also lacked the interest or the incentive to support NRS on a large scale. By 1987, when the majority of NRS projects became operational, the building societies had begun to retreat from their cautious involvement in housing renewal during the early 1980s. Deregulation and measures to stimulate competition between the societies, the banks, insurance companies, and other financial institutions, led them to concentrate more of their energies on developing and expanding their commercially-orientated financial services at the expense of less profitable or even loss-making renewal activity. Furthermore, although the neighbourhood reinvestment legislation in the USA, which requires financial institutions to show that they are providing a full range of services in their localities, may seem weak and ineffectual, there is no equivalent legislation in the UK to place financial institutions under any obligation to make loans available locally. Most financial institutions in the UK, including the majority of the building societies, operate nationally or regionally and have few local connections.

Table 3: **Comparison between NHS and NRS**

	NHS	NRS
Context	Reduction in federal/local government involvement in urban renewal programmes. Grants more rarely available. Neighbourhood Reinvestment Act placing pressure on local financial institutions to lend/sponsor.	Local authorities responsible for renovation strategy and able to declare improvement areas and provide grants to home owners to finance renovation work.
Area	Basically sound neighbourhoods of 1,000-2,000 houses with more than 50% home ownership and strong residents' group.	Areas of mainly pre-1919 terraced houses given priority by local authority for renovation grants, not necessarily with any residents' group involvement.
Project structure	Autonomous projects managed by local board of residents, business, financial institutions and local government. NRC developed projects and provided support. NHSA managed secondary market for revolving loans.	Unitary structure, with project staff employed by, and responsible to, central NRS coordinator and board. Local committees advisory role only.
Project staffing and funding	Executive director, financial adviser, and rehabilitation specialist all employed by local board and funded by cash contributions from local financial institutions, businesses, and government.	NRS core staff small: project manager plus administrative support. Technical service provided by independent fee-charging building agency. Sometimes financial advice provided by building society staff.
Funding building work	Commercial loans from local lenders plus low interest loans from revolving loan fund capitalised by NRC, foundations, community development block grants, or business sources.	Allocation of renovation grants by local authorities topped up by contributions from owners' savings or formal commercial loans at market rates.

Second, the areas selected for NRS projects differed from those in the USA. As a result of pressure from local authorities, and as condition for obtaining an allocation of renovation grant finance, the areas selected in the UK were in poorer condition than those in the USA and the majority of properties were built before 1919. Residents tended to have lower incomes than people living in the equivalent neighbourhoods in the USA and the scope for residents to afford to pay for their own repairs and improvements was correspondingly much less.

Third, the NRS initiative as it was established in the UK differed in organisation from the NRC-NHS network in the USA. In the UK, the local project staff were employed by the NHIC and managed directly by a central NRS management team. The NHIC was primarily a representative body with few staff, relying heavily on voluntary inputs from its membership, and it proved difficult to provide the administrative support for more than 50 new employees as the NRS initiative developed. In addition, there was a reluctance to delegate financial decisions to local level, stemming from the often precarious nature of funding arrangements and from the need to be accountable to the government for the financial support which it provided.

Although the Urban Renewal Task Force which supported NHS projects in the USA was very small at the outset, this was less problematic because the organisation was not responsible for the direct management of projects, and in any case staffing levels were rapidly expanded after its transformation into the NRC. The main burden of project management in the USA was carried by the local management committees. In the UK, each project formed a local committee at the outset to oversee operations, which included representatives of local businesses, financial institutions and local residents. But the committees were essentially advisory rather than managerial and their influence declined rather than increased over time. They did not play the key role in raising finance to meet project running costs, arranging funding for building work including a revolving loan fund, and involving local residents and businesses in the management of projects which they did in the USA. In the UK the most significant external influence at local level was exerted by local government officers and politicians who were providing an allocation of renovation grants to fund building work.

As a result of a shortfall in the funds raised by the NHIC's national appeal, project staffing levels were also limited. The core of NRS-funded staff was small, comprising only a project manager, administrative support, and in some areas, staff provided free of charge or at a low cost under government sponsored training schemes, often to perform clerical tasks. Most private sector contributions to running costs took the form of offers to second staff or to provide premises, office equipment, or materials such as advertising. Financial advice to clients was generally limited to referrals to a building society on an ad hoc basis. The key function of providing technical advice was subcontracted to an independent surveying or architectural practice which provided services on a fee charging basis in order to cover its costs. The split of responsibility between the NRS staff, who carried out the initial promotional and advisory work, and the independent building agency, which undertook surveys, specified work, and supervised its execution, often made it difficult to coordinate work, and as a result clients were often uncertain as to who had overall responsibility.

In the USA one of the key contributions of NHS was to develop new mechanisms for financing the costs of housing renovation, but surprisingly no attempt was made to develop similar arrangements for NRS clients in the UK. Instead agreements were negotiated with local authorities to secure earmarked allocations of renovation grant finance for use by project clients, and these became the main source of funding for building work. Such grants did not cover the whole costs of work and in some cases individual owners were assisted to raise loans to cover the additional costs, but these loans were at normal commercial rates and from traditional lending sources such as building societies and banks.

The use of renovation grants was initially intended as a pump priming exercise to encourage other households to invest their own resources, but it soon became a permanent and essential feature because residents were deterred from investing their own resources when they could see their neighbours getting public subsidy. In addition, project staff were unable to devote time to negotiating with local financial institutions to develop new financial mechanisms because they came under pressure to ensure that they spent the grant allocations that they were given by their local authorities. In the UK, the NHIC and the NRS central managing organisation also failed to develop any significant new sources of funding in the way that NRC and NHSA did in the USA and there were no arrangements for low cost loans.

Conclusions

The problems experienced by NRS, therefore, stemmed in part from factors which were specific to the way in which the initiative was organised in the UK and in part from differences in the context of housing renewal in the UK and the USA. As a result, it is possible that an NHS-type initiative could enjoy more success in the UK in the future if it were to be organised differently and if there were to be changes in the financial and legislative framework for renewal.

In terms of organisation, it is clear from both the US experience and from other UK initiatives to help older people with home repairs, such as Staying Put or Care and Repair projects, that alternative approaches to the provision of an NHS-type service can be more successful. Experience suggests that approaches are required which involve either local projects managed by a strong central organisation such as a non-profit housing association, or independent projects with a well-developed local management presence. There is also a need for a well-resourced national support organisation and for adequate funding at local level to enable the project to employ its own technical staff to advise on building work. The USA experience makes it clear that the majority of the funding for the national body must come from public sources. In the UK, the majority of funding for local project staff also comes from the government or local authorities because of the absence of incentives to persuade the private sector to contribute.

There are also some signs that the context of renewal policy may be changing. After a long period of review, the 1989 Local Government and Housing Act introduced some significant changes to the framework for housing renewal policy in the UK. Although local authorities retain overall responsibility for housing renewal strategies, the system of renovation grants has been radically altered. Grants are now subject to a test of the applicant's income, increasing the resources available to poor households but making many middle or higher income households ineligible for state aid. In the longer term, this change may make those who can afford it more likely to take on a loan to pay for renovation work than they were in the past when it was possible that they would eventually receive a grant.

In addition, limits on the overall amount of resources available to local authorities are forcing many to limit the types of work which they will provide grant aid for, again forcing home owners to look for other ways to finance work. This could increase the need for financial institutions to become involved in renewal programmes and increase the likelihood that they would support an NHS-type project working outside the renovation grant system. However, if private sector organisations are to play a greater role in housing renewal, other changes will be needed, such as a legal requirement on financial institutions to help local communities, the provision of tax benefits to companies making contributions to project running costs, and the provision of financial incentives to home owners to invest in repair, improvement and maintenance work. To date, the government has not shown any interest in introducing any of these new ideas.

The framework for area-based housing renewal has also been altered and local authorities are being urged to take a broader view of housing renewal through new powers to declare and implement renewal areas in order to attract private sector investment. In practice this means incorporating commercial redevelopment opportunities into renewal area proposals on a larger scale than in the past, perhaps by increasing levels of housing clearance, and this may lead to conflict rather than cooperation with local residents. The current recession in the UK has so far prevented any significant progress but in the longer term, housing renewal initiatives may become more closely integrated within broader urban renewal projects.

The majority of houses in poor condition in the UK are now owner occupied (Department of the Environment, 1988). Many home owners have low incomes as a result of unemployment or a reduction in income associated with retirement. Almost one in five home owners had an income of less than £150 per week in 1989. More than 50% of older people are now home owners and many are experiencing difficulty in managing or affording the repair and improvement of their homes in old age. Whether through approaches such as NHS, or by other means, it is clear that the need to provide home owners with help in improving their homes can only increase in the future.

Note

The authors would like to acknowledge the information and help provided by a number of organisations and individuals, including David Boelke and Tom Adams at the NRC in Washington, Bill and

Lynn Whiteside, Bruce Gottschall, Sean Heath and Mike Reardon of Chicago NHS, and Mike Braswell of NHS Baltimore. They also wish to thank the Nuffield Foundation, the Joseph Rowntree Foundation, and the Building Societies Association for financial support with the research in the USA on which this paper is based and the Department of the Environment who funded the work on NRS in the UK.

References

Building Societies Association (1985) *Helping owner occupiers improve their homes*, London: BSA.

Department of the Environment (1988) *English house condition survey 1986*, London: HMSO.

Gibson, M. and Groves, R. (1986) *Neighbourhood revitalisation services*, unpublished report to the NRS monitoring and evaluation advisory group, 8 October.

Hambleton, R. (1990) *Urban government in the 1990s: lessons from the USA*, Bristol: SAUS Publications, School for Advanced Urban Studies, University of Bristol.

Huntley, J. (1980) *Neighbourhood revitalisation*, Occasional Paper no 4, Reading: School of Planning Studies, University of Reading.

Kintrea, K. (1987) *Arresting decay in owner occupied housing? The neighbourhood revitalisation scheme*, Glasgow: Centre for Housing Research, University of Glasgow, Discussion Paper 13.

Leather, P. and Mackintosh, S. (1990) *Monitoring assisted agency services, part I: Home improvement agencies - an evaluation of performance*, London: HMSO.

Leather, P. and Mackintosh, S. (1992) *Performance of home improvement agencies 1990*, report to the Department of the Environment.

Leather, P., Mackintosh, S., Hoyes, L. and Holmes, R. (1990) *Monitoring assisted agency services, part III: the detailed case studies*, London: HMSO.

Mackintosh, S. and Leather, P. (1992) *Home improvement under the new regime*, Bristol: SAUS Publications, School for Advanced Urban Studies, University of Bristol.

National Home Improvement Council (1983) *Report of the capital steering committee on neighbourhood revitalisation services (NRS)*, London: NHIC.

Neighborhood Housing Services of America (1990) *Better to light a candle: the NHS/NeighborWorks Network 1968-90*, Washington: NHSA.

Thomas, A. (1986) *Housing and urban renewal*, London: George Allen and Unwin.

twelve

CITIZENS AND HEALTH CARE

Penny Morris

In the UK, it seems the peoples' voice is sought high and low throughout the land: policy makers are urged to seek 'public opinion' to help make difficult decisions about budget priorities (Dixon and Welch, 1991); hospital managers want patients to tell them how to improve their services (McIver, 1991); and, when the chips are down, citizens on run-down estates are chivvied to speak their mind to the miscreants in their midst, take responsibility for health in their community and pull their community socks up.

We are moving on from the notion of people as clients who are excluded from the evaluation of solutions offered by professionals, and from the idea that only the professionals do that. We now have people as consumers who can evaluate solutions, but the range is still narrow (this Vauxhall or that Ford? This carpet in the waiting room or a video? A friendly doctor or an unfriendly one?).

A true citizen role in health care is rather to take part in the setting, monitoring and evaluating of the health agenda and its outcomes, in identifying problems and priorities, in determining and evaluating solutions (Arntson, 1989). While we are beginning to develop people as consumers in health care, this alone will not be sufficiently 'capacity-building' to ensure effective citizen input to the solving of problems. In this chapter, I describe a community initiative in the USA which aims to find, strengthen and make heard the voice of its people in the improvement of their community's health, and offers a lesson for us here in the UK.

Why is the people's voice in health care and promotion regarded as important on both sides of the Atlantic? Researchers and consumer groups claim that patients should be involved in the audit of medicine (Hughes and Humphrey, 1990; College of Health, 1990): why? Perhaps the answer is simply that patient opinion can be an accurate measurement of health: in a survey of 10,000 people US research found that patient opinion of health status is the best predictor of mortality and quality of life we have (New York Times, 1991). A parallel argument, that communities have the answers and hold the key to the promotion of health in their community, is also well established (Bracht, 1991), and efforts are being made by policy groups, funding bodies and health planners to ease the path to more consumer involvement (Department of Health, 1992; Annenberg Center, 1992; Boston City Council, 1991).

Jackie Reed is one of the leaders of the US community initiative that I shall describe in this chapter, the Westside Health Authority in Chicago. She said in a video interview:

> There are so few resources available and so many different things have been tried. We've had people coming out here into the community who are so smart, they're so sharp about what to do with those people, how to help those people ... it has not worked and lots of dollars have been spent. This is the time when policy makers are recognising the fact that unless they hear the community ... well, they no longer have the choice, they have to find the best use for the dollars.

But it is often citizen acquiescence that is sought in hard choices about resources (Morris, 1993). In many cases, certain decisions have already been made by experts and policy makers before the citizen is involved.

So there is a gap between the rhetoric and the reality, and between what is intended and what is achieved. Sometimes this is because of the tenacity of old ways of seeing the role of the citizen in health, even within efforts to change: for example, the Greater London Association of Community Health Councils (GLACHC) has reported on the Audit Commission's description of the patient's view of day surgery. The Commission refer to the health professional's views on improvement in health status, while the patient is credited only with knowledge about a "perceived" improvement in health. GLACHC comments despairingly:

> If the patient is not given equal status in knowing whether or not their health has improved, what hope is there for

involving health service users on an equal basis with the professionals? (Levenson and Joule, 1992)

In addition, a report by the King's Fund on medical audit has called for priority to be given to "developing truly patient-centred audit". They add:

All too often patients are used as just another source of information. If patients participate in identifying problems, setting standards and assessing practice, there is a far greater chance that audit will result in real improvements in patient care. (Hughes and Humphrey, 1990)

We have been assured by our government that the thrust of their reforms of the public services is "to give real power to citizens and communities - a bottom-up approach" (*The Guardian*, 15 October 1991). But the secretary of a local community health council believes that when health authorities and managers talk of seeking the lay voice "they mean public relations, they don't mean public involvement". In an article in the *Health Services Journal*, highly critical of the process of public consultation on the first wave of hospital trust applications, consultation procedures were cast as half-hearted, shrouded in secrecy and short on information-giving: "Informing and involving the public in the running of the health service appears to be increasingly seen as a waste of time and resources" (Martin and Marks, 1991).

Nevertheless, the voice of the citizen is invoked in political battles between authorities, managers and professional workers: "Everybody is raising the flag of the patients' champion: the government, management, consultants, GPs, nurses ..." (Nikki Joule, Research and Information Officer of GLACHC, in an interview). The patient's interest is claimed in territorial debates among hospital managers and clinicians (*The Observer*, 6 August 1991), and a report I gave on the activities of the community group to an official in the US Department of Health and Human Services was met with: "Splendid! Neighbourhood initiative, that's what we need! Now, how can we get rid of 10,000 social workers?".

Why the citizen voice is being canvassed affects the way it is sought and what is heard. In this chapter I shall concentrate on what might happen if the value of its contribution is trusted, and all the effort of intervention is put into effective seeking and strengthening of that resource.

Building the citizen voice in the USA - the Westside Health Authority

The image of Chicago's Westside is of a place where some of the city's poorest citizens live and where drug abuse, crime, alcoholism, and illiteracy are rife. According to the US Department of Health and Human Services report *Healthy People 2000*, which contains the national health promotion and disease prevention objectives, the most critical and unrelenting health problems facing inner city communities are caused by risk-related behaviours. The leading cause of death among African American men between the ages of 15-34 is homicide, while cancer, heart disease, hypertension and diabetes rank as among the major causes of premature and excessive mortality and morbidity and are aggravated by poor diets, lack of exercise, smoking and so forth. The people are labelled as 'unmotivated', and are seen as the problem.

The Westside Health Authority (WHA) is a community advocacy group on the Westside of Chicago which consists of community organisations, community-based health providers and churches. It was set up to involve community residents in policy decisions about health care. The mission of the WHA is:

> to empower Westside residents to improve the community's health status and to preserve health institutions serving the Westside through the organising and sharing of resources. As the name reflects, the people within the community are the 'authority' on how to create a healthier environment on Chicago's Westside. Solutions for health problems will come from people who live on the Westside. (Westside Health Authority, 1992)

The groups first came together in 1988 as a coalition with the aim of developing the community's input into resolving its health care problems. The initiative came from provider groups running local clinics. But the activists did not manage to arouse community interest in their work until the sudden closure of St Anne's hospital, the third hospital to close on the Westside within five years. Large public meetings and general indignation encouraged two of the provider groups to work together to try and build something positive from the loss of this hospital. These provider groups were individually backed by funds from federal, county, and city programmes, and private foundations. With extra fundraising from rich churches outside the neighbourhood, and judicious planning and borrowing, they managed to acquire parts of St Anne's hospital site for each group to provide primary health care and social services.

The involvement of the grass-roots community with the activities of the coalition was not ensured, however, until the threatened closure of another local hospital, Bethany. This time the groups, now sufficiently emboldened by their own ability to take charge of some major resources, declared their coalition to be the WHA. They responded to the community's anger by undertaking to fight the closure.

I was in Chicago in September 1990 during this crucial period of the organisation's development as a participant observer of the successful campaign to keep the Bethany hospital open. The WHA organised a candlelit prayer vigil, encircling the hospital to protect it, led by churches and involving 500 local people. They undertook a number of other protest actions at the offices of major players in the future of the hospital: the state public aid office, the county board, and the foundation which owned the hospital.

But the key to their success was that they did not just protest and react. With demonstrated community support they went back to the institutions offering to broker an agreement for an effective formula to keep the hospital open: increased state support for each non-paying patient at the hospital in return for measures aimed at increasing patient throughput, adding to the number of nurses who had been difficult to recruit, further fundraising efforts and increased management efficiency. The WHA undertook to recruit extra nurses through the churches. They also organised a collection drive for a monthly $1,400 donation from local church congregations, and set up a system for the clinics among their own provider groups to ensure increased referral rates to Bethany.

Throughout this period, the WHA operated as an ad hoc group of volunteers without funding, responding to crises. They felt having money as a coalition would only hamper their ability to work together, as all their member organisations had struggled with issues of like boundary disputes and competition for funds.

During 1991, they had worked out a way of cooperating and were keen, as with the Bethany fight, to move from reaction to action, from protest to planning. Jackie Reed from the WHA commented:

> The Bethany prayer vigil was fine - it called up the 1960s for
> the rich white folk who had power over us - but it's an old

song. That old song won't continue to play: what's the new song we're going to play? When are we going to stop begging from white people, when are we going to define our lives? (in an interview; *all following unattributed quotes are from interviews with her*)

This phase of the group was supported by membership dues and development funds from foundations which provided for a director and some office expenses. The central idea was to develop a community-driven agenda:

Whoever sets the agenda, drives the vision, drives the discussion, drives the action.

The community was to be the catalyst for this agenda, drawing on its own expertise and using provider and institutional groups as resources to assist, not plan for them. Working groups were set up consisting of community participants, with outsiders serving these committees as technicians - public officials, health professionals, and academics from the Universities of Chicago and Northwestern.

The components of their health agenda were: the setting up of a 'mega-clinic' in the community to replace the old St Anne's hospital; expanding health coverage for uninsured workers in the community; increasing job opportunities for Westsiders in health careers; developing health related industries on the Westside and a Community Wellness Plan. This last project holds the key to what makes the WHA tick.

The Community Wellness Plan: an alternative to needs assessments

I was a provider for 20 years. I was a social worker by training and I worked very hard in those years to make a difference in peoples' lives but it was never a permanent kind of thing, very transitional, you know. How do you make a difference that's going to be permanent?

The Wellness Plan challenges the health research that has focused on the use of professionals to address community deficiencies. In that model, it is the professionals who have the answers and the power, and the community's role is to cooperate with the professional. Planning for the use of professional services has acted as a catalyst for community intervention, justified by needs assessments, which become more frequent as the needs and subsequent use of professionals continue to increase.

The WHA claims that this model neglects to affirm the value of the community's non-professional providers or community residents who live productive, healthy, rewarding lives. They planned a demonstration project aimed at identifying and utilising existing 'gifts' and 'strengths of community residents to improve the community's health. This work is based on a successful community model which does not focus on 'deficiencies' as a means of organising its efforts: the African American church, where congregations with little or no staff organise themselves around the various levels of skills that each member can volunteer.

> Most providers start with a premise of needs. Somehow when you are writing for money and trying to get dollars to do a particular programme, you focus in on what somebody needs. Somehow you paint them as poor, deprived, needy etc etc, and that justifies your programme. I don't think that it allows much room in the programme for focusing in on the individual strengths and gifts that each of us have.

> We're not a community without resources. We're a community with tremendous resources, tremendous talents and gifts and human resources are much more valuable than we have been led to believe.

The WHA is working with one of its academic affiliates, the Center for Urban Affairs at Northwestern University, to develop an inventory of health strengths, as opposed to a health needs assessment. The centre has been developing a 'neighbourhood assets map' which shows the strengths of a locality, such as citizens' associations, gifts and talents, religious and cultural organisations, businesses and locally based institutions. The assets map is contrasted with a 'neighbourhood needs map', showing slum housing, child abuse, gangs, truancy, broken families and so forth (McKnight and Kretzmann, 1990).

This group of academics is committed to working as a resource for the community, rather than merely using community resources as its laboratory. For a community with a deep sense of exploitation by outside researchers and organisations who have received enormous sums of money to investigate problems and propose solutions for the community, this new relationship is vital. The Kellogg Foundation agree that: "Professionals must rebuild their credibility with communities by establishing long-term collaborative relationships based on mutual respect and trust" (Annenberg Center, 1992) and have awarded a substantial grant to the WHA to run its own wellness experiment, and invite technical help from the universities.

How is the Westside Health Authority effective?

Accountability to its members and the wider community

The WHA works carefully to try to make a real difference by driving its own agenda, and keeping that agenda of and with the community.

The first task was to make the coalition effective. From the beginning, each group's representative at the coalition meetings had to be the executive director, or empowered to speak and vote for him or her, so that decisions could be taken and acted upon. Other community members are encouraged to attend and join the debate, but the coalition's ability to act quickly and forcefully has been ensured by this insistence that the group means business.

These meetings are held monthly and constitute the main decision-making body of the authority. They are two hours long, begin and end with a short prayer, and have a packed agenda in between. They are prepared by the staff who ask members to report on key projects and political moves, and can be a regular litmus test of who is being involved and how. There are rarely less than 20 people attending and sometimes as many as 40, including major organisations from outside the community: heads of hospitals, funders, and members of city and county health boards.

By keeping its community advocacy groups involved, the WHA has a built-in watch dog against slipping into a professionalisation of its role and a neutralising of its policies. The balance of power between the professional, provider groups and the lay, advocacy groups is weighted towards the lay groups. Early on, a committee consisting of providers only was set up to suggest a constitution for the authority. They came up with a plan that would have allowed an equal voice to the professionals in and around the group. But in recognition that "in any group, the professional voice is the loudest", the main meeting of the authority agreed to ensure that the lay members and advocacy groups had a built-in majority. There is a creative tension in this mix of provider and consumer groups:

> The best thing is we're always on the verge of major conflict in our group. You know, everyone around the table primarily operates from some sense of self-interest, with the providers basically trying to manipulate the grass-roots organisations because they need their support to get the particular piece they want. At the same time, the community organisations are trying to control to make sure the providers don't manipulate them. I think it creates sufficient tension to offset any real problem.

As a coalition, the groups are careful to avoid competing for funds. The authority does not run programmes as such. The largest grant received, from the Kellogg Foundation for the Wellness initiative described above, is administered by the authority, but the money for community health organisers is shared between the appropriate groups. The groups meet, along with the technical advisers from Northwestern University and others from the authority, in a working committee to hammer out how these new kinds of organisers should work. Each group has their own way of setting up their part of the project in the context of basic agreed principles.

A key to their successful collaboration is a commitment to try new ways of working: the professionals trying the community development approach and looking at strengths, and the community organisers trying ways other than fire-fighting. Building on the Chicago-based tradition of Alinsky radical organising, they are trying for something new: their 'new song'. They are getting information, joining the debate, insisting on partnership, not just relying on intimidation and humiliation of the enemy with well-placed demonstrations, as in the earlier tradition:

> We're not afraid of confrontation, we confront them when we need to, but we don't want to be out there just protesting.

As well as the monthly meetings of the authority, there is an executive committee to which the staff are accountable for managing budgets, and small working groups for each project who coopt other community members and outside professionals as technical resources. A regular community newsletter is produced and distributed. Most importantly, wider community meetings of various kinds are held:

> The community organisers do insist on having regular community meetings. At first, with a provider history like me, I thought that - well, that's going to be very time-consuming, and it's going to slow the process down, people will clearly not understand the information we bring. I mean, I've read those big thick books, and even when we bring information, the people around the table haven't read it, the minutes and so on - how in the world will the people who work in the simple jobs and come home tired, how will they understand what is going on? And how will you maintain their interest in these issues? ... Well, that's what I learned, I learned it's all our jobs, working in the community, to make sure that information is plain, that people understand what we are saying - because people can make a contribution.

These community meetings can be small discussion meetings of key groups: for example, the pastors of the member churches have met in short successive bursts to thrash through their role in the communities' health. Regular retreats are held, perhaps just for a few hours, occasionally over two days. All these meetings are helped by the sharing of food.

In March 1993, I was with a small group of elderly women who met over lunch. They were supporters of authority demonstrations led by the oldest authority activist, the 88 year-old Mary Alice Henry. They talked about past healthy habits they remembered from their Mississippi communities, and how they wanted to share these with the young people on the Westside who were not aware of these traditions. They followed this with a gathering over pizza at which a dozen or more students from the local high school attended. This joint group now works together teaching students from Chicago's medical schools how to relate to patients. Their unique contribution is ensured by their sharing of community health values.

A main focus for keeping the WHA close to its roots is the large open community meeting for which "we always struggle for turnout - like everybody else". These meetings will be summoned around an issue, and time taken to talk again about the community health agenda and how people might make a contribution. The largest meetings happen when there is a threat to existing provisions or resources. Once the collective energy is aroused ("like a mother rescuing a baby from a burning building, you find you can do anything"), the authority offers the opportunity to people who are always giving their voice to someone else to do more than protest.

One meeting held in January 1992 about the proposed state cuts in health benefits to single welfare claimants attracted over 1,000 people. This was partly because of what was at stake and partly the hard work of the community organisers. The WHA undertook to support the ensuing actions against the Illinois state authorities, and offered its offices and encouragement to a group from the meeting who wanted to help the claimants get the benefits they were entitled to. But the developing role of the authority is not to protest, nor to organise programmes, but to involve more people in planning. So the meeting was asked "If you had the dollars, what would you do about health out here on the Westside? What can you do right now, and what do you need to do it?" One man ventured that the sight of green around the poor housing projects would result in an improvement in the community's health, and worked out that he needed seed, nerve, and moral support to begin to sow grass himself.

The big meeting was the right place to ask the question about the dollars, but it has turned out that another forum is needed to find the answers. So, for example, the mothers on welfare group meet in small discussions where the women can make their own decisions. The usual way that the community organisers would run such a group would be to have one large meeting, chaired by one organiser, while another organiser wrote up the women's suggestions on a bulletin board. To Jackie Reed, that way of running the group, where numbers are the main aim, can smack of manipulation not empowerment: "the same old thing with different players".

The challenge is to help more people see that they can influence outcomes, and the authority is committed to experimenting with approaches within a faith-driven framework:

> What are the various strategies and mechanisms available to ordinary, everyday community people to help them work for a common vision? How can you mobilise? Well, firstly through love - love is a powerful, healing thing, love is sustaining, love, it lasts, ... now that's difficult to talk about to those who want rebellion, to kick arse. But hate cannot set you free. We don't want just to switch the paradigm around, we want a society where relationships between people will be different.

Another temptation for the leadership is to feel that it's easier for the more accomplished and experienced members to get on with it rather than continue to develop people. An exercise that has kept the group's faith with their intentions has been the working through of some guiding steps toward community wellness: they used the 12 step approach of the self-help group, Alcoholics Anonymous, as a basis for their discussions:

> The first step is *awareness*: we admit that we have community problems which we have contributed to. Each of us is a part of the problem, since we did not address the issues before they became situations which adversely affect community wellness.

This insistence on the self-help model, that the best source of help is someone else who shares the problem, came into focus while I was at the first retreat about wellness held by the WHA. During this exercise one group was given the task of coming up with some suggestions for developing community wellness. There was only one professional in the group, a nurse, yet all their suggestions became peppered with professional idioms: distancing, 'doing-to' language, full of talk about 'modelling' behaviours, setting a curriculum, and 'contracts' between a healthy person and an unhealthy one. In contrast, the language of the youth and senior discussions described above is rather of 'how have we survived, what strengths do we have, what can we learn from each other?'.

Two more steps exemplify the collective self-esteem building: *unity* which stresses that each member of the community has unique gifts, each as significant and needed as another, and *collective work and responsibility* which emphasises the sharing of resources for the good of the whole community. These contrast starkly with the top-down, self-esteem building approach of the trainers of welfare women in California's GAIN programme, a state-run programme aimed at getting women on welfare to work. These women were urged to believe in themselves, but also to surround themselves with positive-thinking people in order to be in the best position to compete for the few jobs available. "You cannot all be a winner", they were told, "you owe it to yourself to be the best" (programme leader during training session I witnessed). Jackie Reed commented:

> We affirm our own value and purpose, and ways we can find our gift and give it away.

So a lot of attention is paid to encouraging people to speak up:

> We get everyday people around the table, to build
> relationships.   They might clam up in meetings, so we
> encourage them to speak up. We're careful to give credit to
> people for saying what's on their minds, to help them struggle
> to see how their idea fits the agenda, or to change the agenda,
> by finding a couple of people to support their ideas, then
> building on that.

The WHA's own struggle is to keep its leadership at one with the
grass-roots, not to fall into the same trap as some outsiders of
thinking of themselves as the holders of the answers, or knowing
the way to the answers. The recent history of many community
activists encourages that kind of thinking. They applied for funds
on the basis of being the key to reaching the community, of being
the people who could cope while others could not. They felt
controlled by policy makers and funders, who offered funds for an
agenda driven by outside interests (cutting resources, containing
crime), to which community plans had to fit. In turn, community
leaders tended to manipulate the 'powers that be', by stressing the
deficits of their community and agreeing, in effect, that answers
would have to be provided for them.

There is an essential difference between the meetings of the
WHA and those of the local district health council, on which many
of the same community leaders sit. The district health council was
set up by the county board:

> It seems a good idea to empower community people and give
> some inroads into planning on health care, but their agenda is
> clear - rationing. Any time dollars get scarce, all of a sudden
> they want to talk to the community. They have to close
> clinics so they need supporters to help them choose which to
> close. People know when they are being manipulated and
> controlled. People aren't stupid enough to be real in those
> meetings, so they manipulate back, and the lack of
> communication continues. You can tell from who keeps
> going to their meetings: the real community people don't go
> any more.

Staying as the driver of the community's agenda

One of the most effective markers of the WHA's effectiveness has been its ability to act as broker to disputing agencies. 'The community is the grease' and has proven to be an effective problem-management tool. After the Bethany victory, all four remaining local hospitals were threatened by cuts in Illinois state aid. The executive directors of those institutions met for the first time around a table, called together by the WHA. They undertook to present a joint response to the proposed cuts, to avoid the public aid department pitting them against each other.

Once the community's strength has been felt by managers of local systems, there can often be an attempt to harness that strength by incorporating it. One hospital director announced his invitation to the authority to send a representative to his board: their courteous but firm reply was that they were the community health board, his hospital was welcome to join, and the fee for institutions was $500. The hospital joined.

This community had learned years earlier, following a successful campaign to 'capture' their local hospitals, that having community people on hospital boards makes not a jot of difference to the health of their area (McKnight, 1978).

The leadership of the WHA are now invited to all the key planning meetings of the city and county as the voice of the community, but in turn, the WHA insists that the major players have to come out to the community. The president of Cook County Board is one of the leaders expected to come out regularly to the Westside to respond to the community's questions about plans for their area. The authority also presses for those in power who wish to involve the community representatives in their meetings ('the downtown meetings'), to do more than use them to legitimise plans that have already been made. They want the power brokers to 'join our table', to come out to the Westside, to WHA committee meetings, and cooperate in planning together. So far, some professionals and planners have acted as sources of information and technical support. This process has helped keep the process of planning for the area rooted amongst and accountable to the people of the Westside. But at a recent retreat for major funders and policy makers, Jackie Reed's call for them to join the WHA's table was met with an invitation to another out-of-town policy devising meeting.

Of all the threats to the WHA's effectiveness, coopting is the most potent. At the beginning, some thought it would be inevitable, and that one day another group would rise to challenge the dead hand of the bought-off authority. That may yet happen, but they have given themselves just five years from 1992 to make a difference: this means that they are not putting energy into infrastructures that could hinder the dynamic and organic growth of the group. But money may yet be getting in the way, as feared in the early months of the coalition:

> Since we got the Kellogg grant, the preachers haven't met once. When we didn't have the money, we got on with our plans anyway, we had great, inspiring meetings. We were freed up, not dependent on anybody. We needed each other, that kept us together.

The test will be if, in a few years time, the community has managed to develop its power without being incorporated into depowering structures.

The setting for citizen involvement in health care

The dire state of health provision in poor areas of the USA means that the community is often fighting to preserve institutions it would prefer to replace, for example, an acute hospital with primary care provision. However, the sheer openness and anarchy of the system means that people can be quite creative in their response. It is relatively easy to organise extra service provision through community-based provider groups, and with the changes in the UK government's attitude in the 1980s this will become more common here too. The challenge in both countries is to find an authentic citizen input to strategic health planning, not just to take the opportunity to plug a few gaps.

In the USA there has been a history of profound disillusionment with government funding of community-based initiatives: the spectre of millions of dollars going to services for the poor and doing no good has only served to confirm the image of the community as hopeless and worthless. There is a growing feeling in the community that federal funds were just creating more jobs for researchers and service workers and professionals. Resources were being given to those who exploited the community's problems, and systems were shored up with funds ostensibly for the community which would inevitably create more dependency by the community. So there is a fierce independence in the approach of the citizen groups which is mirrored by the radical republicans' repugnance for spoon-feeding the poor with services. Our own government has similar feelings. The need for the agenda to be shared, for the community to own the plans to ensure effective citizen input, is the same in both countries. For people to have a real say and to change things, they need to be brought in at the beginning of the process, at the agenda-setting stage. They need support to build on their own capacities to contribute; they need information and resources. The confidence and energy resulting from community organising has been a key to the WHA's development.

In Chicago, building 'community capacity' grew from the community organising tradition of the 1930s and 1940s. The civil rights movements of the 1950s and 1960s in Mississippi formed the bed-rock for the black community to work within this tradition. This means their immediate work is recognised as being rooted in a strong set of shared values and ideas.

In the UK, there is a tendency to look at these traditions as alien to ours, but our most effective consumer groups also come from a radical base. The user groups in mental health care and the childbirth activists have been boosted by their shared history in the wider mental health and women's movements. The growth of black groups looking at health issues in the UK, most notably the Manchester Action Committee for the Health of Ethnic Minorities (Mohammed, 1993), will involve the invoking of exploitation and spiritual history similar to the Chicago group.

The old systems on which both the US and UK groups were formed to put pressure are collapsing. In the same way as the WHA is experimenting with new ways of organising, consumer advocacy groups in the UK are being urged to build new approaches (Pfeffer and Coote, 1991) for this new situation.

The Chicago group's efforts are enlivened by their faith which gives them the nerve for their high profile actions. We have similar faith-driven groups in the UK, such as the group Communities Organised for a Greater Bristol. Their activities have been carefully chosen to boost the community's confidence. The Reverend John Bishop of St Paul's said it was hard to accept direct action "but it's been proved to work - quite voiceless people suddenly become confident". Neil Jameson, organiser of the Bristol group, commented "It's not the detailed issue that matters but people's power. This is a real Pentecost thing: people receiving power". Reverend Neville Bounty, Vicar of Cotham, Bristol, stated people's power had no limits: "In time we could challenge the whole budget priorities of the city" (*The Guardian*, 6 June 1991).

While the Bristol group is mainly middle class, the poor black community in Chicago and the joy riders of our run-down estates share the negative images of themselves as weak victims or evil miscreants. In both countries, there is a demand for action to change those communities, not least because of other peoples' fear of them. But the resources for action are often not given directly to those in the heart of the community: capacity building does not take place effectively in the setting. Instead, here in the UK, we have the example of the local health authority advertising for volunteers from a Sunderland housing estate to join a group to help with health planning and promotion. When I asked whether existing community groups had been contacted and given resources to help them create their own planning forum, the puzzled reply was that there really were not any groups in that community. The fact that all communities have some sort of cooperative groups may be more recognised in the USA, and the groups on the Westside of Chicago may be more vociferous, but the image of poor and minority communities as disorganised and incapable is endemic in both countries, and the raising of the true community voice a challenge.

How can we build citizen capacity in health care in the UK?

> In order to develop communities' ability to respond, you've got to invest in the process. It's like digging foundations before you build the wall, you need to spend two-thirds of your time empowering people and enabling them to speak for themselves, to have the information they need. You can't have a robust user voice without resources. (Margaret Martin, ex-secretary of Cambridge Community Health Council, in an interview)

The two main themes of citizen capacity building are information, which entails openness, and resources (Pfeffer and Coote, 1991). The WHA is empowered by its access to information. During its agenda-setting stage, the authority went around in small groups talking to professionals and planners, and inviting them in, asking all the time for information, for facts around which to build their own ideas. The authority approached these meetings with an agenda, a list of their own priorities. The people they met with would say "how can I help?" and they would say "we need information - from that we'll make our own recommendations".

It is vital not only to have access to information, but also to know how to make the best use of the information. Dissemination of the information is not enough: we also need standing interactive mechanisms between our health authorities and institutions, and the communities they serve. The Cambridge Community Health Council commented:

> We're seen as confrontational but we're only asked for our views at the end of the line when everything is a *fait accompli*, so our only response can be confrontational and a challenge.

The National Health Service changes have been attacked for reducing the accountability of our health system. Comparing the makeup of the Cambridge Community Health Council with that of the Family Health Services Authority (all of whose members live in a house with a name in a village, The Red House, The Rectory and so forth), the community health councils are the nearest we have to a voice representing a broader community. Resources should therefore be given to community health councils to help them carry out a careful self-audit, and prepare themselves for a more responsive and accountable role.

The Department of Health has suggested in some detail how health authorities should ensure that they "give people an effective voice in the shaping of health services locally" (Department of Health, 1992). It is acknowledged that this "will call for a radically different approach from that employed in the past". Effort and resources have been put into turning the bureaucracy towards the community: posts have been created and projects set up to "involve the consumer".

So we have a situation where our health authorities are already grappling with working with local people. Looking for a role, the authorities are clear that 'champions of the people' is one they want to espouse, and we may begin to consider what differences in practice might result from these projects. So far, informal discussions I have had with those involved in this work indicate that it is likely to have had two main effects: first, to have enabled authorities to develop ways to have citizens engaged in debates about how to spend scarce resources (rather than arguing for larger budgets to begin with) and, second, to have convinced some people in the authorities, to their surprise, of the ability of people in the community to contribute to planning.

However, within the bureaucracies, consumer involvement work is just another competitor for funds and influence. The investigation into 'hard' edges of practice, such as audit and outcome research and policy, is unlikely to be substantially affected. This is an argument for integrating outreach community work into the main programmes of authorities.

But a lesson that can be drawn from the Chicago experience is that authentic community contribution is achieved only through basing work within communities. Projects which engage community residents in arguing through and pursuing their own agenda are in themselves positive. They also have more chance of uncovering how to build our community's health than any outside plan. Expansion of bureaucracies to incorporate this work means more energy into the status quo, and the risk of a repeat of the cycle of exploitation and disillusionment described above. A more effective use of resources would be to give them to community groups, who could then work on the difficult questions arising: how does consumer involvement affect outcomes? What difference can it really make? How shall we plan for health together?

The principle of the importance of the eliciting of the citizen and patient voice in health care and promotion is well established, but examples of good and successful practice are harder to find. Using the positive community development model, an inventory of strengths in this area in the UK should be undertaken and collaborative networks of user, patient and self-help groups, together with voluntary, community organising groups and community health councils, should be encouraged.

The challenge then for the researchers, planners and providers who are reading this chapter is: how are we to change our professional role? How do we act as a resource for people in our community?

I am suggesting that there is a role which can emerge, phoenix-like, from the ashes of defunct professional practice. It will entail trusting the community voice, not supplanting it. It will involve giving up control of the agenda and not dominating it. Thereby we will be acting in a true partnership offering professional expertise in the service of a democratically decided agenda. Here, the example of the Westside Health Authority can act as one model of our efforts. This is not a demeaning of the professional role; rather, by working together with the community, respect for, and understanding of, the contribution of those working in health will be enhanced.

In recent years, the experience of doctors learning to listen to patients has taught us that professionals who trust what patients have to say, and who help them to speak their concerns and discover how to take care of their own health, find that their own work becomes more productive and rewarding. This is a healthier outcome for all.

Note

I am grateful to Professor Paul Arntson of the Department of Communication Studies at Northwestern University where I was based during my Harkness Fellowship, and to Jackie Reed, the executive director of the Westside Health Authority.

References

Annenberg Center at Eisenhower (1992) *Challenges in personal and public health promotion*, Executive summary of conference of the same title in 'Medicine for the 21st century' series, Eisenhower, Palm Springs, February.

Arntson, P.H. (1989) 'Improving citizens' health competencies', *Health Communication*, vol 1, pp 29-34.

Boston City Council (1991) *Building health through community: an international dialogue*, Report of conference of the same title, Boston, March.

Bracht, N. (ed) (1991) *Health promotion at the community level*, London: Sage.

College of Health (1990) *Report on activities*, London: College of Health.

Department of Health (1992) *Local voices: the views of local people in purchasing for health*, London: HMSO.

Dixon and Welch, H.G. (1991) 'Priority setting: lessons from Oregon', *The Lancet*, 13 April.

Guardian (1991) 'Building from the bottom up', 15 October.

Guardian (1991) 'Christian militants barrage Bristol', 6 June.

Hughes, J., and Humphrey, C. (1990) *Medical audit in general practice: a practical guide to the literature*, London: King's Fund Centre.

Levenson, R. and Joule, N. (1992) *Listening to people*, London: Greater London Association of Community Health Councils.

Martin, P. and Marks, P. (1991) 'Listen to the people', *Health Services Journal*, 4 April.

McIver, S. (1991) *Obtaining the views of users of health services*, London: King's Fund Centre.

McKnight, J. (1978) 'Politicising health care', *Social Policy*, November/December.

McKnight, J. and Kretzmann, J. (1990) *Mapping community capacity*, Chicago: Center for Urban Affairs and Policy Research, Northwestern University.

Mohammed, S. (1993) 'Black people as users of the health service', in J. Copperman (ed) *The public as partners: a toolbox for involving people in commissioning health care*, published by the Healthgain Conference and available from the East Anglian Regional Health Authority.

Morris, P. (1993) 'Prioritising health services with local people', in J. Copperman (ed) *The public as Partners: a toolbox for involving local people in commissioning health care*, published by the Healthgain Conference and available from East Anglian Regional Health Authority.

New York Times (1991) 'Patients' opinions say all', 3 March.

Observer (1991) 'Doctors' orders may not be best for us', 6 August.

Pfeffer, N. and Coote, A. (1991) *Is quality good for you?*, Social Policy paper no 5, London: Institute for Public Policy Research.

Westside Health Authority (1992) Publicity leaflet.

thirteen

REFLECTIONS ON TRANSATLANTIC POLICY TRANSFER

Robin Hambleton and Marilyn Taylor

Introduction

Since the autumn of 1991, when we held the People in Cities conference, the world has moved on. Cities in both the UK and the USA have boiled over into urban unrest, focusing, as has been the case before, on police activity. In the USA this has been strongly linked with racial discrimination; in the UK it is as likely to be a phenomenon of white unemployed youth as black, reflecting the different composition of city populations in the two countries. In the UK, too, the flash points are as likely to be found on the margins of cities, in peripheral estates where disadvantaged and poor people have been rehoused over the decades. A common factor in both the USA and the UK is the spatial concentration and ghettoisation of people without choices and their increasing separation from the rest of society combined with a demonstrable widening of the gap between rich and poor. These divisions, which are all too visible to the poor through the media, are increasingly invisible to the people who still have jobs and wealth, except where homelessness brings the poorest back to the haunts of the better-off.

Notwithstanding the 'back to the city' movement found in many US urban areas, the centres of the cities have largely been deserted by the middle classes, with the flight to the suburbs described in several of the chapters in this book. These chapters also point to the pitfalls of the welfare reforms now being implemented by central government in the UK. The development of two-tier systems in, for example, health, education and housing - with the public sector increasingly concentrating on those who cannot afford to choose - has gone much further in the USA. Critics of US public policy argue that the stigmatisation of particular groups has helped to create a dependent underclass, which no longer conforms to the rules of the rest of society (Murray, 1990). This is the kind of transatlantic policy transfer that is unwelcome in the UK, as are the rising levels of crime and alienation that are causing so much concern as we write in 1993.

But these chapters also demonstrate a greater freedom to act at local level in the USA, as well as a greater willingness on the part of business and citizens to invest in their local community. The US public sphere is strengthened by foundations which provide resources on a scale undreamed of in the UK. There is a new administration in the USA in 1993 and a potential for new directions which is more difficult to find in the UK. Certainly the major cuts in the Urban Programme, announced in November 1992, coupled with continued cutbacks in local government budgets give little cause for optimism. But, as Lavery reminds us, cities in the USA have had to face a fiscal squeeze much tougher than in the UK - with huge financial crises and even bankruptcy (see Chapter 4). Some of our authors talk about the view there that the cities are 'obsolete', a view which we have not yet heard so much in the UK. The impression is that relatively little has changed in downtown Los Angeles, despite all the wringing of hands following the urban unrest in April 1992. The Clinton administration has to contend with a huge budget deficit and miracles cannot be worked overnight. Nevertheless President Clinton is on record as intending to pursue a strategy of "putting people first" (Clinton and Gore, 1992). There appears to be a growth in concern about the plight of US urban communities - time will tell if this concern is translated into practical action in US cities.

In this final chapter we offer some general reflections on the possibilities for successful transatlantic urban policy transfer in the future. To structure the discussion we return again to the three part framework, developed by Wolman (1992), which we introduced in Chapter 1. This poses three critical questions:

- Are the problems to which the policy is to be addressed in the UK similar to those to which it was addressed in the USA? If not, are the problems to which the policy is to be applied in the UK nonetheless susceptible to the policy?

- To what extent was the policy 'successful' in the USA?

- Are there any aspects of a policy's setting in the USA which are critical to its success there, but which are not present, or are present in a different form, in the UK?

We now examine briefly each of these dimensions in turn.

Similar problems?

In Chapter 1 we suggested that, notwithstanding the existence of substantial differences, many of the 'problems' experienced by people living in cities are similar in both the UK and the USA. Many of the contributors to this volume have also drawn attention to similarities in their respective fields. At the same time, discussions at the conference stressed the importance of taking great care over problem definition. Anderson has described the concern eloquently:

> Problems can be appraised in the light of many different political principles. We talk frequently about the 'common' problems of all industrialised societies, but these so-called shared problems - inflation, inequality, environmental deterioration, social conflict, participation and the like - may have a wholly different kind of significance from one nation to the next, not only because of economic and social differences but because of the way such problems are evaluated and analysed. ... Public problems are not just 'out there' waiting to be dealt with. Policy making is not simply problem solving. It is also a matter of setting up and defining the problem in the first place. (Anderson, 1978, p 20)

Wolman uses the example of local economic development to show how problem definition is crucial and, by implication, how policy confusion is likely to arise if this aspect is neglected (Wolman, 1993). He points out how local politicians and officials in the USA usually see the problem which local economic development policy addresses as primarily fiscal: the need to strengthen the local authorities' tax base by increasing the amount of economic activity located within their boundaries. In contrast, political leaders and local government officers in the UK see the local economic development problem more as one of unemployment: the need to provide decent job opportunities for the area's residents. These divergent problem definitions flow from institutional, historical and policy differences. Wolman concludes:

> given the differences in problem definitions, it is quite possible that a successful local programme in the American context (for example, one that increases the local municipal tax base) may be quite unsuccessful from the British perspective (for example, if new employees commute to the area from outside and the unemployment rate of residents in the local authority is not affected). (Wolman, 1993, p 22)

This insight is echoed in various chapters.

Whilst recognising the need to avoid loose definitions, many of the chapters have suggested that the 'problems' in both countries are similar and could become even more so. There are significant differences that need to be taken into account, notably in relation to the even closer interweaving of race and alienation in the USA, where in many cities the 'minority' communities are in fact the majority. In both countries, however, there is a sense in which the way in which the 'problem' is defined may serve to reinforce it. It is arguable that neither country has come to grips with the way in which previous policies themselves along with the relatively free rein given to economic forces may have created the 'problem'. Still less has there been an objective rather than an ideological assessment of the success of past policies (for example, the widespread belief that the US Great Society initiatives of the 1960s were a failure when some, like the Headstart Programme for pre-school children, were very successful; or the withdrawal in the UK of the apparently successful Urban Programme). Nor has enough been done to reverse the labelling of inner cities - to focus on the considerable assets in these areas rather than the 'problem' (see Morris, Chapter 12).

Policy evaluation

How successful have past policies been? This is always difficult to establish. Against what criteria should the policy be evaluated? In the context of cross-national policy transfer the task is more complex than assessing the policy on its own terms. Whether or not the policy achieves its stated intentions, whilst important, is not the primary focus of interest. Rather, the central question revolves around the extent to which the policy has successfully tackled the problem as defined in the UK. As noted earlier, this may or may not be the same as the stated US policy objectives.

The research and evaluation task has somehow to accommodate the fact that stakeholders in a given policy may have a vested interest in showing it to be a success. For example, in Chapter 1 we referred to the phenomenon of 'civic boosterism' encountered in many US cities. As cities become increasingly concerned to market themselves in a global market-place for inward investment they, perhaps unavoidably, have a tendency to be 'economical with the truth'. Similarly, politicians and professionals associated with particular policy initiatives tend to have a stance which veers towards enthusiastic endorsement rather than dispassionate analysis. Moreover, the information needed to assess policy performance may simply not be available. For example, Meyer has pointed out not only that different nations classify data in different ways, but that standard statistical sources are not up to the job. Critical distinctions are often not made and the geographical units of analysis may be unhelpful (Meyer, 1993). These various obstacles to cross-national policy evaluation should not be underestimated. Having said that, what do we know about US policy performance?

Bright (Chapter 8) questions whether there has been a policy at all in the USA, given the resistance to central planning. But several chapters do highlight central policy initiatives which have significantly changed the options open at local level. For example, as Falk explains, the Community Reinvestment Act and the Home Mortgage Disclosures Act, which were introduced to stop red-lining of areas, have been influential in making business locally accountable and encouraging financial investment on the doorstep (Chapter 5). Various chapters also describe a much wider range of local initiatives, some of which are repeated across the country, which represent pockets of excellence and from which we can learn. Some of these successes have, however, been explicitly targeted on the not-so-badly off (see Leather and Mackintosh, Chapter 11) and, while this has its own value not least in terms of prevention, it is not clear whether such policies could be transferred beyond this group.

But the knowledge that has been gained of what does not work is also important. A particularly pertinent example, in view of current debates in the UK, concerns deterrence. Bright (Chapter 8) argues that it is not working even on its own terms, having produced a criminal justice system in the USA that is in danger of collapsing under its own weight. Relying on self-help alone in communities which have no resources is another danger, as are woolly community initiatives which are too unfocused to do good, or the often ill thought out mega-initiative which fails completely to meet the expectations it raises (see Singh, Chapter 9). Even where policies have been demonstrated to work, they have not necessarily been learned from even in the USA: the Headstart Programme for pre-school children being one of the main examples quoted.

The policy setting

What aspects of the policy setting are crucial to policy success or failure? Wolman (1992) has identified three hurdles which need to be overcome if policy transfer is to be successful. It must be capable of adoption through the political system. Once adopted it must be effective: that is, it must address the problem it is expected to solve in the recipient country. Third, it must be capable of survival: that is, of attracting sustained support to enable it to continue to exist and to operate effectively. He points out that different aspects of a policy's setting might be relevant to each of these hurdles. Moreover, some features of the policy setting will reflect aspects of the host society as a whole, whilst others may be specific to particular policies, or even to particular cities.

The greater willingness of business and philanthropy to invest in US cities is undoubtedly an important factor (see Norman, Chapter 10). For example, business in the USA has been more prepared to see the future of local education as affecting its own future (see Bolsin, Chapter 7). The churches have made a contribution which is all the more significant there because of the higher level of church membership (see Newton, Chapter 6; Morris, Chapter 12). The tax exemption available to donors is another important factor, but there is also a cultural dimension to this in a country which has always been more distrustful of government than is our own in the UK. Tax policies have also encouraged potential investors and developers (see Falk, Chapter 5).

Ironically, the distrust of federal government has also created local administrations which are much stronger than our own vis-a-vis the centre. The US citizen would never tolerate the central interventions experienced at local government level in the UK. Compare the fact that there was no federal department of education before the Carter administration with the extraordinary centralisation of power in Whitehall which has taken place in the years since 1979. There are costs and benefits to this. Several authors (Norman and Bolsin, for example) attest to the greater fragmentation this produces, to the difficulty of spreading good practice, and to the obstacles to driving change across the USA. But the greater freedom of local government, for example to raise taxes locally and to raise money through bonds, has provided resources for new initiatives and also, according to a number of contributors, gives business more of a stake in the community. On the other hand, whilst US local authorities have more policy freedom, we are usefully reminded of the enormous fiscal pressure that city governments in the USA experience. Rose-coloured spectacles are not in order. It is in the USA that city governments have gone bankrupt, not the UK.

There is, as mentioned in Chapter 1, great variation across the country and different levels of government are responsible for different services. But it is interesting to note that, in a country that is supposed to have less government, US municipalities can be found running services viewed, at present, as being outside the scope of UK local government, such as the public utilities. US local authorities have more choice over what they do and over what services they can run. For example, Seattle's mayor decided to raise a special education levy to support the city's schools even though the city itself is not an education authority (Hambleton, 1993). The mayor and the council took the view that improving education was vital to the city's future prosperity. Seattle also has its own electricity company, City Light.

Having said this, the US distrust of government stretches to local government too and there is suspicion of the political machine and political appointments. This is reflected in Schmoke's mission to widen involvement in the running of public services through new kinds of partnership arrangement (see Chapter 2). This is a particularly interesting area for policy exploration, given current shifts in the UK. In Chapter 1 we referred to the idea of the 'enabling local authority' and many of the chapters (going beyond those in Part 2) have explored ways in which councils are increasingly 'working across the boundaries' of the public, private, voluntary and community sectors. Schmoke, for example, outlines four ways in which the city collaborates with the private sector: the Community Development Financing Corporation; school-business partnerships; privatisation of nine schools; and bringing minorities and women into the economic mainstream through, for example, pairings between new minority-owned businesses and established businesses in mentoring relationships.

Lavery (Chapter 4) runs in more detail through the differences between local government in the USA and the UK, which also featured in Chapter 1. Some government ministers, noticeably Michael Heseltine when he was at the Department of the Environment, have been attracted by US models of local government management. Certainly the government's consultation paper on the internal management of local authorities was influenced by US ideas. It included some options - for example, the mayor-council form and the city manager form - which were straightforward copies of the arrangements found in thousands of US city halls (Department of the Environment, 1991). It is encouraging to note that the recent report of a working party on the internal management of local authorities in England recommends that the Secretary of State for the Environment should take powers to enable individual authorities to experiment with entirely new forms of internal management (Department of the Environment, 1993). It is to be hoped that these powers will be made available and that the opportunities provided by the local government reorganisation in the UK will be used to develop a variety of new forms of governance.

The traditional uniformity of local government management in the UK looks increasingly strange given the diversity of needs in different areas and the rapid changes now taking place in the policy environment. Why do some councils not try out a variant of the strong mayor model adapted to the UK context? Why do some councils not consider experimenting with the city manager model? Lavery (Chapter 4) shows that both these models have characteristics which would be worth importing, provided they were adapted to the UK policy setting. Those concerned with local authority policy making and management in the UK could undoubtedly learn a good deal from their US counterparts. This is starting to happen at the city level. Some cities - for example, Cardiff and Baltimore - have commenced a process of public policy exchange.

The greater autonomy at local level in the USA has its impact on other institutions too. Local negotiations in education have, according to Bolsin, freed trade unions from their national preoccupation with terms and conditions and given them a greater role locally in professional development and nationally in policy making. In the areas Bolsin has studied he notes that teaching commands higher wages and, by implication, greater respect (see Chapter 7). Whether this is a country-wide phenomenon is another question; all the areas Bolsin studied were areas of good practice. Before endorsing the idea of local negotiations, it would be useful to know how the less enlightened cities and states are faring.

Another important difference in the policy setting is the emergence in the USA of significant intermediary bodies which can lever funds, provide support, spread good practice and generally provide the infrastructure on which community-based and other initiatives can be run. Falk argues that a well-resourced intermediary operating in the grey area between commercial and charitable objectives is invaluable in enabling local aspirations to be fulfilled at minimum risk or cost. Two major examples in this book are the Local Initiatives Support Corporation (see Chapter 5) and the Public Education Funds (see Chapter 7). The foundations have had a significant role to play, notably in providing the all-important pump-priming role (the Ford Foundation was instrumental in kick-starting both these initiatives). Because of the level of funds involved it is difficult to see who, apart from government (or possibly the European Commission), would be in a position to play a similar role in the UK.

The possibilities for policy transfer

Given these differences in policy setting, what are the lessons that can be learned? Specific lessons can be found in each chapter and we do not intend to repeat them here. Singh (Chapter 9) has argued that the aim should be not to transfer policies wholesale, but to ask: 'Can the USA provide insights which would be helpful within a UK context?' It is to this question that we address ourselves in these conclusions.

The first is a plea to policy makers in both countries that it is essential to start from the point of view of people in cities and the assets that they represent. Focusing on needs and problems is in the end a negative message which encourages dependency. Focusing on assets, as Morris argues in Chapter 12, is to start from strengths. But this does not mean leaving people in cities entirely to their own devices, or wringing our hands over the inevitability of welfare dependency. Far from it. It means taking stock of the potential capacity of the community, listening to what people have to say and providing the support and resources that will allow people to build on their potential.

Both Norman and Morris (Chapters 10 and 12) reinforce this message by showing what people can achieve for their communities. But they and others underline the fact that building capacity takes time - there is no 'quick fix'. Indeed, Schmoke (Chapter 2) and others point to the fact that it took more than 20 years to turn the central area of Baltimore around. Such timescales needed federal investment in the USA and are likely to demand a significant long-term investment of central government funds here too.

The more diverse the communities the more important it is to take the time to involve the different communities and encourage cooperation between them. Expecting city governments to consult their communities over new initiatives in a period of a few weeks, as the initial City Challenge bid process did in 1991, is misguided. Investing in patient capacity building so that the community is ready to take up these challenges when they arise is the better option, so long as initiatives recognise the capacity that is there rather than going for political capital (see Chapter 10).

This also argues strongly against pulling the plug on successful small-scale initiatives like the Urban Programme, which has been the seed-bed from which community capacity has grown in the past and could continue to be so in the future. Newton (Chapter 6) stresses the role churches have played in giving people a way out of the welfare cycle, in preparing them for training and supporting them, through child-care and other means, as they move back into employment. Arguing for a recognition of the limits of policing, Bright describes a range of pre-school, teenage pregnancy prevention, family support and anti-drug initiatives which do the same (Chapter 8). The activities of many community-based organisations are in this vein. They are not the stuff of which headlines are made. As we have already suggested they work incrementally, with no overnight miracles. But they are at least as successful as many of the more trumpeted initiatives and considerably more effective than some which have been far more expensive.

As Singh (Chapter 9) argues, multiple problems need multiple solutions. Cooperation and partnership are themes which have been emphasised in numerous chapters. Popular words these, but they often stick at the rhetoric. For central government, this requires a recognition that there is a need for a democratic intermediary at local level. In the educational field, for example, Bolsin argues that a vision is needed that is wider than the individual school, but more localised than the government or its regional agency. Self-governing islands operating in isolation from each other will not deliver what cities need. Businesses and universities will rarely be interested in investing in just one school (see Chapter 7).

It is difficult to avoid the conclusion that local government, however structured and organised, is essential to make a multi-agency approach work. Falk (Chapter 5) argues that the collapse of the property market in the UK means that neither developers nor financial institutions are in a position to take a lead. Others argue the need, through such measures as the Community Reinvestment Act, to make business accountable. But this requires a significant change for local government as well as for central government. Central government needs to recognise that under current financial provisions which, as Bullock suggests, magnify the cost of any local decision to the local taxpayer, local government is being set up to fail (see Chapter 3). But local government needs to move away from the concept of service provision as its *raison d'être*, even if it continues to provide a wide range of services. City Challenge has set an important precedent for the kind of partnership that is needed and this vision needs to spread beyond the Challenge areas. As Bullock argues: "Efforts to provide leadership for a whole community without first seeking to establish a relationship with other leaders in the community are doomed to fail. This means reaching out rather than consolidating and reorganising within".

Falk (Chapter 5) argues for local government as theatre director or animateur. In another context we have argued for the role of local government as 'orchestrator' (Hambleton, 1992; Stewart and Taylor, 1993). As Norman (Chapter 10) suggests, the ideological gulf that separates the civic and business cultures needs to be bridged. The future lies not in hierarchical bureaucracies nor, we would argue, in free markets which in their pure form exist only in the imagination and have little to do with the real world. It lies in joint agreements, in the development of cooperative networks involving the wide variety of actors on the city stage, underwritten by the legitimacy of the democratic system. But that legitimacy can only be secured by widening citizen involvement in urban affairs.

Such a strategy requires investment from government and from other institutions to develop and use a varied institutional framework which, in concert, can deliver and develop public respect. Schmoke (Chapter 2) argues, for example, for the development of a strong minority business community which would give minority communities a stake in the future of their city. And although Newton (Chapter 6) is disappointed at the level of involvement of black churches in training, it is clear from Morris (Chapter 12) that these are institutions which can reach minority communities more effectively than most and need to be involved. Bolsin (Chapter 7) argues for investment in schools and housing as a basic need in city communities and points to the fact that, even in the USA, citizens have been prepared to pay more taxes in order to guarantee that investment.

Several of our authors remind us that the UK has useful lessons for the USA. The strategic planning that is still possible in our less fragmented system must be seen as an asset. Youth training and help with business start-up are examples given of policy transfer in the opposite direction, while the technical and vocational strands in mainstream education are nowhere near as well developed in the USA. The planning mechanisms available here offer opportunities not available in the USA. And the flight of middle class urban families from state education in the USA should give us pause for thought in this country. As Bolsin reminds us, in the UK, partnership with parents and local communities is much more developed than in the USA (see Chapter 7). Different forms of local government in the USA provide the opportunity for lateral thinking way beyond the concept of unitary authorities, but we should be wary of throwing out the baby with the bath water. We need to learn from what has not worked in the USA where, as Bright has argued, the problems are much deeper and where the concentration of joblessness and disadvantage in city ghettoes has gone much further (see Chapter 8). But both countries need to look elsewhere - to learn from Europe in particular about approaches to urban living that stem from different cultures and different political histories.

It is interesting to note that the broad thrust of our conclusions resonates well with recent cross-national studies of economic restructuring. At a theoretical level, Walton (1990) has developed a set of hypotheses about progressive urban responses to economic restructuring. He suggests that cities in a number of countries that have effectively developed policies aimed at averting local economic decline or defended themselves against uneven economic development are characterised by three features:

- a historical tradition of popular action, experience and memory whether in the form of populism, labour militance, civic action or environmentalism;

- a current and extensive network of community-based organisations that participate in politics and provide, among other things, a left opposition;

- regional autonomy in the sense of geographical independence, decentralisation, and intergovernmental cooperation.

(Walton, 1990, p 251)

Whilst, in our view, these variables do not tell the whole story (we believe, for example, that Walton underplays the significance of governmental form) they do tie in with many of the themes set out in this book.

In conclusion, the evidence of this volume is that transatlantic cross-national policy transfer in relation to urban issues is on the increase. The likelihood of success depends on a wide range of factors. We have stressed, in particular, the need to be clear about the nature of the problems to be addressed and to be aware of the policy setting. If the approach is handled thoughtfully and carefully and if policy makers are able to widen their horizons, the potential for further fruitful cross-national exchange is very promising.

References

Anderson, C. (1978) 'The logic of public problems: evaluation and comparative policy research' in D. Ashford (ed) *Comparing public policies*, Beverly Hills: Sage Publications.

Clinton, B. and Gore, A. (1992) *Putting people first: how we can all change America*, New York: Times Books.

Department of the Environment (1991) *The internal management of local authorities in England: a consultation paper*, London: HMSO.

Department of the Environment (1993) *Community leadership and representation: unlocking the potential*, Report of the working party on the internal management of local authorities in England, London: HMSO.

Hambleton, R. (1992) *Rethinking management in local government*, Papers in Planning Research 130, Cardiff: Department of City and Regional Planning, University of Wales.

Hambleton, R. (1993) 'Enabling US style', *Local Government Chronicle*, 12 March, pp 16-17.

Meyer, P.B. (1993) 'Defining and measuring urban policy impacts: a comparative assessment', Paper to the Annual Meeting of the American Urban Affairs Association, Indianapolis, April.

Murray, C. (1990) *The emerging British underclass*, Choice in Welfare series no 2, London: IEA Health and Welfare Unit.

Stewart, M. and Taylor, M. (1993) *Local government community leadership*, Luton: Local Government Management Board.

Walton, J. (1990) 'Theoretical methods in comparative urban politics', pp 243-257 in J.R. Logan and T. Swanstrom (eds) *Beyond the city limits: urban policy and economic restructuring in comparative perspective*, Philadelphia: Temple University Press.

Wolman, H. (1992) 'Understanding cross-national policy transfers: the case of Britain and the US', *Governance: An international journal of policy and administration*, January, pp 27-45.

Wolman, H. (1993) 'Cross-national comparisons of urban economic programmes: is policy transfer possible?' in D. Fasenfest (ed) *Community economic development. Policy formation in the US and the UK*, Basingstoke: The Macmillan Press Ltd.

INDEX